MASTER DRAWINGS
IN THE ALBERTINA

MASTER DRAWINGS
IN THE ALBERTINA

European Drawings from the 15th to the 18th Century

by

OTTO BENESCH

in collaboration with Eva Benesch

London: Evelyn, Adams & Mackay

Published in 1967 by Evelyn, Adams & Mackay
9 Fitzroy Square, London W. 1

Printed in Austria

Clichés by Beissner & Co., Vienna.

Printed by Salzburger Druckerei, Salzburg.

Acknowledgments

This book was originally published in Austria in 1964 in the German language by Verlag Galerie Welz Salzburg.

The translation into English prepared by R. Rickett and M. Schön in Vienna was revised for this edition by Felice Stampfle and Ruth Kramer. The editors have endeavored to keep the translation as close as possible to the German text. The bibliographical references were brought up to date by Eva Benesch.

CONTENTS

PREFACE

Notwithstanding the fame of the Albertina, there has never been a publication that serves as a popular introduction to its collection of old master drawings. There are a number of scholarly catalogues of the collection; the comprehensive volumes of plates by Schönbrunner and Meder, and the series of Albertina-Facsimiles give some idea of its riches. But these works, insofar as they are not out of print, do not find their way to a large circle of art lovers because they are either too learned or too expensive. It was essential to create an instrument which, through a selection of illustrations and the accompanying text, would do justice to the collection in all its variety, and allow the most important masters, trends, and schools to speak for themselves. Peter Halm and his collaborators have accomplished this task in an exemplary manner for the Staatliche Graphische Sammlung in Munich. Something similar, although on a larger scale, has been attempted here for the Albertina. The choice of the examples encompasses the time from 1400 to 1800. In making the selection, quality was the first consideration, then the representative character of a drawing within the collection. Thus the art lover – and hopefully the reader – will find not only the celebrated names of those artists who are the subjects of the innumerable art publications flooding the market today, but also the names of those artists who, though less familiar, nevertheless created works of high quality. Consideration was given not only to the interests of the layman but also to those of the expert, who will find many an unpublished sheet along with everything requisite for its scholarly discussion in the commentary and bibliographical notes, the latter necessarily in restricted form.

My thanks are due first and foremost to my wife who has been my tireless collaborator, then to my publisher, Mr. Friedrich Welz, without whose enthusiasm for art and selfless devotion this long-entertained plan could never have been so beautifully realized.

Vienna, July, 1964   Otto Benesch

The Empress Maria Theresa is shown drawings brought from Italy by her son-in-law, Duke Albert von Sachsen-Teschen, and his consort Marie Christine. Miniature on vellum, 40 by 36.5 cm., by Friedrich Heinrich Füger. 1776.

Oesterreichische Galerie, Vienna

THE DRAWINGS COLLECTION OF THE ALBERTINA

Its History

More than any other collection of drawings in existence today, the Albertina is a personal achievement, reflecting the character of its founder. Duke Albert Casimir August, the son of August II, Elector of Saxony and King of Poland (where he reigned as August III), was born on July 11, 1738, at the hunting lodge of Moritzburg near Dresden. His mother, Maria Josepha, was a daughter of the Emperor Joseph I. As the eleventh child, the young prince could not look forward to any great prospects in his native Saxony. Since Saxony was allied with Austria in the Seven Years' War, it is hardly surprising that he, along with his younger brother Clemens, later Archbishop of Trier, aspired to a career in the Austrian army. In the autumn of 1759, the two princes reported to the headquarters of Field Marshal Daun, who took them into his entourage. After the recapture of Dresden, the two princes made their way to Vienna in January, 1760, in order to present themselves to the Emperor and Empress.

Their reception was most cordial, and Maria Theresa invited Albert to join the Austrian army. At a concert he made the acquaintance of the Empress' second daughter, the Archduchess Marie Christine, born on May 13, 1742, a meeting which was to lead to a marriage of rare harmony and happiest understanding. Although he regarded himself as destined for a military career, the Duke already as a young man was of a decidedly artistic turn of mind. He had a fine example of a collector in his father, under whom the Dresden Gallery enjoyed its most brilliant program of acquisition. The dawning age of idealism in German intellectual life meant that some degree of artistic education was virtually indispensable. People began to take pleasure in paintings and sculpture, in drawings and the graphic arts. One dabbled in art just as one studied music or read the classical poets. The Duke's tutor was a Wessenberg, a member of a family whose name is associated with the establishment of an art collection in Constance. Marie Christine had similar interests. When Liotard visited Vienna in 1761 and made colored chalk drawings of the Empress' children[1]), most of the girls were portrayed at their needlework or writing, but Marie Christine was shown drawing, with her watercolor box beside her – evidently her favorite occupation. Some samples of her work are still today preserved in the Albertina. The wedding of this eminently well-suited couple took place in the chapel of Schloßhof Castle on April 8, 1766.

The private ducal archives provided abundant documentary evidence relating to the biography of the ducal pair and to the origin of the collection, including five volumes of the Duke's memoirs up to the year 1798 and a mass of letters, records, catalogues, and accounts. It was

---

[1]) Now in the Musée d'Art et d'Histoire, Geneva (Insel-Bücherei 613).

from these archives that the ducal pair's biographers, Wolf[2]), Malcher[3]), and Vivenot[4]), drew their material, but by 1863 two volumes of the memoirs had already been lost. Another important document was the Duke's detailed report of his trip to Italy with his wife in 1776, which was presented to the Empress as a special volume. Unfortunately, this wealth of material was used by historians only to attest the unusually attractive and sympathetic personalities of the ducal couple; there is no account of their activity as collectors. Thausing[5]), Schönbrunner[6]), Meder[7]), and Stix[8]) dealt with this activity in brief essays. As far as possible within their limited scope, they give information relating to the history of the collection and the collecting activity of the Duke. In comparison with other great historic collections where there is documentation for every phase of steady growth, facts concerning the history of the Albertina are extremely scarce. It is regrettable that the ducal archives in the Albertina were never explored for the light they could throw on the history of the collection itself. When the collection became the property of the State in 1920, the archives, because they did not come under the law of entail, were restored to their last private owner, Archduke Friedrich. They were stored in the castle of Halbturn in Burgenland where they were inaccessible and unavailable for research. (The memoirs of the Duke which the historians had been able to use were no longer available to Meder.) A great fire at the castle in 1949 reduced the archives to ashes, eliminating forever the possibility of writing a history of the collection. When, from whom, through whose offices, and at what prices the Duke acquired his treasury of drawings will always remain shrouded in darkness. Albert's and Christine's ample family correspondence preserved in the Haus-, Hof- and Staatsarchiv in Vienna reveals no clues. Information can be laboriously gleaned at second hand, but the result is scant as the following account shows.

The Empress Maria Theresa was intent on insuring that her favorite daughter and her husband should be well provided for. Albert, the son of an extravagant father who had brought his country to bankruptcy, had been born poor. The ducal couple, however, was liberally endowed from the imperial coffers. Albert was given the Duchy of Teschen, which he added to his title, and he and his wife received the domains of Mannersdorf and Ungarisch-Altenburg. The dowry amounted to 666,821 florins. Albert was named Field Marshal, Captain-General, and the Empress' Governor in Hungary, with a residence at the castle in Pressburg (Bratislava). This latter office, which he held from 1766 to 1780, was highly remunerative. The ducal pair was thus *ex superabundanti* provided for, and the financial basis for collecting was established

[2]) Adam Wolf, Marie Christine. Erzherzogin von Österreich, 2 vols., Vienna, 1863.

[3]) F. X. Malcher, Herzog Albrecht zu Sachsen-Teschen bis zu seinem Antritt der Statthalterschaft in Ungarn 1738 – 1766, Vienna, 1894.

[4]) Alfred Edl. v. Vivenot, Herzog Albrecht von Sachsen-Teschen als Reichs-Feld-Marschall (January 1794 – December 1795), Vols. I and II (1, 2), Vienna, 1864 – 1866.

[5]) Moriz von Thausing, La Collection Albertine à Vienne, son histoire, sa composition. Gazette des Beaux-Arts, 1870/1871, Vol. 29 (II Serie 4), p. 72 ff., p. 147 ff.

[6]) Joseph Schönbrunner, Die Albertina. Ein Vortrag gehalten am 17. Dezember 1886 im Alterthums-Vereine, Vienna. Berichte und Mitteilungen, Vol. 24, 1887, p. 190 ff.

[7]) Joseph Meder, Herzog Albert von Sachsen-Teschen. Zu seinem hundertjährigen Todestag. Die Graphischen Künste, 45, Vienna, 1922, p. 73 ff.

[8]) Alfred Stix, Herzog Albert von Sachsen-Teschen. Die Zeichnung, No. II, Vienna, G. Nebehay, 1927.

on a scale unmatched among the Hapsburgs since the time of Albert's predecessor, Leopold Wilhelm. The ducal couple had also been promised the reversion of the governship of the Netherlands.

The earliest written evidence of the Duke's activity as a collector is provided by the entries in the diary of Johann Georg Wille[9]), engraver, collector, and art dealer in Paris, who supplied engravings to the Duke. The entries begin with August 14, 1768, and continue until December, 1774. There is a short addendum as late as April, 1784, by which time Albert was already governor at Brussels. In the eyes of the eighteenth-century collector, prints took precedence over drawings, and the Duke's collection developed at first as a print collection. In 1774, he commissioned the imperial ambassador in Venice, Count Jacopo Durazzo, to assemble as complete a collection of Italian engravings as possible. Within two years, Durazzo managed to comply with this tall order and when the Duke visited Italy, he presented the collection to him with a beautiful title page, etched by Bartsch, for the individual portfolios. During the same visit to Italy, the Duke received as a gift from Pope Pius VI the complete etched works of Piranesi.

The Italian trip of the ducal pair, which lasted from the end of December, 1775, to the middle of July, 1776, contributed to their growing enthusiasm for art. As the guests of the Archduke Leopold, Regent of Tuscany and the brother of Marie Christine (see No. 119), they spent considerable time in Florence admiring the city's many churches and galleries. In Rome, a certain Herr von Reiffenstein, a disciple of their much admired Winckelmann, was their guide. They also enjoyed the association of art lovers like Sir William Hamilton, the British ambassador. A visit to the Court of Naples aroused their enthusiasm for classical antiquity. From King Ferdinand, his brother-in-law, the Duke received permission to visit at any time his collection of antiquities, which included the finds of the latest excavations at Herculaneum and Pompeii. At the gallery in Turin, he showed himself receptive to the charm of the early Netherlandish masters. There is a souvenir of this journey in the Österreichische Galerie at Vienna, a large miniature on vellum by F. H. Füger representing the reception of the returning ducal pair by Maria Theresa's family. Albert and the high-spirited Marie Christine show her mother the Empress the works of art they have accumulated – apparently drawings – amid an admiring circle of brothers and sisters: the Co-Regent Joseph II, the Archduke Maximilian (later Prince Bishop of Cologne), and the Archduchesses Maria Elisabeth and Maria Anna. The miniature was obviously commissioned by the Duke, who favored the young artist on other occasions as well. The Albertina is particularly rich in Füger's drawings (see No. 120). The Duke commissioned further miniatures from this portrait painter of international rank[10]).

Such documentary evidence as we possess refers only to the purchase of engravings in these early years, but there must have been a parallel program for the acquisition of drawings. When the Duke once again took the field against the Prussians in 1778, his wife sent drawings by Mieris (see No. 203) and Teniers to his camp for his pleasure, not forgetting to enclose the

---

[9]) Mémoires et Journal, publiés par Georges Duplessis, 2 vols., Paris, 1857.

[10]) See the fine double-portrait of the ducal pair on the cover of a box in the Vienna Kunsthistorisches Museum (A. Stix, H. F. Füger, Vienna, 1925, Catalogue 11).

bill from the dealer Artaria. As a collector of graphic art, the Duke definitely led the field. He seems to have had an advantage over even the rich imperial print cabinet of the Hofbibliothek, which had taken shape after the acquisition of the collection of Prince Eugene of Savoy. While there is an abundance of evidence concerning the growth of the imperial collection[11]), the sources are silent concerning the formation of the Duke's drawing collection. The still extant handwritten catalogue of the collection of drawings (the so-called "Cahier"), compiled during the Duke's last years and augmented by subsequent owners, gives no acquisition dates. Provenance is noted in only a few cases[12]). While there are lists of prices for the prints, there are none at all for the drawings.

On the death of Carl, Duke of Lorraine, in 1780, Albert and Christine succeeded as governors of the Netherlands, a post occupied in the early seventeenth century by Rubens' patrons Albrecht and Isabella. From 1781 to 1792, the couple resided in Brussels. At nearby Laeken, Albert commissioned the neo-classical architect Montoyer to build the palace that became their favorite residence. The Duke was now much nearer to the great centers of the art market than he had been in Vienna. In 1786, the ducal pair paid a visit to Paris, from which they returned laden with presents from those who knew them to be passionate amateurs. The visit also provided the opportunity to expand the collection of drawings on a grand scale. Between 1783 and 1792, the Duke spent 14,000 florins a year on his collection. There were a number of other like-minded collectors in the vicinity, for instance, the young Prince Charles de Ligne at Beloeil Castle, who had appointed Adam Bartsch as his adviser and teacher in the art of etching. There was scope for friendly rivalry. When in 1792 the Prince de Ligne fell in the fighting against the French Revolutionary army, his collection of drawings was sold at auction at the Theresianum in Vienna in 1794. The detailed catalogue was compiled by Bartsch, secretary ("skriptor") and later keeper ("kustos") of the Imperial Library and keeper of the imperial collection of prints[13]). Prince Albert, too, availed himself of Bartsch's advice for his own collection. In both collections the arrangement and classification by schools were almost identical. The Italians were listed under the Roman, Florentine, Venetian, Lombard, and Genoese schools (in the Albertina the last two were combined), a procedure that undoubtedly goes back to Bartsch's scholarly system. It is, therefore, hardly surprising that at the auction a large part of de Ligne's drawings passed into the possession of Duke Albert[14]).

In the absence of any documentary evidence one can only indirectly arrive at the sources the Duke drew upon. The previous owners can for the most part be identified by the collectors'

[11]) See Alfred Stix, Pariser Briefe des Adam Bartsch, Festschrift für M. J. Friedländer, Leipzig, 1927, p. 312 ff.

[12]) For the drawings by Claude, there are fairly full indications of provenance: Bernard, Brochant, Crozat, Destouches, De Gouvernet, Joubert, Le Brun, Cardinal Lugné, Mariette, Maurice, Nourré, Sabran.

For the provenance of the drawings by Raphael, the following collections are recorded: Timoteo Viti, Cardinal Santa Croce, Crozat, Mariette, Marquis de Gouvernet, Julien de Parme, d'Argenville, Picart, Destouches, and others. The composition of "Alexander and Roxana" in the nude (red chalk, Cat. III, 118) is traced through the successive ownership of Rubens, Cardinal Bentivoglio, Claude Mellan, Vanrose, and Crozat.

[13]) Catalogue raisonné des dessins originaux des plus grands maîtres anciens et modernes, qui faisoient partie du cabinet de feu le Prince Charles de Ligne . . . par Adam Bartsch, garde d'estampes à la Bibliothèque I. et R . . . Vienna, A. Blumauer, 1794.

[14]) The writer has attempted to make a partial reconstruction of the de Ligne collection from the Albertina and other collections, on the basis of Bartsch's catalogue. See O. Benesch, Die Handzeichnungensammlung des Fürsten von Ligne: Die Graphischen Künste, LVI, Vienna, 1933, Mitteilungen pp. 31 – 35.

marks, or by notations on the drawings themselves. The drawings were originally kept between the pages of portfolios, but in 1822, after the Duke's death, they were unfortunately all pasted onto cardboard by Lefevre so that one can no longer examine the watermarks or the informative notes on the backs of the drawings. Only in rare instances were the notes transferred to the cardboard mount (for example, No. 47). An inscription on a drawing by Fragonard (No. 223) states that it comes from the "Cabinet de M. De Levi." On the back of the mount of "The Bull" (No. 222), there is an inscription noting that it comes from the "Cabinet Puisegur."

Another source of information is provided by the old sales catalogues, which make it fairly easy for a good connoisseur of the Albertina collection to identify drawings from earlier collections. The collections of Crozat, Mariette, and d'Argenville, as well as that of Julien de Parme, emerge therefrom as the principal sources. By and large, they are the same collections which Bartsch cites as sources in the preface to the de Ligne catalogue. Bartsch was already aware that some of de Ligne's sheets came from the earliest systematically classified collection of drawings, that is, from Vasari's five-volume "Libro de' Disegni." In his survey of the drawings that can still be identified as coming from the "Libro," O. Kurz mentions eight mounted sheets in the Albertina that are recognizable as formerly belonging to Vasari by means of their decorative surrounds[15]). They reached the Duke by way of the Crozat, Mariette, Julien de Parme, and Fries collections. Among them are sheets by Carpaccio, Liberale da Verona (No. 11), and Leonardo.

The Duke's great activity as a collector during his years in Brussels is all the more admirable when one considers that it was crowded into a life that had become unsettled and full of anxiety because of political confusion and war, a life so very different from the idyllic days in Pressburg. Joseph II's radical reforms in Belgium had turned the country into a hotbed of discontent, culminating in open revolt. At the end of the year 1789, the Governor and his wife had to flee while the "United States of Belgium" were constituted. They stayed in the Rhineland as guests of Marie Christine's brother, Prince-Bishop Maximilian of Cologne. In spite of the troubled times, Albert was able to enjoy the treasures of the Düsseldorf Gallery. The death of Emperor Joseph II in 1790 and the succession of Leopold II, the former Regent of Tuscany, a ruler who was as conciliatory as he was enlightened, brought about a turn for the better.

The restoration of the estates of the realm led to the temporary collapse of the independence movement. The Governors returned to Brussels, but only for a short time. The Revolution in France broke loose and its armies advanced on the Austrian Netherlands. Following the disastrous battle of Jemappes in 1792, Albert and Marie Christine left Brussels for good. It was only with considerable losses that the Duke was able to bring his art treasures to safety. A shipload consigned to Hamburg sank off the Dutch coast[16]). The next few years were a time of instability, spent mainly in Münster, Vienna, and Dresden. In 1794, Albert was appointed Supreme Commander of the Allied Forces against the advancing French; meanwhile, Marie Christine sojourned at Schwetzingen and Heidelberg. The lack of unity among the Allies precluded any hope of military success, and, when the Austrian Netherlands were finally lost, the Duke in a mood of profound resignation laid down his command in 1795. The only ray of sunshine during these

---

[15]) Giorgio Vasari's "Libro de' Disegni," Old Master Drawings, 45 (June, 1937), 47 (December, 1937).

[16]) The cargo included twelve cases of books, two cases of drawings and prints, a case of paintings, also some pieces of sculpture, coins, and valuable furniture.

years was the growing fame of their adopted son, Archduke Carl (the son of the Emperor Leopold II, who had died in 1792), who proved himself a brilliant military commander.

In 1795 the ducal pair took up permanent residence in Vienna. The Emperor Francis II, who in the meantime had succeeded to the throne of Austria, assigned them as residence the Palais Sylva-Tarouca, which stretched eastward from the Imperial Library and the Augustinian monastery on the Kärntnerbastei. This baroque palace had originally been acquired by Maria Theresa, and the Duke had lived there as a bachelor during his stay in Vienna. The Imperial Office of Works occupied part of the building, and Minister Hatzfeld and some members of the imperial household also had quarters there. The project of moving the print collection of the Imperial Library to this compound of buildings had first been considered as early as 1787[17]). By this time the collection, augmented extensively by the acquisition of Prince Eugene's collection in 1737, had grown to 250,000 sheets in 717 cartons, albums, and portfolios with an estimated value of more than a half million florins. The proposal to transfer the collection was submitted by the Prefect Freiherr van Swieten – no doubt at Bartsch's instigation – and was approved orally by Emperor Joseph II. In 1795, the ducal pair established their residential and ceremonial apartments in the palace. For their collection and library they rented and adapted the top floor of the adjacent Augustinian monastery, which by breaking down the partitions between the former monks' cells was converted into a single long room, the home of the "Old Albertina" and the heart of the present one, which is still preserved in its original form under the protection of the Monuments Commission.

Having now retired from all military and political affairs, Albert devoted himself first and foremost to his collections. In 1796, he made the most important acquisition of his career as a collector: the drawings from the Hapsburg imperial and private collections, famous for an incomparable block of sheets by Dürer.

Without the benefit of scholary method as it developed in the eighteenth century, here was a highly important collection of drawings assembled as imperial property through the enthusiasm of individual princes and through occasional acquisitions. Its origin goes back to the passionate collecting zeal of the Emperor Rudolf II. The Emperor's favorite artist was Dürer, and he would make any sacrifice to acquire Dürer's works.

One of the famous collections the Emperor was interested in was that acquired from the Dürer family by Willibald Imhoff at Nuremberg. After Imhoff's death the Emporer entered into negotiations with his widow and sons, offering them the domain of Petschau in Bohemia in payment. The correspondence (1588) was accompanied by a number of detailed lists[18]). In addition to paintings and prints, the collection included a great number of drawings[19]). Many of them can be identified with drawings in the Albertina and in other collections like the Print Room in Berlin, for example, the early "Self-Portrait" (No. 68), the portraits of Dürer's wife, his mother, his brother Andreas, and the Emperor Maximilian, the "Hare" (No. V), the "Violet," the "Old Man of Antwerp" (No. 71), the "Nuremberg Women in Costume," the "Imperial Triumphal

---

[17]) Haus-, Hof- und Staatsarchiv O. Me. A., S. R. 372.

[18]) Reprinted in Joseph Heller, Das Leben und die Werke Albrecht Dürers, Vol. 2, Leipzig, 1831, p. 71 ff.

[19]) A "Buch" with "Dessins von Albrecht Dürer und andern guten Meistern," and another containing drawings by Dürer (numbered 37 to 130, with titles, among them the most famous ones) are mentioned in these lists.

Chariot," and many others. The Emperor's negotiations with the Imhoff family obviously were crowned with success.

Another of Rudolf's great Dürer acquisitions was the collection of Cardinal Granvella[20]). On the Cardinal's death on September 21, 1586, Rudolf instructed the imperial ambassador in Spain, Count Khevenhüller, to take steps to acquire the collection. From December 13, 1586 onward, the correspondence mentions a volume containing around two hundred fifty drawings by Dürer. By July, 1587, Khevenhüller had the volume in hand and held the first option to purchase it. On September 21, the Emperor wrote that he "was now as eager as ever to have the deceased Cardinal Granvella's book of drawings by Durrer [sic]." We know from the list of Dürer drawings in the imperial collection that in this case also the Emperor was successful.

At first this treasure trove of drawings was probably kept in Prague, but after Rudolf's death it found its way to the Kunstkammer in Vienna, where Ferdinand III is known to have himself shown it to Joachim von Sandrart during the latter's visit to Vienna. Sandrart mentions the "Green Passion" and sketches from the Netherlandish sketchbook (of which only the one with Charles V's lion remains in the Albertina).

The collection was eventually deposited in the Schatzkammer, from which it was transferred to the Imperial Library in 1783. By this time it had grown to eleven folio volumes, two of which contained 371 drawings by Dürer. Another volume contained 111 drawings by Hoefnagel, Bruegel, and others, and there was also a volume of 100 drawings by Stradanus. Moreover, there are cited without specific names 361 drawings from the "best and famous old masters," 125 drawings by "miscellaneous masters," and 379 "lesser" and "ordinary" drawings. In short, the drawings were carefully separated according to their quality, and there was an obvious awareness of the importance of the collection. But some drawings had found their way to the imperial collection even before the transfer from the Schatzkammer. Between 1765 and 1787, the Imperial Library had amassed from various other sources a further "9,000 engravings and drawings," in addition to the *Atlas Stosch* with its large collection of architectural drawings, particularly by Borromini, which was acquired in 1769.

In 1796 Duke Albert proposed to the Prefect of the Imperial Library, Gottfried van Swieten, "to exchange some of the drawings in the Imperial Library for engravings." In a report to the Lord Chief Steward, Van Swieten recommended the exchange on the ground that the imperial collection of drawings had neither a complete set of masters nor even any particular value. In view of the collection's renown, the latter reason sounds so absurd that it cannot have been advanced in good faith. Even if the Duke's collection of prints was superior to the Emperor's, the difference cannot possibly have been equal to the value of the whole Dürer collection. We have no list of what the Duke was offering in exchange, but it is hardly likely that he would dispose of important prints of which he had only a single impression. Although Bartsch's main interest was prints, he was too experienced a connoisseur of drawings not to be aware that the deal represented a very poor bargain for the Emperor. It seems more probable that the Emperor

---

[20]) Ludwig Urlichs, Beiträge zur Geschichte der Kunstbestrebungen und Sammlungen Kaiser Rudolfs II, 3. Die Sammlung Granvella, Zeitschrift für Bildende Kunst, 5, 1870, pp. 136, 137.

Urkunden und Regesten aus dem K. und K. Haus-, Hof- und Staats-Archiv Nos. 9465, 9485, 9509, 9514 (Jahrbuch der Kunsthistorischen Sammlungen des Allerhöchsten Kaiserhauses, Vol. XIII).

Francis II was anxious to make some seigneurial gesture of compensation to the Duke for all his severe disappointments in his military and political career, including the loss of part of his collection. At all events the exchange was duly effected, and officially approved and confirmed on July 8, 1796.

The Albertina had made an acquisition of incalculable value. From the time of Duke Albert there date two handwritten catalogues ("Cahiers"), an earlier one which remained unchanged, and a later one, which was brought up to date by Duke Albert's successors. The earlier one prefaces the Dürer collection with the words "Oeuvres d'Albert Dürer. Cette Suite vraiment unique ainsi que tout ce qui se trouvera ci-après de Desseins d'Albert Dürer, vient à quelque peu de Pièces de la Bibliothèque Impériale et Royale," and goes on to list 136 original sheets and eight copies.

From the same source come some of the early German drawings such as "The Martyrdom of St. Ursula" by Schongauer (No. 67). On the "Bathsheba at her Bath" (Albertina Cat. II, 63) by an Antwerp master of the Bles group, the catalogue remarks: "Ce Dessin ainsi que la plus grande partie de ceux des Maîtres allemands qui le suivent, viennent de la Collection Impériale et Royale."

We also know that it was from the same source that the Duke acquired his finest Rembrandt drawings. A separate folder contained in the "Cahiers" referred to above bears the inscription: "Dessins de Rembrandt provenant de la Bibliothèque Impériale" and lists twenty-six drawings, among them some of the finest in the whole collection[21]). The Rembrandt drawings seem not to have come from the volumes that were transferred from the Schatzkammer in 1783, but were probably by that time already in the Library, along with a number of Italian drawings. Bartsch made etchings of some of them, not only of works by Rembrandt himself but of his school as well, which were all lumped together under the name "Rembrandt," including the "Woman at her Spinning-Wheel" by Nicolaes Maes (No. 180). On his etching of 1782 after this drawing, Bartsch gave the provenance as the Imperial Library. This was a year before the collection was transferred there from the Schatzkammer. How did these drawings find their way into the Emperor's possession? Their outstanding quality points to an informed collector. As a mere assumption, it might be suggested that they formed a supplement to Prince Eugene's collection of engravings, which he started in London as early as 1712, years before P. J. Mariette classified it.

Whether the imperial collection of drawings was handed over to the Duke *in extenso* we do not know. The Duke certainly received the greater part of it. The entail inventory dated May 5, 1822, lists 238 drawings by Dürer. This inventory, together with the catalogue, was still in existence in 1920, but then disappeared[22]), so that once again the history of the collection is

---

[21]) They included the "Young woman at her Toilet" (No. XVII), the two drawings of elephants (No. 170), the "Beggar Family with Dog" (No. 173), the copy after Lastman's "Joseph Distributing Corn in Egypt" (Benesch 446), "Nicodemus with Christ" (Benesch 889), "The Holy Family" (Benesch 888), the "Cottages Before a Stormy Sky" (Benesch 800), and the landscapes in black chalk from the sketchbooks (Benesch 805–808, 1275, 1277, 1280 and 1281).

[22]) "In 1920 the original inventories of the Duke Albert of Sachsen-Teschen entail kept among the documents of the family archives, together with the catalogue of the Albertina forming a separate section, were taken from the *Staatsamt für Inneres und Unterricht* (The Ministry of Education), where they were lost" (L. Bittner, Inventar des Haus-, Hof- und Staatsarchivs, Vienna, 1937, Vol. 2, p. 7).

An inventory of the Duke Albert entail made by Rechberger, which is in the Albertina's possession, lists only 158 drawings by Dürer (including copies and works of his "school"). They are all identifiable in the present collection.

shrouded in mystery. The discrepancy between the number of Dürer drawings contained in the volumes of Emperor Rudolf II. and those in the Albertina (Meder estimates 145, Winkler "about 150") is disquietingly large. "Losses," reports of which go back a hundred years, may be attributed partly to war conditions, partly to misappropriations by employees of the Court. The "dessinateur" Lefevre, a mediocre watercolorist whom the Duke had employed earlier in Brussels, seems to have played a particularly dubious role in this connection. Schönbrunner already states that out of the mass of Dürer drawings a selection was made in accordance with the taste of the times, and that the rest was disposed of. In view of the fairness, correctness, and devotion of a character like the Duke's, the present writer regards such a procedure as unlikely. Even if the Duke had declined to take all of them, he would never have hawked around possessions from a source as sacred as the imperial family. He made, of course, occasional gifts to friends[23]), but how highly Albert prized the imperial collection is attested by the older of the two "Cahiers."

It is possible that some of the drawings were left in the Library. In 1809, Vienna was occupied by Napoleon, and on June 11th of that year, the French Governor-General Andreossy, in Napoleon's name, ordered Bartsch to place certain items, to be specified, at the disposal of the Director-General of the Museums of France, Vivant Denon. The simultaneous order to Denon included virtually the entire collection of prints. Although there is no definite mention of drawings, it is quite possible that they, too, fell victim to this general requisition. In 1815, Austria re-claimed and recovered from Paris five cases of prints and codices. How much disappeared into the portfolios of the authorities can be estimated when one realizes that after his Viennese mission Andreossy emerged as a collector of drawings in the grand style. Most of the hundred Dürer drawings in the Sir Thomas Lawrence collection came from Andreossy[24]), and some of them, including Dürer's famous portrait of his mother, now in Berlin, are identifiable as coming from the imperial collection. Hausmann in his Dürer catalogue already referred to the activities of this plunderer. The drawings from Dürer's Netherlandish sketchbook in the Bonnat collection at Bayonne came from Vivant Denon; Sandrart had seen them in the Emperor's collection.

Of the 238 Dürer drawings of the ducal entail, nearly one hundred are no longer in the Albertina. After the Duke's death in 1822 a great number of Dürer drawings were sold by Lefevre to a Viennese dealer named Grünling, who in turn sold them to the print cabinets in Bremen and Hamburg[25]). It is quite possible that after the Duke's death there were irregularities in connection with the entail, since Archduke Carl did not share his uncle's passion for col-lecting[26]). Albert, on the contrary, sought to augment his collection of Dürer drawings up to

---

[23]) Count de la Gardie of Borrestad, Skåne, Sweden, owns some drawings which Duke Albert presented to his friend the Swedish Ambassador, a De la Gardie, on his departure from Vienna. Among them is Rembrandt's study for the Portrait of Sylvius (Benesch 762a), which Duke Albert had acquired from the Prince de Ligne's collection.

[24]) Frits Lugt, Les Marques de Collections de dessins et d'estampes, Amsterdam, 1921, p. 456.

[25]) See J. Meder, Die Handzeichnung, ihre Technik und Entwicklung, Vienna, 1919, p. 646. In a letter dated August 22, 1827, Grünling offered 77 drawings by Dürer for which he could tender purchase certificates signed by Lefevre.

[26]) On pages XV – XVII of the first volume of his Dürer corpus, Friedrich Winkler presents a rather pessimistic picture, maintaining that practically all the great nineteenth century collections of Dürer drawings, especially that in the "Kunsthalle" in Bremen, were indebted to the dispersed imperial collection. Similar views are held by E. and H. Tietze in the preface to Vol. IV of the Albertina Catalogue, pp. VII and VIII, and by Anton Reichel, Zur Geschichte der Dürer-Zeichnungen in der Albertina, Fest-schrift für Josef Strzygowsky, Klagenfurt, 1932.

the day of his death. In the "Cahier," the charming study of Dürer's bride, "Mein Agnes," was annotated "du dernier achat du Duc."

In 1798, Albert's beloved wife Marie Christine died, and he honored her memory with Canova's impressive tomb in the Augustinian church in Vienna. From then on he devoted himself exclusively to the care and expansion of his collection, spending between 1783 and his death in 1822 no less than 1,265,992 florins. The Dresden collector W. G. Becker had amassed in Italy an exceedingly rich collection of Italian drawings, and this the Duke acquired *in toto*[27]). In 1820 Count Moriz von Fries, embarrassed by financial difficulties, began to dispose of his collection, and again the Duke succeeded in obtaining many of the finest items, including drawings by Dürer; a number of the drawings in the Albertina are marked with the Maltese cross, which was the collector's mark of Count von Fries (Lugt 2903). Reports of the Duke's enthusiasm for his collection, to which he devoted practically all his waking hours, were transmitted like legends from mouth to mouth, from generation to generation. In 1801, he had his palace rebuilt in the neoclassical style (illustration on page 29) by the Netherlandish architect Montoyer, who had earlier constructed the palace of Laeken near Brussels, but the collection itself remained in its original modest quarters.

Duke Albert von Sachsen-Teschen died on February 10, 1822. His heir, Archduke Carl, inherited the collection, which by now amounted to about 15,000 drawings and 166,000 prints. In the following years there ensued the shady episode involving Lefevre, who was replaced in 1827 by Franz Rechberger, the former curator of the collection of Count von Fries. Rechberger was a practicing artist who, like Bartsch, had become an expert connoisseur through practical museum experience. Activity was now concentrated on the arrangement and systematic classification of the collection. Few drawings of importance were added to the collection; a list of new acquisitions included names of Netherlandish artists like Heemskerck, Crispin van den Broeck, Jan Brueghel, Soutman, and Saftleven. The acquisitions for the print collection were more important (the Italian *chiaroscuri* of the Fries collection). In Albert's lifetime the collection had only been shown to a privileged few; now it was enjoyed by a wider public. On Carl's death in 1847 the collection passed to his elder son, Archduke Albrecht. The acquisition of new drawings remained within the modest limits set by Carl, although more Italian and German works of an earlier date began to make their appearance (Dürer, Cat. IV, 115; Baldung, heraldic designs for stained glass; the Master of the Coburg Roundels; Campagnola). The most important addition was the sketchbook of Stefano della Bella. Attention was chiefly concentrated on nineteenth-century Austrian artists. In 1873, the year of the World's Fair, the rooms in which the collection was housed took on the appearance still remembered by visitors to the "Old Albertina." At the same time the name "Albertina" came into use. It was now a museum, open to the public at large, and with changing exhibitions of its holdings. Now, too, began its important role in art education. The Dürer specialist Moriz von Thausing, Professor of History of Art at the University of Vienna and the teacher of Franz Wickhoff, was the first of a series of directors of the Albertina who were at the same time scholars by profession.

---

[27]) Lugt, op. cit., pp. 30 and 58; Supplément, The Hague, 1956, p. 410.

On Albrecht's death in 1895, the collection passed to his nephew, Archduke Friedrich. His era was distinguished by the activities of Joseph Meder, the pioneering scholar and connoisseur in the field of drawings. With relatively modest resources, the collection was systematically enlarged by a number of important acquisitions, including a Dürer drawing (Winkler 434). Unfortunately Meder's acquisitions, apart from what Stix re-purchased, were lost to the collection because, since they were not included in the entail, they were returned to their owner when the collection became state property in 1920.

After the Albertina was nationalized, there followed the gigantic task of amalgamating its collection with that of the Print Room of the National (formerly Imperial) Library, an idea first put forward by Hans Tietze in his capacity as adviser to the fine arts section of the government. The result was a collection which in size, completeness, and importance surpasses any other graphic collection in the world. The whole of Albert's lovely old palace was used to house the new enlarged "Albertina." The collection of prints was brought to a unique degree of completeness while the duplicates yielded an acquisitions fund of almost unparalleled amplitude. The sale of the duplicates was begun by Joseph Meder and largely carried out by Alfred Stix; it was completed by the present writer whenever commercially justifiable. By the end of these brilliant decades of acquisitions the collection had attained its present wealth of over 34,000 catalogued drawings. Furthermore, an important collection of nineteenth- and twentieth-century prints was formed, including Julius Hofmann's collection of Goyas and Lessing's Menzel collection. The most extensive and important acquisitions were made while A. Stix was director (1923 – 1934), comprising, for example, the early Italian collection of Luigi Grassi acquired through the good offices of F. Lugt, with works by Ghiberti (No. 4), Stefano da Verona (No. 2), Pisanello (No. 3), and Paolo Veronese (No. 39); the collection of Dürer drawings (mostly studies of hands and drapery for master works like the "Feast of the Rose Garlands") which are presumed to have come from the dispersed imperial collection; the Count Salm collection of drawings, with works by Cranach (No. VIII), and Wolf Huber (No. 91); and a great many Italian and Austrian Baroque works, among them entire blocks of drawings by Volterrano (No. 51), Maulbertsch (Nos. 117 and 118), and M. J. Schmidt (No. 116). The collection of nineteenth-century drawings was systematically built up, from the German Romantics to Menzel, Leibl, and Marées. Simon Meller assisted in the accumulation of a representative collection of French drawings, from Delacroix to Cézanne, while the main trends of the twentieth century, Fauvism, Cubism, and Expressionism (with special emphasis on Austrian artists like Klimt), are also richly represented.

It should be stressed that during the era of the three "connoisseur directors" mentioned above, many important acquisitions were due to prompt action and to the purchase on favorable terms of unrecognized masterpieces (for instance, the Rembrandt No. 172), which, by increasing the value of the Museum many times over, also made a substantial contribution to the national wealth.

In addition to purchases, the Albertina has benefited from legacies. Dr. Oswald Kutschera-Woborsky, a pupil of Wickhoff and an eminent connoisseur of the Venetian Baroque, left the Albertina his important collection of Italian drawings.

From 1934 to 1938, the Albertina came under the supervision of the Director of the National Library, and it was during these years that the extensive collection of Austrian Baroque drawings was acquired from the firm of Artaria.

The years of the National Socialist regime from 1938 to 1945 were as inglorious in the history of the Albertina as in that of the other Vienna museums. The new authorities ordered the removal of all Expressionist works of art, which for the German museums meant decimation, but in Vienna the execution of the decree was averted by the deliberate procrastination of the Austrian authorities. The only enrichment resulted from transfer from the Österreichische Galerie of nineteenth- and twentieth-century drawings and watercolors, as well as of a choice selection of portrait miniatures, particularly works by Füger. The collection itself suffered no war damage, but a considerable part of the old palace was destroyed by bombing.

In 1947 the laborious task of reconstruction began. The writer was director of the Albertina from 1947 to 1961, and during the first years it was work under the most difficult circumstances imaginable. Wars invariably lead to considerable shifting of property. The writer took advantage of this situation as had his predecessor Stix in the past. Among the many important additions were works by Altdorfer (No. IX), Huber, and other masters of the Danube school (No. 88) from the dispersed Liechtenstein collection; drawings by Strigel (No. 77) and Burgkmair (Nos. 78 and 79) from monastic holdings; and designs for church windows by Jan de Beer (No. 126a and b) from the Ritter von Gutmann collection. For the first time an original drawing by Hans Holbein the Younger (No. 94) found its way to the Albertina, and the collection of Rembrandts was increased by three. Although the Albertina could no longer count on the ample funds provided by the sale of duplicates that the Stix era had enjoyed, a number of important acquisitions were made in many fields, notably in the art of the Romantic period, as represented by the considerable Rudolf Alt collection, and in the field of Expressionism in the assembling of a comprehensive collection of drawings and watercolors by Egon Schiele and by acquisition of the Alfred Kubin Foundation.

Such in broad outline has been the history of the Albertina's collection of drawings. In details of secondary importance it could be expanded at will, but of further basic facts there is no documentary evidence whatsoever[28]). The collection has preserved the stamp of its founder: universality and quality, irrespective of period. Its most successful directors have been and will continue to be those who embody the qualities of its founder: a passionate love of the field, tireless industry in research, a comprehensive knowledge of the whole domain, and an unerring feeling for quality in works of art of all schools and periods.

*The collector's mark
of Duke Albert von Sachsen-Teschen
(enlarged).*

---

[28]) Some informative documents are published in the Appendix.

The collection of old master drawings in the Albertina attracted critical research at a relatively early date. In the second part of his work "Die vornehmsten Kunstdenkmäler in Wien" (1866), G. F. Waagen devoted considerable space (pp. 124–197) to the Albertina, commenting on the drawings one by one in the order of the portfolios.

The first complete critical catalogue of the Italian drawings was published by Franz Wickhoff in 1891 and 1892 (see Bibliography), and is the only one in existence. In his sound comment this great scholar arrived at the correct attribution of many of the drawings or pointed the way to it. Wickhoff maintained that the study of drawings was especially important for the development of Giovanni Morelli's objective method of identification of works of art, and he systematically encouraged its use in his teaching. His Albertina catalogue is, as it were, a model of this method.

All distinguished connoisseurs in the field have studied the drawings in the Albertina and passed authoritative judgments upon them. As in many old collections, their opinions are frequently found in the form of short notes in their own handwriting on the front or reverse of the mount; these are veritable mines of information and belong to the collection's historical cachet. There are notes by connoisseurs such as Morelli, Rooses, Bredius, Hofstede de Groot, Meder, and Glück, and by more recent connoisseurs such as Lugt, Parker, Hind, Burchard, Schilling, Byam Shaw, Winkler, Van Regteren Altena, and Morassi, who all have contributed scholary clarifications.

The activity of Joseph Meder, who through constant work with the material became a profound connoisseur, was of the greatest importance for the collection. Having begun his career as a student of German language and literature, he had, like his predecessors Bartsch and Rechberger, attained through practical experience the stature of a scholar and museum man whose activity was of fundamental significance in the field. Between 1895 and 1908, he published the series "Handzeichnungen alter Meister," which in twelve volumes made known the riches not only of the Albertina but also of all other important European collections[29]). This was the first publication of its kind devoted to drawings and served as a model for later publications such as those of the Vasari Society and the Prestel-Gesellschaft. It served not only as an instrument of research, which even today has not lost its importance, but also helped to kindle an interest and delight in old master drawings among the wider public.

Another publication that took shape during Meder's years at the Albertina was his historical and systematic work entitled "Die Handzeichnung, ihre Technik und Entwicklung," which first appeared in 1919 and which is still the standard work on the subject, indispensable to critical research dealing with technical and historical problems.

A series that made a substantial contribution towards familiarizing the public with the Albertina's drawings was the series of "Albertina Facsimiles," which Meder began to publish in 1922. The early editions, which were issued under Meder's personal supervision, represent a model of painstaking reproduction. The reproductions, which were also available individually,

---

[29]) There was to have been a sequel entitled "Neue Folge," but only two volumes were issued.

found their way to all parts of the globe and made the Albertina more widely known than almost any other collection in the world.

Under Meder's successor Alfred Stix, the project of a critical catalogue of the whole collection was begun, the first volume appearing in 1926. Stix himself dealt with the Italian drawings in collaboration with Lili Fröhlich-Bum. He followed a principle generally adopted at that time for the re-arrangement of painting collections: the separation of the material into one collection for exhibition purposes and into another for study only.

All drawings that were deemed to be of the highest quality, especially characteristic of the artist, or of unusual visual appeal were assembled in the "Erste Garnitur," which was systematically re-arranged according to styles and period, and listed in the new catalogue. This novel method of classification represented a complete departure from the alphabetical system adopted by most other collections, and was suggested by the old Albertina system of classification based on the artists' dates of birth. It has the advantage of presenting the collection as a lively illustration of the historical scene. It also has resulted in a reappraisal of many drawings, and a more precise classification. But the division into "Erste und Zweite Garnitur" was often arbitrary and subjective, and led to the neglect of many classifiable and even important master drawings which, together with inferior copies and mediocre works, were relegated to the "Zweite Garnitur"[30]).

The authors of the catalogue volumes devoted to the Northern Schools (see Bibliography) avoided such a separation on the basis of personal taste and relegated to the "Zweite Garnitur" only truly inferior material and outspoken copies. The surprising result was that the "Zweite Garnitur" dwindled to a minimum, a proof of how unerring Duke Albert's judgment had been in constantly subjecting his collection to rigorous sifting[31]). Only in the case of his contemporaries, the "petits maîtres" of the eighteenth century, did he display more leniency, and even their acceptance was very often due to the interest in subject matter, especially in the case of some of the vedutists.

Simultaneously with the re-studying of the drawings of the Albertina, a critical reappraisal of its comprehensive collection of architectural drawings was undertaken. Its core was the famous Atlas Stosch with Roman architectural drawings acquired in 1769 for the Imperial Library by Freiherr Gerard van Swieten. The work was begun[32]) by Hermann Egger and continued by Dagobert Frey[33]) and Oswald Kutschera-Woborsky. The collection had subsequently been

---

[30]) Subsequently this procedure was rejected by scholary opinion. See W. Vitzthum, Seicento Drawings at the Cabinet des Dessins, Burlington Magazine CII (1960), p. 75: "Disregarding Wickhoff means that the part of the Albertina which the compilers of the modern catalogue very erratically classed as 'Zweite Garnitur' and which they completely omitted from their volumes will sink even deeper into neglect . . . That an investigation of Mariette would have to take this situation into account may be pointed out in passing: a considerable number of his drawings at the Albertina unjustifiably found their way into the 'Zweite Garnitur' . . ."

   The exhibition of Venetian drawings which the writer, in collaboration with Konrad Oberhuber, organized at the Fondazione Cini, Venice, in 1961, included a number of masterpieces from the "Zweite Garnitur." The Albertina's Parmigianino Exhibition of 1963, which was organized and catalogued by Oberhuber, showed that more than twenty of the former attributions to Parmigianino are correct, although only one of the drawings had been placed in the "Erste Garnitur" and thus had secured a place in the new catalogue.

[31]) Inferior drawings were discarded or relegated to an appendix entitled "Diverse Schulen."

[32]) Kritisches Verzeichnis der Sammlung architektonischer Handzeichnungen der Hofbibliothek in Wien, Part. I, Vienna, 1903.

[33]) Die Architekturzeichnungen der Kupferstichsammlung der Österr. Nationalbibliothek, Österreichische Kunstbücher 19, Vienna, 1920.

enlarged by a great many designs of northern (including Russian) masters, especially designs for court buildings by the great Austrian Baroque architects which were eventually discussed in a comprehensive handwritten catalogue by Justus Schmidt. The Italian drawings still await cataloguing. The drawings by Borromini were incorporated in Eberhard Hempel's monograph on the artist (1924). A catalogue in the form of a corpus by Heinrich Thelen is ready for publication and excerpts from it have already appeared in the catalogue of the Albertina's Borromini exhibition in Rome in 1959.

The Albertina in its present scope has been the subject of a number of critical catalogues and corpora, ranging from Bartsch's "Peintre Graveur" and Rembrandt catalogue to Meder's catalogue of Dürer's graphic work, and from Lippmann's, Meder's, and Winkler's corpus of Dürer's drawings to the corpus of Rembrandt's drawings by this writer, which, together with his service to the Albertina's incomparable collection, he considers his lifework.

The move into the new premises in 1920 meant that the Albertina now had plenty of room for exhibitions so that the results of scholary research could be presented to the public at large in a readily comprehensible form. Handy and inexpensive catalogues, issued in large editions, contained in compact form not only a general summary of established facts but frequently new scholarly findings as well. During the writer's term as director, exhibitions tended more and more to include loans from other collections, both private and public, especially from abroad. This procedure had the great advantage of making it possible to compare the Albertina's holdings with those of other collections at first hand. From this confrontation came many new scholarly insights so that also in this respect the Albertina has been fulfilling its purpose as a living organism.

Palace of Duke Albert von Sachsen-Teschen (today the Albertina). Watercolor by Jakob Alt. 1816.
Albertina, Vienna

Hans Freiherr von Khevenhüller to Emperor Rudolf II.

El libro de Alberto Durrer, que fue de Granvela, tiene de docientas y cinquanta pituras o por mejor dezir boradores; ariva de su propria mano; los de la arte lo estiman en mucho y essi me dieron de intender, que los herederos de Granvela lo tenian quando en menos en quingentos ducados; yo hasta a hora no les dy de entender, que es para vuestra magestad, porque no lo saben mas. — Madrid den 20 julli 1587.
Haus-, Hof- und Staatsarchiv, Wien, Nr. 9509 (Jahrbuch d. Kunsthistorischen Sammlungen d. Ah. Kh. XII)

Joachim von Sandrart, Academie der Bau-, Bild- und Mahlerey-Künste, Nuremberg, 1675, Chapter III. on Albrecht Dürer.

Ihre Käyserliche Majestät haben in dero Kunstcammer zu Wien eine Taffel nur anderthalb elen hoch, worauf er überaus fleißig die Marterung von 300 Christen gemahlt, imgleichen ein anders Marienbild etwas größer. Auch ein Buch in Quart, darinn der ganze Paßion auf grün Papier mit der Feder gezeichnet und Bleyweiß gehöcht, welches von allen seinen Paßionen für die bäste zu halten. In selbiges Buch habe ich auch gesehen von seiner Hand gezeichnet viele Sachen nach dem Leben gerissen, als die Kirchenthür zu Antorff und Leyden, samt vielen andern zu Utrecht noch befindlichen Gebäuden, welche er alle mit der Feder nachschraffirt, die Ihro Majestät Käyser Ferdinand der dritte höchstlöblichen Angedenkens, mir selbst in diesem Buch gezeigt, worüber ich mich dann billich verwundern und schliessen müssen, daß er in Niderland zu Dienst des Käysers Maximiliani gewesen.

Records of the Administration of the Imperial Library from 1575 up to and including 1825, collected, arranged, and indexed by J. F. Edlen von Mosel, 1829 – 30. Österreichische Nationalbibliothek, Vienna.

1783, 292, IV

Verzeichniß

Deren Manuscripten, und Zeichnungsbücher, so aus der K:K: Schatzkammer in die K:K: Bibliothek übersetzt worden. A. Do. August 1783.

No. 9. Ein grosser Foliant im grün Pergament gebunden, mit 125. Stück Zeichnungen von verschiedenen Meistern.

No. 10. Ein grosser Foliant im grün Pergament gebunden mit 144. Blätter verschiedene geringe Zeichnungen.

No. 11. Ein Foliant im grün Pergament gebunden, in 128. Blättern meistens ordin: Zeichnungen bestehend.

No. 17. Ein Foliant in schwarzen Leder gebunden, mit verschiedenen Zeichnungen von alten besten Meistern. 69. Blätter.

No. 20. Ein Foliant mit weissen Leder gebunden in 186. Blätter meistens origl. Zeichnungen von Albrecht Dürrer.

No. 21. Ein detto, der zweyte Theil, ebenfalls mit Origl. Zeichnungen des Albrecht Dürrer. 185 Blätter.

No. 23. Ein Buch im rothen Atlas gebunden mit 100. Stück Zeichnungen Köpfe und Helm. (Dazu eine Bleistiftnotiz von späterer Hand: „Jac. d Strada Galearum antiqq. cristatarum formae atque imagines Toms. I. s. Miniat. no. 45. Jetzt umgebunden").

No. 24. Ein Foliant im grünen Pergament mit verschiedenen Zeichnungen von besten Meistern 128. Blätter.

No. 25. Ein Detto, Detto mit Zeichnungen theils von Hufnagel, Breugel, und andern Meistern. 111 Blätter.

No. 26. Ein Detto, Deto, verschiedene Zeichnungen von alten berühmten Meistern 164 Blätter.

No. 27. Ein Deto. Verschiedene geringere Zeichnungen 107: Blätter.

The corresponding document found among the Schatzkammer records of the Haus-, Hof- und Staatsarchiv was published by H. Zimmermann in *Jahrbuch der kunsthistorischen Sammlungen d. Ah. Kh. 16* (1895), No. 12658.

1796, VIII

Dem Durchlauchtig-hochgeborenen Herrn Fürsten
von Starhemberg Ritter des goldenen Vliesses,
Großkreuz des Königl: St. Stephansordens, S.K.K.M
wirklichen geheimen Rathe, Conferenzminister,
und obersten Hofmeister.

Euer Fürstliche Gnaden

    Des Herzogs Albert von Sachsen-Teschen Königl: Hoheit haben gegen mich den Wunsch geäußert, von den Handzeichnungen welche sich bey der K.K. Hofbibliothek befinden, einige durch Tausch mit Kupferstichen zu erhalten.

    Da nun einerseits die bey der Bibliothek vorhandenen Zeichnungen weder die für eine ordentliche Sammlung nöthige Folge von berühmten Meistern darbiethen, noch überhaupt genommen einen vorzüglichen Werth haben, und also weder zum Vorzeigen, noch zum Gebrauche dienen können, andererseits aber jede Erwerbung, welche dem bereits ansehnlichen, und herrlichen Vorrathe an Kupferstichen vielen Zuwachs bringt, der Bibliothek und dem Publicum nützlich ist, so könnte meines Erachtens dem Verlangen Sr. Königlichen Hoheit ohne Anstand gewillfahrt werden, worüber ich mir also von Eurer fürstlichen Genaden die Genehmigung erbitte.

Wien den 4ten Julius 1796

Fhr van Swieten

    Seine Majestät haben das Verlangen des Herzogs Albert von Sachsen-Teschen Königl: Hoheit, die in der Hofbibliothek vorfindigen Handzeichnungen gegen Kupferstiche umzutauschen, gnädigst begnehmigt.

    Wovon Sr. röm: kais: apostol: Majtt wirkl: geheimen Rath und Hofbibliothekpräfekten Herrn Gottfried Freyherrn Von Swieten Commandeur des St: Stephansordens auf den Bericht vom 4ten dieses zu dem Ende die Eröffnung gemacht wird, um hienach den Tausch gehörigermaßen zu besorgen.

    Starhemberg

Vom kaiserl: königl: Obersthofmeisteramt.
Wien den 8. July 1796

1809, 1031

    Sa Majesté l'Empereur et Roi ayant chargé Monsieur Denon, Directeur Général des Musées de France de lui presenter le Tableau des objets d'art qui se trouvent à la Bibliothèque du Chateau, et qui méritent d'être choisis et séparés, M. Barch-Garde de la Collection d'Estampes à ladte Bibliothèque voudra bien donner à M. Denon, rigoureusement, tous les renseignemens convenables, et mettre à sa disposition tous les objets qu'il designera. Celle est la volonté expresse de Sa Majesté.

    Vienne le onze Juin 1809

Le Gouverneur Général
f. Andreossy

Haus-, Hof- und Staatsarchiv, Vienna
O Me A
S R. 372
Nr. 15
1787 Vermehrung an Manuscripten, gedruckten Büchern und Kupferstichen

Beilage

Aus derselben zeigen sich dreyerlei merkwürdige Gegenstände und zwar von A° 1765 bis 1787 erhielt die Hofbibliothec theils von denen aufgehobenen Kloster Bibliothecen, Archiven, vorgefundenen Verlassenschaften und Licitationen theils durch außerordentliche Wege, theils durch ihren Fond zur Vermehrung an Manuscripten um 780 Stück, an Diplomen um 5089 St. an gedruckten Büchern um 21000 St. und an Kupferstichen und Handtzeichnungen um mehr dann 9000 Stück.

... endlichen befindet sich allda eine Sammlung von Kupferstichen, welche mehr dann 250000 Blätter enthält dafür gehöret die vorbesagte Einrichtung der schon vorhandenen Kupferwerke, Catalogen von Portraiten, Repertorien über Mahler und Kupferstecher usw.

Von dem Hof Bibliothec Prefecten über obigen Bericht und Beylage. /B Die Anzahl der allda aufbewahrten Kupferstiche beläufft sich auf 250000 Blätter, die in 717 Kartons, Bänden und Portefeuilles enthalten sind, und an Werth eine halbe Million übersteigen. Es wäre wünschenswert, dass solche, wie die Manuscripten und Bücher, einen abgesonderten Ort erhielten zu derselben Unterbringung, die im ersten Stock Werk nächst der Bibliothec anstossende, dermahlen von einem Theil des Hof Bau Amts besetze Zimmer bey etwaiger Veränderung füglich umgewendet werden könnten. wozu S:M. dem Vorgeben nach Ihro dießfallige allergnedigsten Beyfall dem Frh v Swieten darüber mündlich bereits zu äußern geruht haben.

ITALIAN MASTERS

Plates 1–60, I–IV

1 MICHELINO DA BESOZZO

2 STEFANO DA VERONA

3 PISANELLO

4   LORENZO GHIBERTI

5　FRA ANGELICO

8   PIERO DI COSIMO

I   LEONARDO DA VINCI

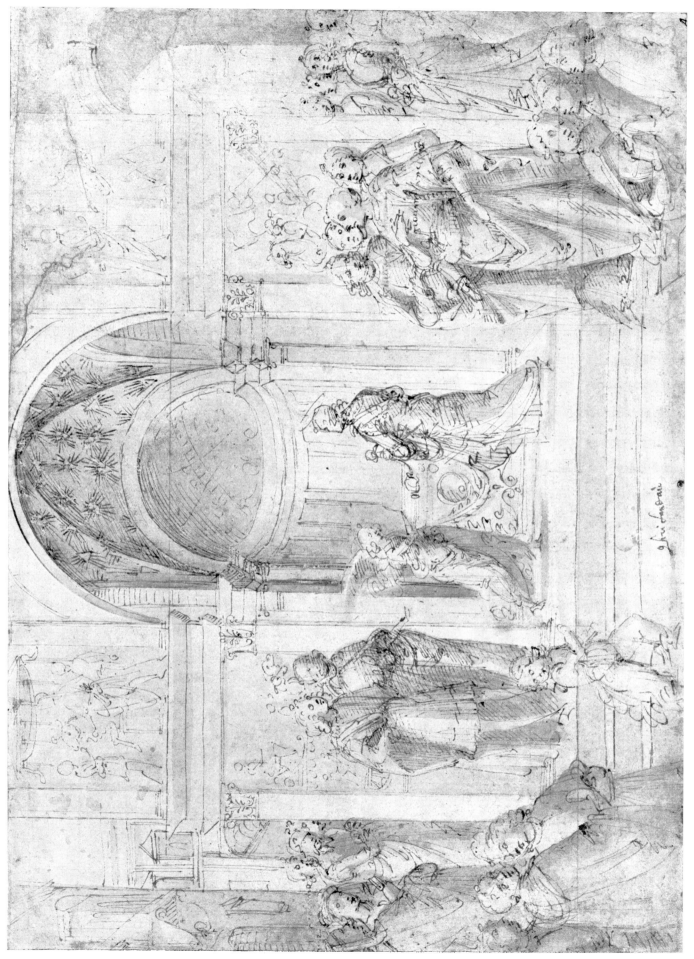

9 DOMENICO GHIRLANDAIO

10 PIETRO PERUGINO

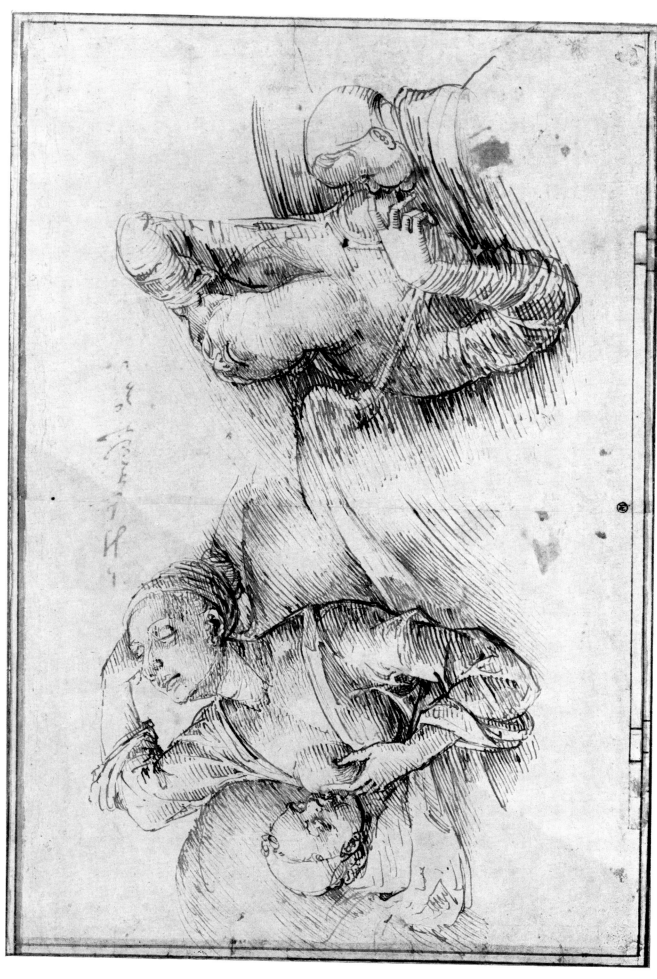

12   ANTONELLO DA MESSINA

13 BARTOLOMEO VENETO

14 LORENZO LOTTO

II BERNARDINO LUINI

15   FRANCESCO FRANCIA

16 GIORGIONE

17 TITIAN

18   GIOVANNI ANTONIO PORDENONE

19 FRA BARTOLOMMEO

20　MICHELANGELO

III MICHELANGELO

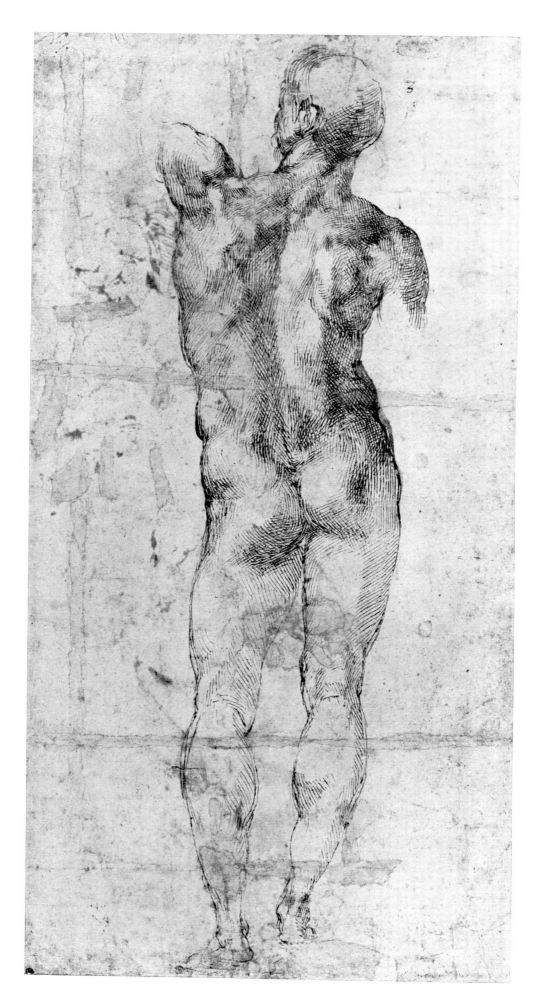

21 MICHELANGELO

22 RAPHAEL

24 RAPHAEL

25   ANDREA DEL SARTO

26   FRANCIABIGIO

27 JACOPO PONTORMO

29 POLIDORO DA CARAVAGGIO

30 PIERINO DEL VAGA

31 CORREGGIO

32   PARMIGIANINO

33   FRANCESCO PRIMATICCIO

34 NICCOLÒ DELL'ABBATE

35 THE MASTER OF THE FLORA

36 LELIO ORSI

La Mater di my e al casso _____ _____ fu lasata della Rei
di S.to gal____ et Anibal fratelli et p____ di d_ medeime

37   JACOPO BASSANO

38 JACOPO TINTORETTO

39 PAOLO VERONESE

41   FEDERICO BAROCCI

42 GIORGIO VASARI

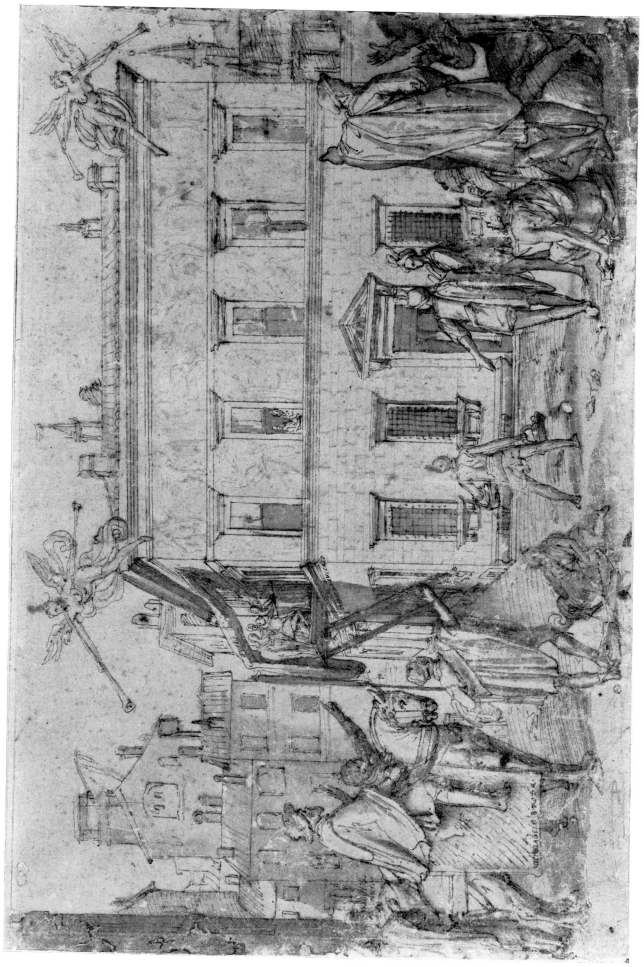

43   FEDERICO ZUCCARI

45 LODOVICO CARRACCI

46　ANNIBALE CARRACCI

47　GIOVANNI LANFRANCO

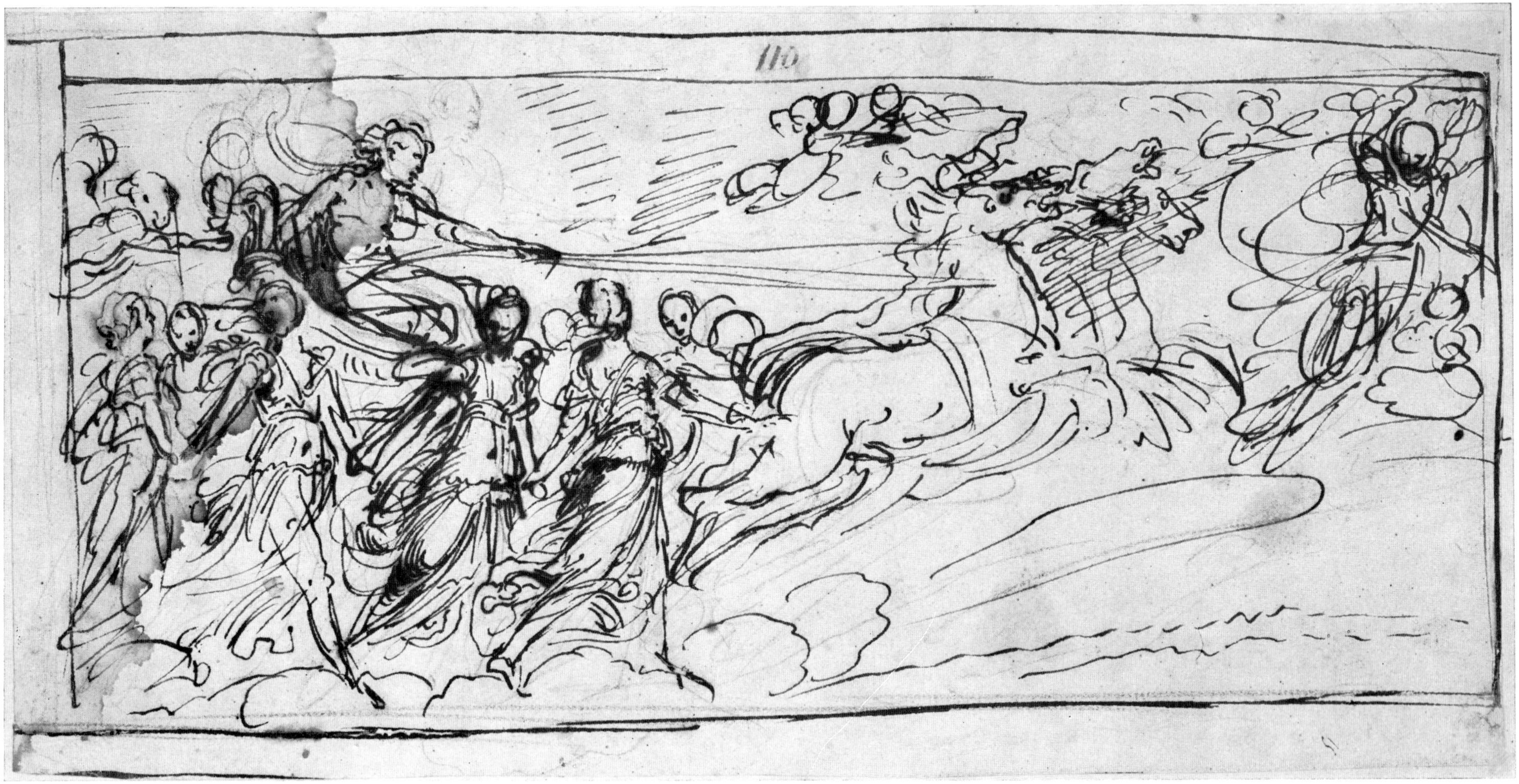

48 GUIDO RENI

49 GUERCINO

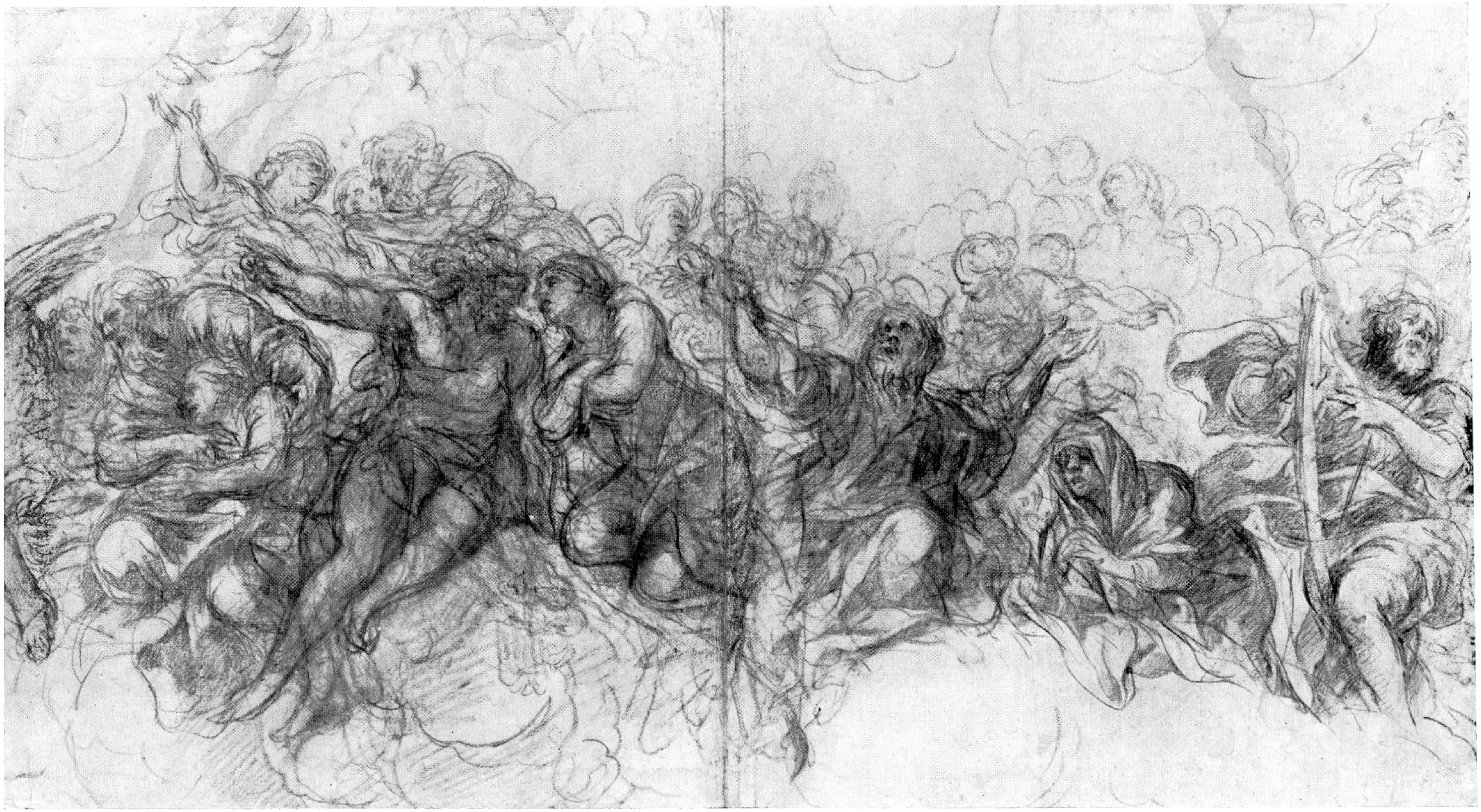

50 PIETRO DA CORTONA

51 BALDASSARE FRANCESCHINI

IV   GIOVANNI BENEDETTO CASTIGLIONE

53 SIMONE CANTARINI

54   FRANCESCO SOLIMENA

io Giò: Batta Piazzetta disegnai di proprio mano
in età d'Anni 52.

A dì 20 Dec.e
1735

55 GIOVANNI BATTISTA PIAZZETTA

56   GIOVANNI BATTISTA TIEPOLO

57   GIOVANNI BATTISTA TIEPOLO

58 CANALETTO

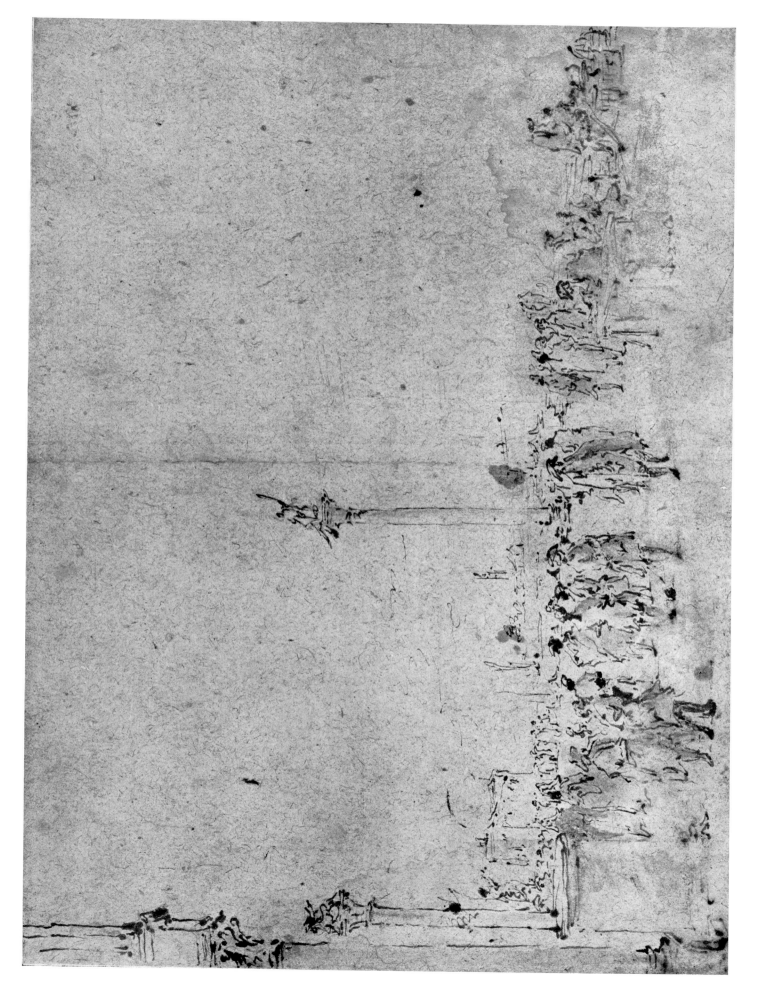

59 FRANCESCO GUARDI

60 GIOVANNI DOMENICO TIEPOLO

GERMAN, AUSTRIAN AND SWISS MASTERS

Plates 61–122, V–XI

61 SCHOOL OF VIENNA ABOUT 1425—30

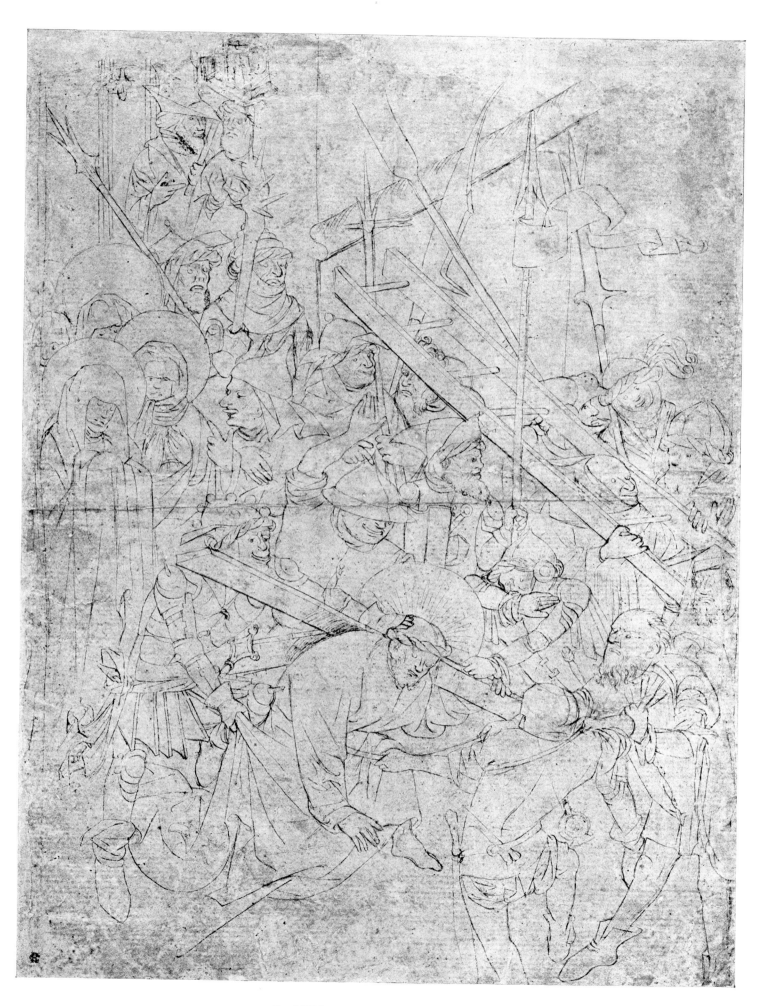

62 SCHOOL OF VIENNA ABOUT 1440

63   ANONYMOUS, SOUTH GERMAN, ABOUT 1445

64   NICOLAUS MAIR VON LANDSHUT

66 ANONYMOUS, SOUTH WEST GERMAN, ABOUT 1440

65 SCHOOL OF STYRIA, BEGINNING OF THE 15TH CENTURY

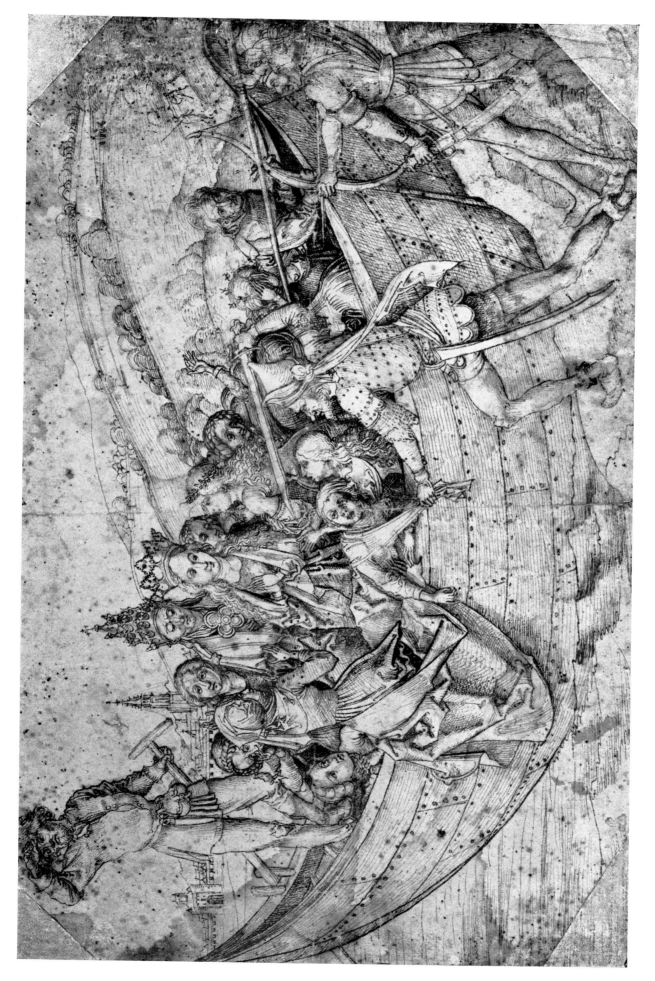

68 ALBRECHT DÜRER

V   ALBRECHT DÜRER

69 ALBRECHT DÜRER

70 ALBRECHT DÜRER

VI   ALBRECHT DÜRER

71   ALBRECHT DÜRER

72 HANS VON KULMBACH

VII HANS VON KULMBACH (CENTRE PIECE, ENLARGED)

73 HANS SEBALD BEHAM

74 HANS BALDUNG GRIEN

75 MATTHIAS GRÜNEWALD

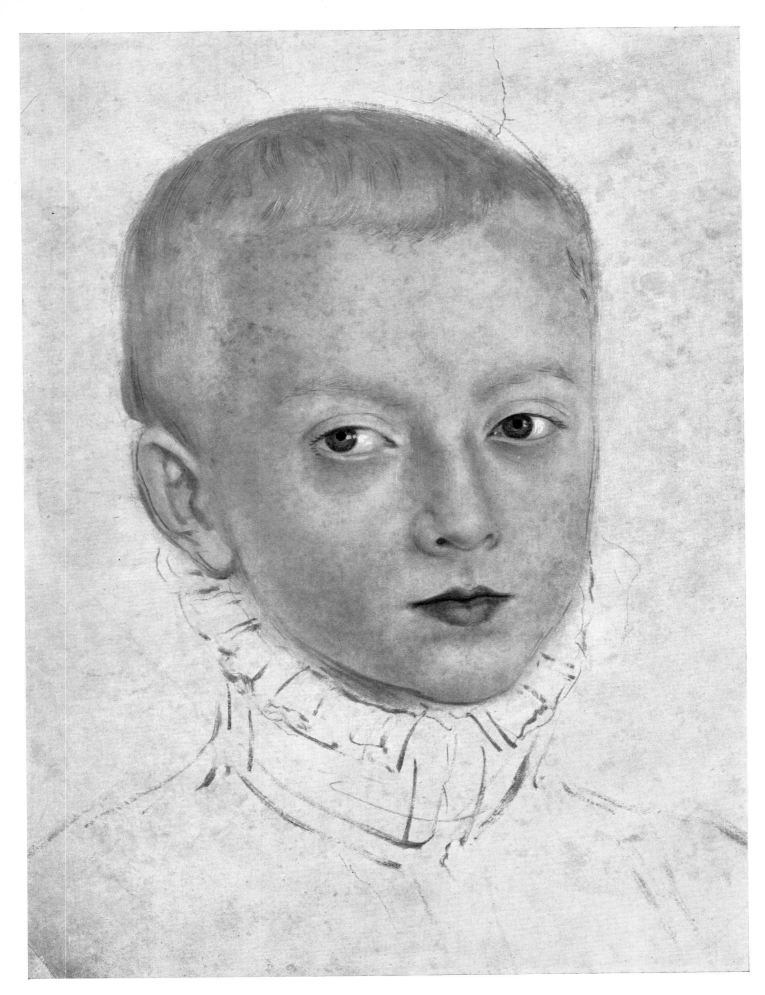

76 LUCAS CRANACH THE YOUNGER

VIII LUCAS CRANACH THE ELDER

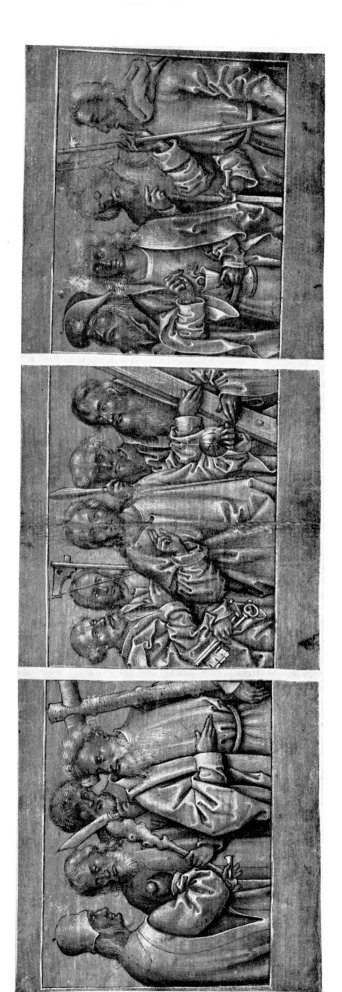

77 BERNHARD STRIGEL

78 HANS BURGKMAIR THE ELDER

79 HANS BURGKMAIR THE ELDER

81 AMBROSIUS HOLBEIN

80 HANS HOLBEIN THE ELDER

82 JÖRG BREU THE ELDER

83 DANIEL HOPFER I

84   ALBRECHT ALTDORFER

IX ALBRECHT ALTDORFER

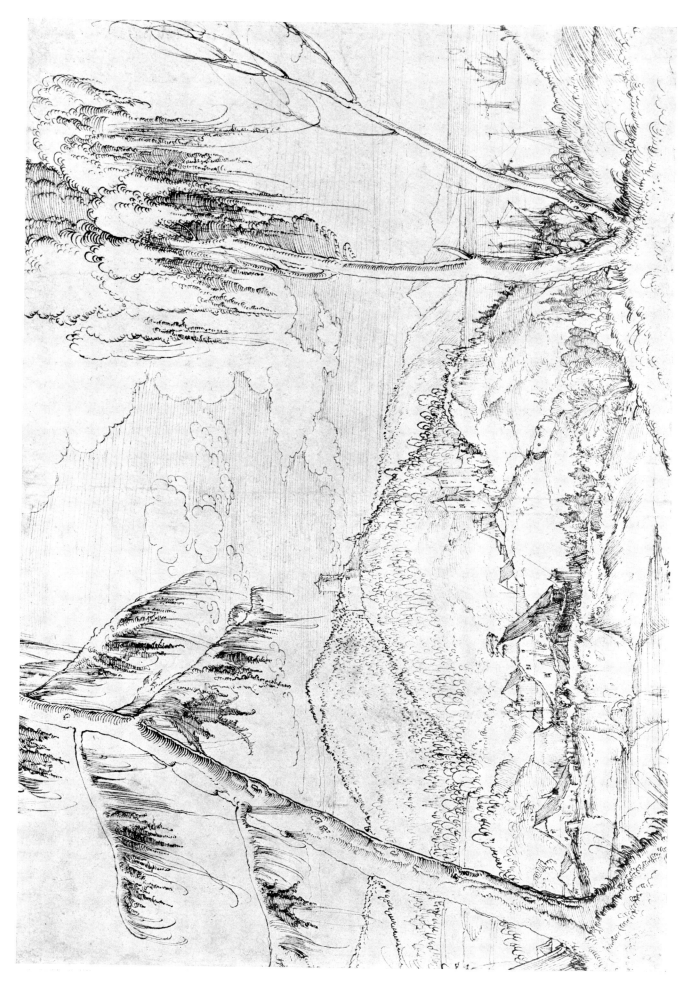

85 ERHARD ALTDORFER

88 MASTER OF THE MATER DOLOROSA FROM SEITENSTETTEN

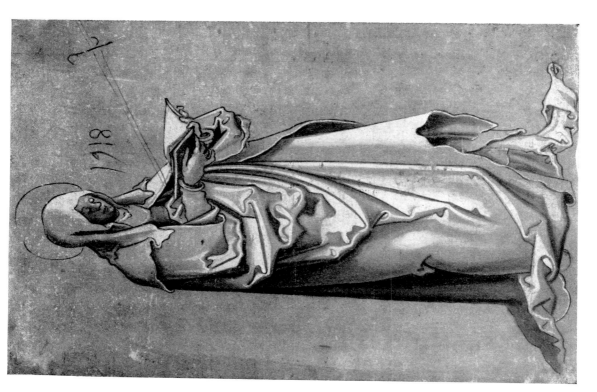

87 MASTER OF THE MATER DOLOROSA FROM SEITENSTETTEN

89 JÖRG KÖLDERER AND HIS SHOP

X   JÖRG KÖLDERER AND HIS SHOP (DETAIL)

90 CIRCLE OF WOLF HUBER

91   WOLF HUBER

1544

W·H·

92   WOLF HUBER

93 URS GRAF

94　HANS HOLBEIN THE YOUNGER

95 HANS MIELICH

96 WENZEL JAMNITZER I

97   HERMANN TOM RING

98 TOBIAS STIMMER

99   CASPAR FRAISINGER

100 HANS VON AACHEN

101 JOSEPH HEINTZ THE ELDER

102 ADAM ELSHEIMER

103 ADAM ELSHEIMER

106 JOHANN HEINRICH SCHÖNFELD

107 MICHAEL WILLMANN

109 WILHELM STETTLER

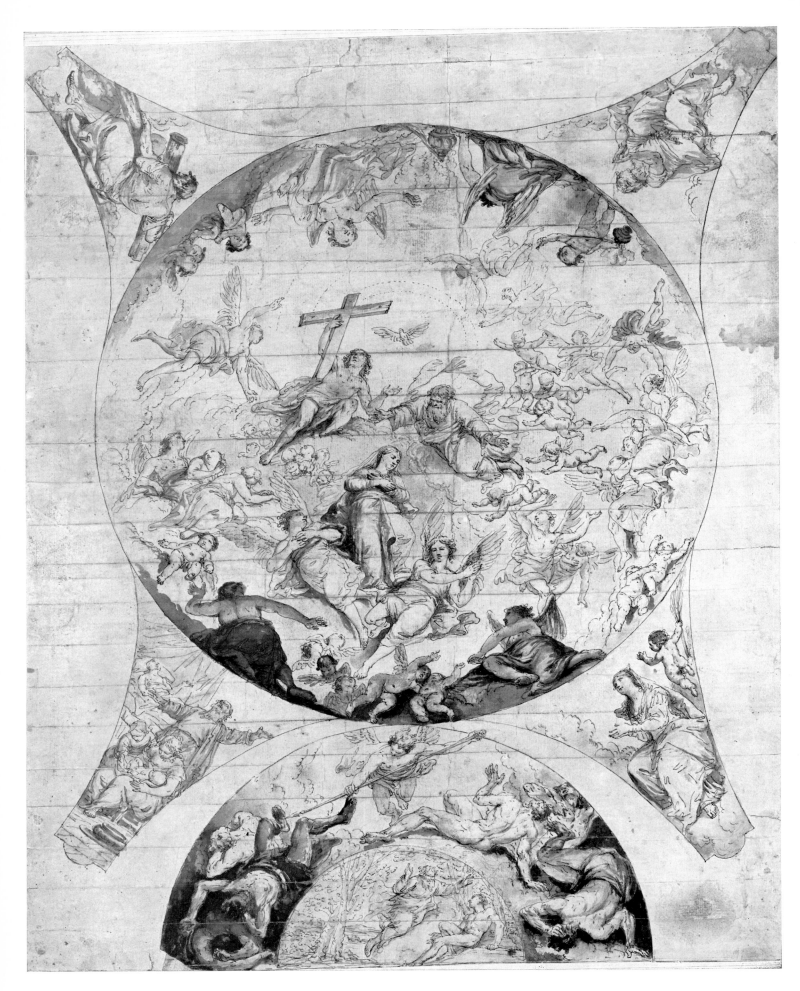

110 MELCHIOR MICHAEL STEIDL

XI JOHANN GEORG PLATZER

111 COSMAS DAMIAN ASAM

112   JOHANN WOLFGANG BAUMGARTNER

113 MATTHÄUS GÜNTHER

114 DANIEL GRAN

115 PAUL TROGER

117 FRANZ ANTON MAULBERTSCH

119 KASPAR FRANZ SAMBACH

120 FRIEDRICH HEINRICH FÜGER

121   ANTON RAPHAEL MENGS

122 ANTON GRAFF

NETHERLANDISH MASTERS

Plates 123 – 204, XII – XVIII

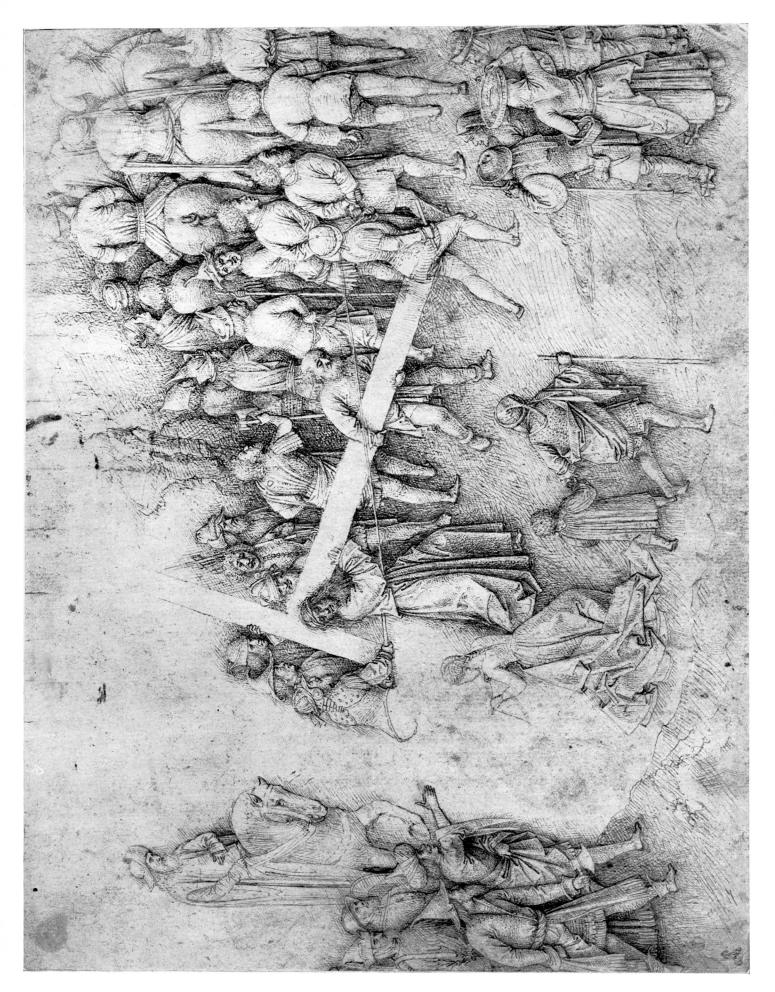

124   PETRUS CHRISTUS I

125 HIERONYMUS BOSCH

126a JAN DE BEER

126b JAN DE BEER

127 JAN GOSSAERT

128   DIRICK VELLERT

129   LUCAS VAN LEYDEN

130   PIETER CORNELISZ KUNST

131 BARENT VAN ORLEY

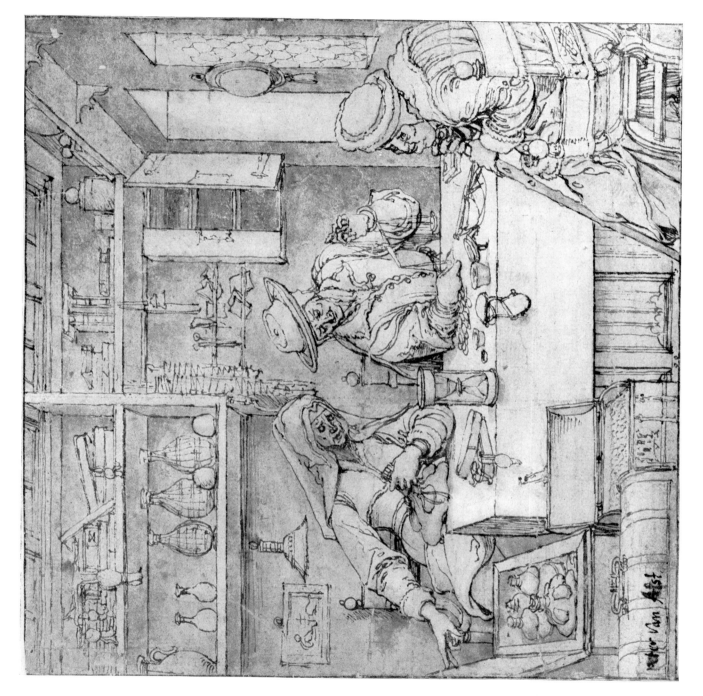

132 PIETER COECKE VAN AELST

133 JAN SWART

Anno Dñi
15

134   DIRCK PIETERSZ CRABETH

136 ADRIAEN THOMASZ KEY

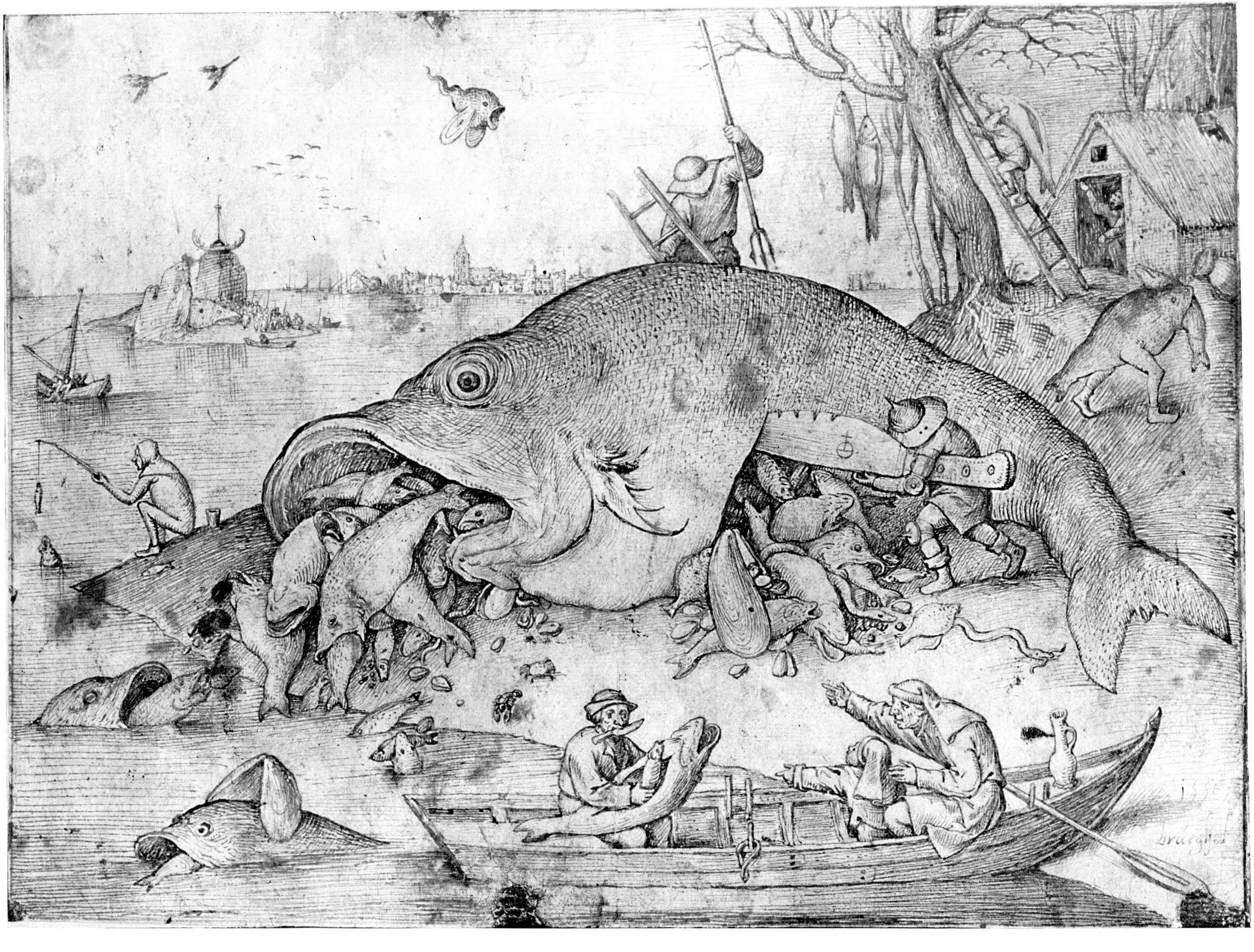

137 PIETER BRUEGEL THE ELDER

138 PIETER BRUEGEL THE ELDER

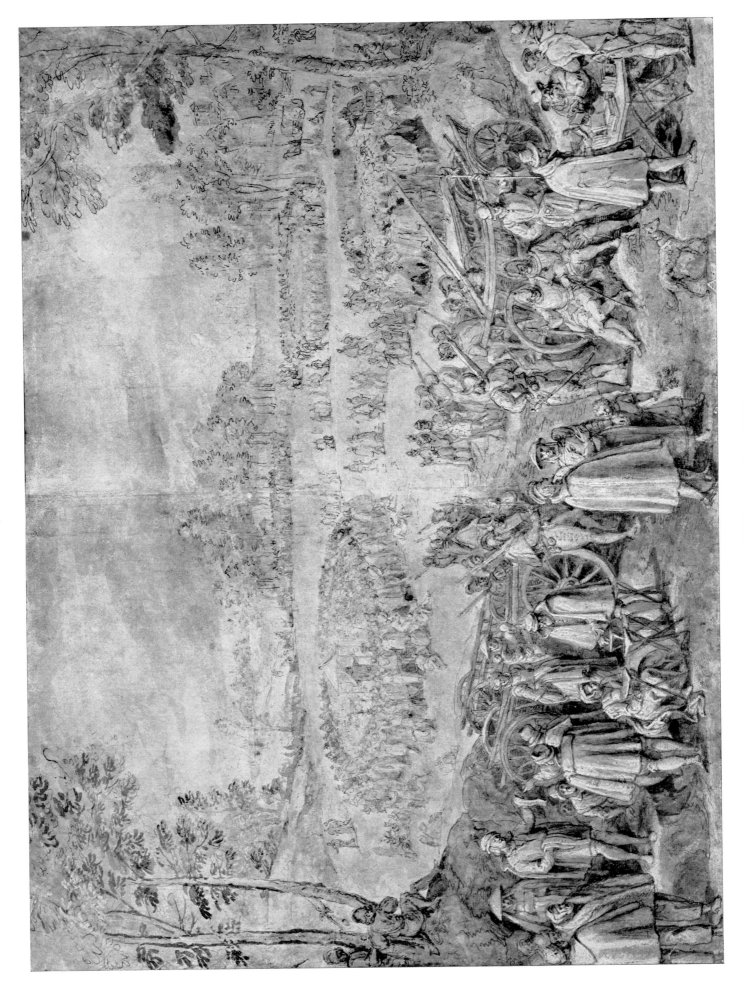

139 CRISPIN VAN DEN BROECK

S·MICHAEL

XII   FRIEDRICH SUSTRIS

140 JOOS VAN WINGHE

141   BARTHOLOMAEUS SPRANGER

142   HENDRIK GOLTZIUS

143 JACQUES DE GHEYN

144 DAVID VINCKBOONS I

145   ROELANT SAVERY

146 JAN BRUEGHEL THE ELDER

147 FRANS FRANCKEN II

148   PETER PAUL RUBENS

149 PETER PAUL RUBENS

XIII PETER PAUL RUBENS

150 PETER PAUL RUBENS

151 ANTHONIE VAN DYCK

XIV ANTHONIE VAN DYCK

152   ANTHONIE VAN DYCK

153　PETER LELY

154   ARTUS QUELLINUS I

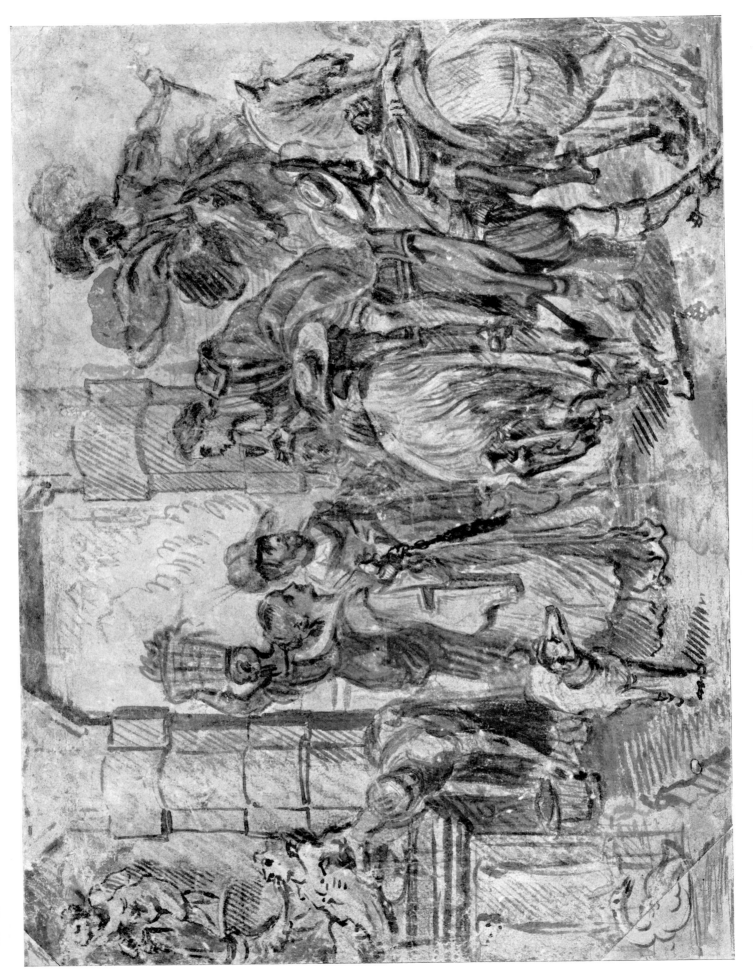

155 THEODOR VAN THULDEN

XV JACOB JORDAENS

156 ADRIAEN BROUWER

158 HENDRIK AVERCAMP

159 ESAIAS VAN DE VELDE I

161 WILLEM BUYTEWECH

162 WILLEM CORNELISZ DUYSTER

163   GERRIT CLAESZ BLECKER

164 JAN VAN DE VELDE II

165 JAN VAN GOYEN

166 SIMON DE VLIEGER

XVI PIETER JANSZ SAENREDAM

168   JAN PORCELLIS I

169   PHILIPS KONINCK

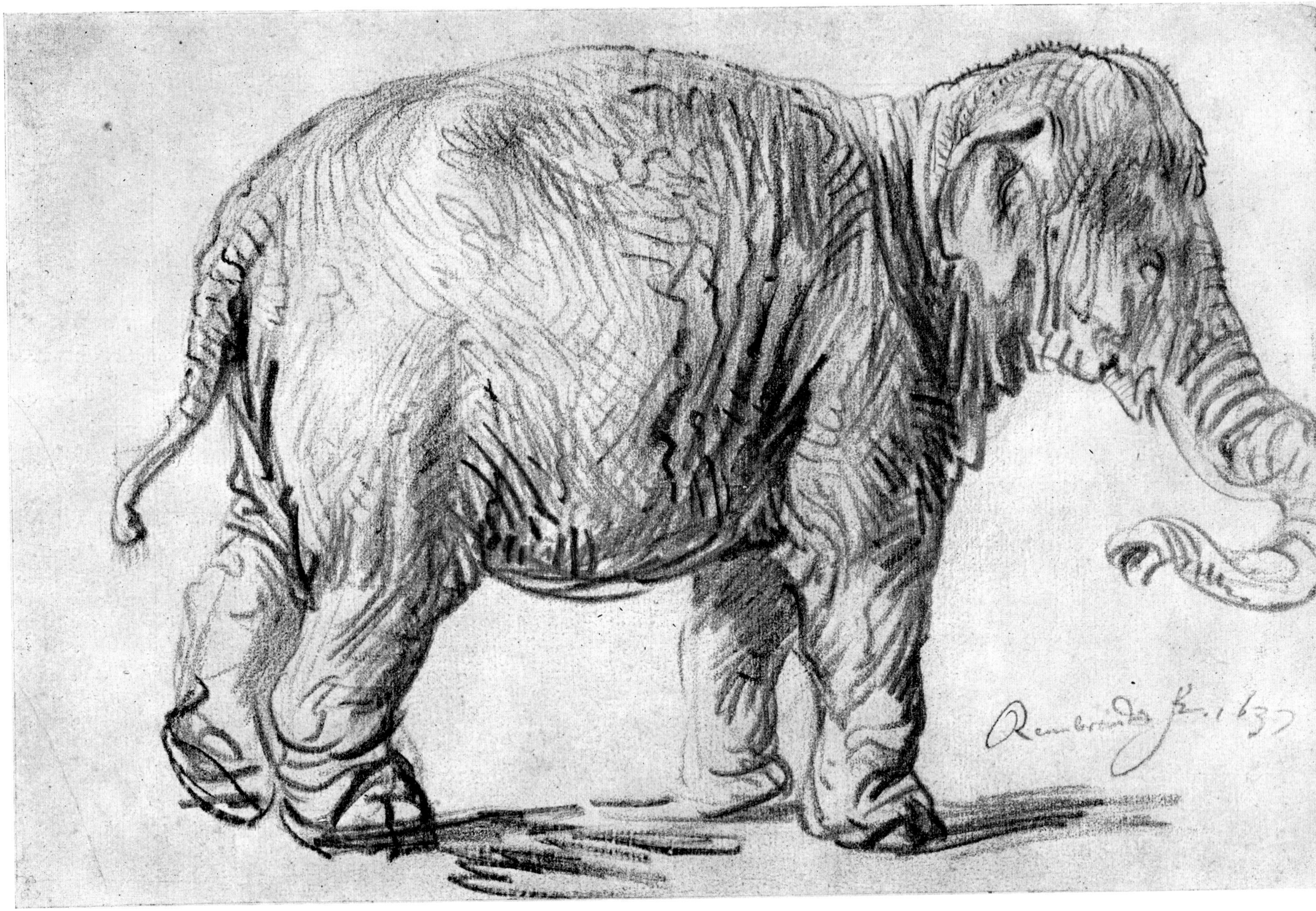

170 REMBRANDT

172   REMBRANDT

173   REMBRANDT

XVII REMBRANDT

174 REMBRANDT

175   JAN LIEVENS

176 FERDINAND BOL

177   JACOB ADRIAENSZ BACKER

178   GOVAERT FLINCK

179 GERBRAND VAN DEN EECKHOUT

180 NICOLAES MAES

181 ABRAHAM FURNERIUS

183 JOHANNES LEUPENIUS

184   ROELAND ROGHMAN

185　JAN VAN DE CAPPELLE

186 AERT VAN DER NEER

187 ADRIAEN VAN OSTADE

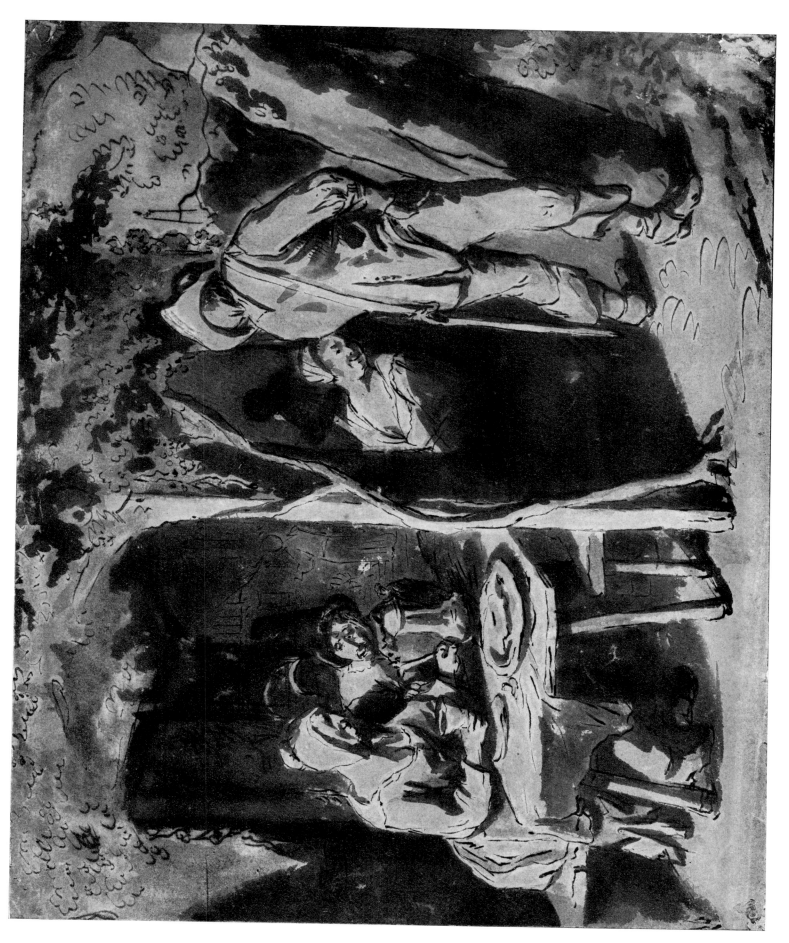

188 JAN STEEN

189   MICHAEL SWEERTS

190 CORNELIS VISSCHER II

192   JAN ASSELIJN

193   ADRIAEN VAN DE VELDE

194   PAULUS POTTER

195 AELBERT CUYP

196   JACOB ISAACKSZ VAN RUISDAEL

197 JORIS VAN DER HAGEN

198 NICOLAES BERCHEM

199   GABRIEL METSU

200 GERARD TERBORCH

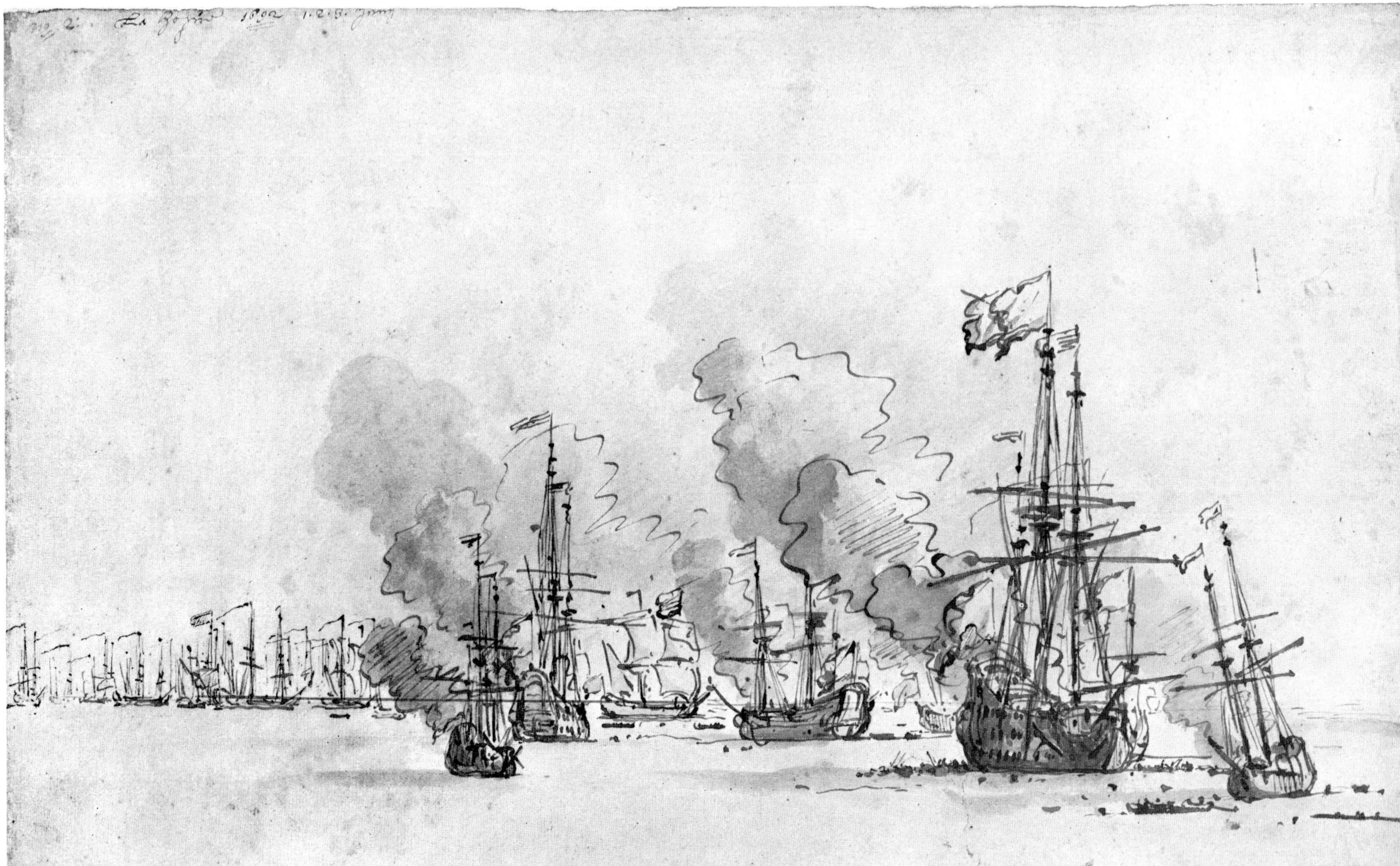

201 WILLEM VAN DE VELDE II

202   JAN DE BISSCHOP

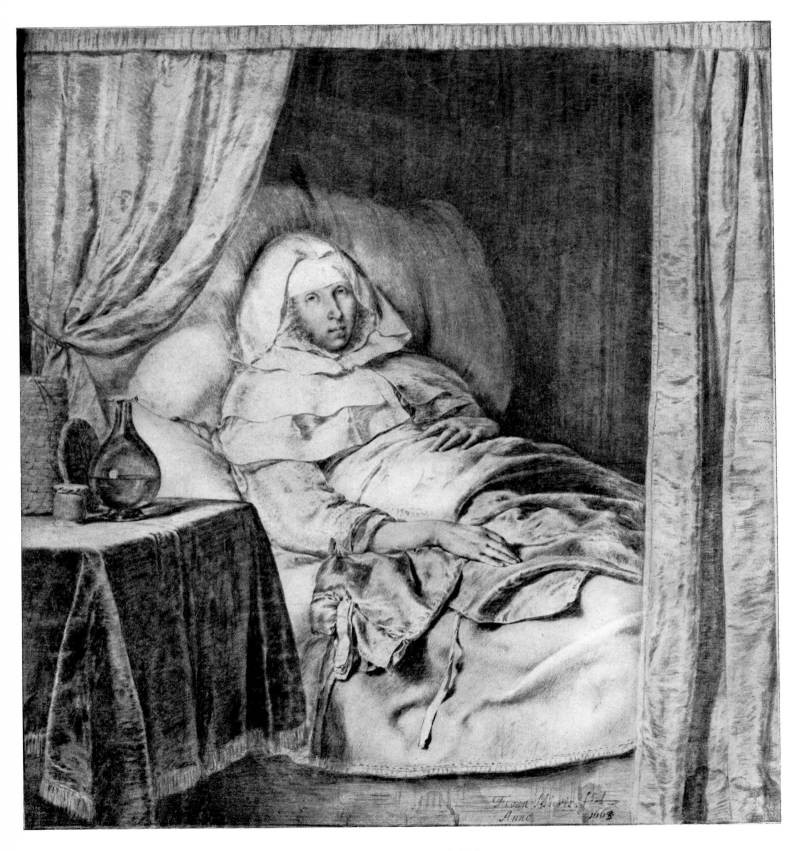

203   FRANS VAN MIERIS I

XVIII   JAN VAN HUYSUM

FRENCH MASTERS

205 FRANÇOIS CLOUET

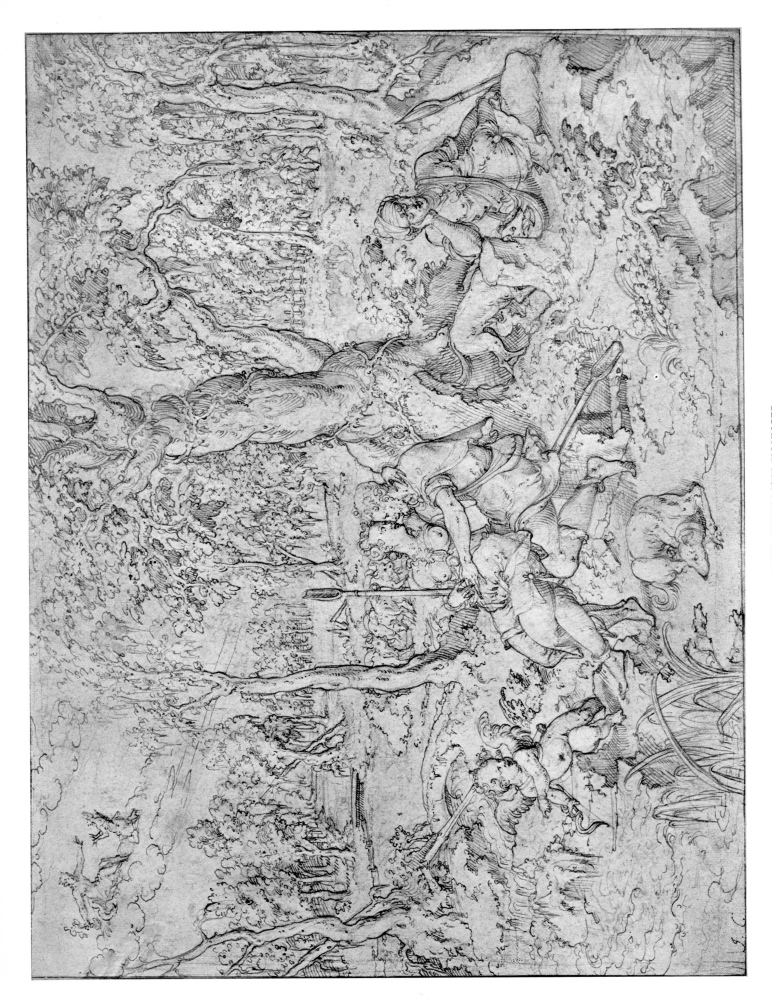

206 JEAN COUSIN THE YOUNGER

Martin Freminet de paris

207   MARTIN FRÉMINET

208 JACQUES BELLANGE

209 JACQUES CALLOT

211 NICOLAS POUSSIN

212 CLAUDE LORRAIN

XIX   CLAUDE LORRAIN

213   SIMON VOUET

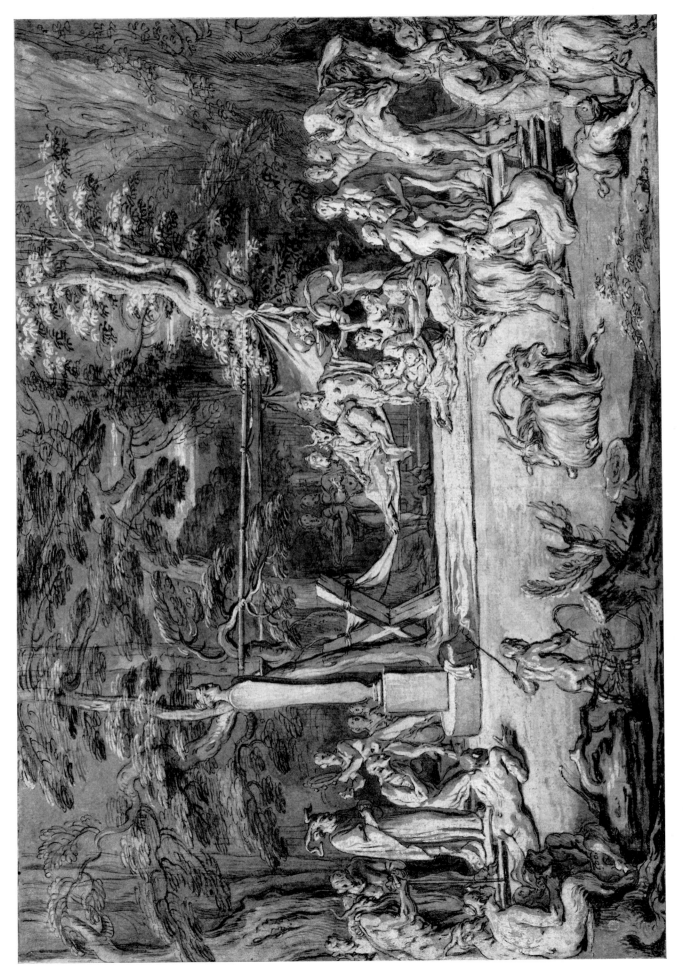

214 CLAUDE GILLOT

XX   ANTOINE WATTEAU

215 JACQUES ANDRÉ PORTAIL

216 JEAN-BAPTISTE OUDRY

G. NATOIRE

monte Porcio al 10 octobr 1758.

XXI   CHARLES JOSEPH NATOIRE

218 FRANÇOIS BOUCHER

XXII   JEAN-ÉTIENNE LIOTARD

219 ÉTIENNE JEAURAT

220　JEAN-BAPTISTE GREUZE

XXIII   FRANÇOIS GUÉRIN

223 JEAN-HONORÉ FRAGONARD

224 JEAN-HONORÉ FRAGONARD

XXIV   JEAN-HONORÉ FRAGONARD

225 JEAN MICHEL MOREAU

226 JACQUES LOUIS DAVID

PORTUGUESE AND SPANISH MASTERS

Plates 227–231

227   NUÑO GONÇALVES

228 VINCENCIO CARDUCHO

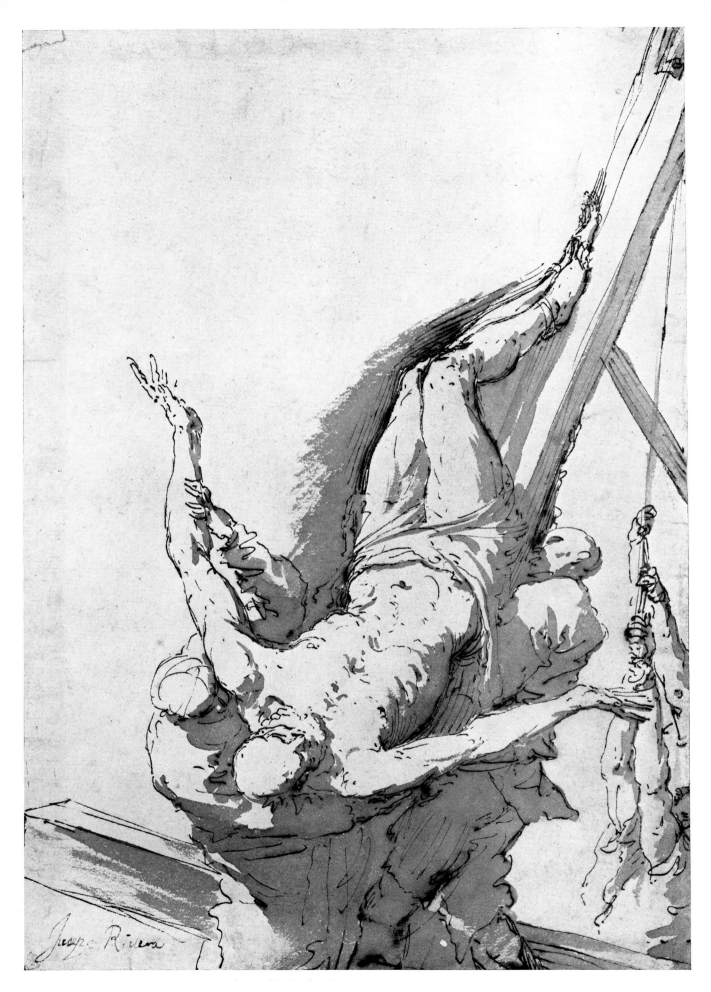

229   JUSEPE DE RIBERA

D. fran.co de Herrera f.t
1664.

230   FRANCISCO DE HERRERA EL MOZO

El ciego trabajador

231   FRANCISCO DE GOYA

BRITISH MASTERS

Plates 232–236

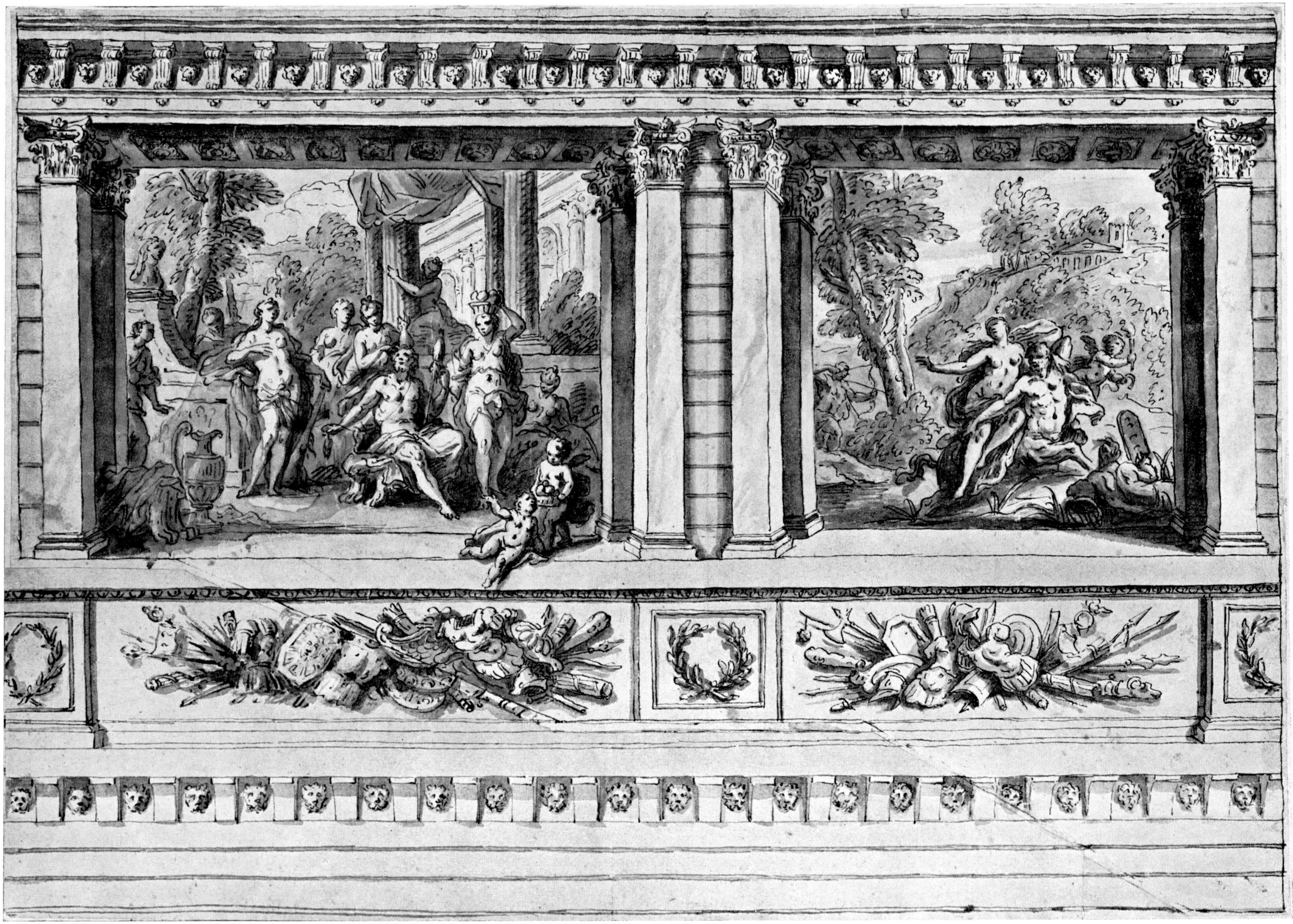

232 JAMES THORNHILL

233 THOMAS GAINSBOROUGH

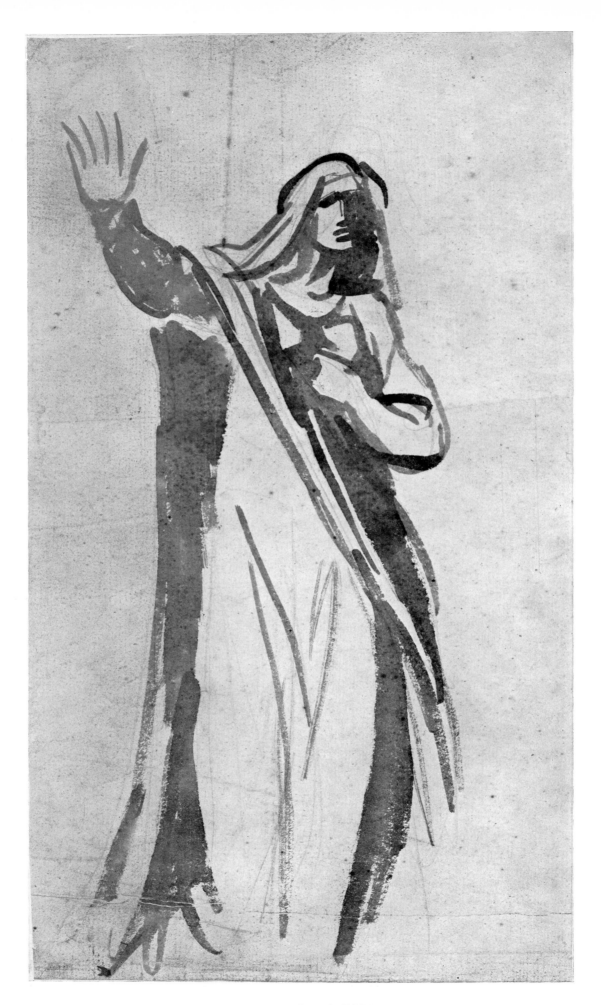

234 GEORGE ROMNEY

235 HENRY FUSELI

236 JOHN HOPPNER

CATALOGUE

BIBLIOGRAPHY

Only a selection of the most important bibliographical and exhibition references has been quoted in full for the individual drawings. General reference is made to the comments on the drawings in the Albertina contained in Die vornehmsten Kunstdenkmäler in Wien by G. F. Waagen, Part II, p. 124 ff, Vienna, 1867.

The Albertina publications referred to have been abbreviated, as follows:

Albertina Cat. I — Beschreibender Katalog der Handzeichnungen in der Graphischen Sammlung Albertina. Edited by A. Stix. I. Die Zeichnungen der Venezianischen Schule, by A. Stix and L. Fröhlich-Bum, Vienna, 1926.

Albertina Cat. II — as above, II. Die Zeichnungen der Niederländischen Schulen des XV. und XVI. Jahrhunderts, by O. Benesch, Vienna, 1928.

Albertina Cat. III — as above, III. Die Zeichnungen der Toskanischen, Umbrischen und Römischen Schulen, by A. Stix and L. Fröhlich-Bum, Vienna, 1932.

Albertina Cat. IV (V) — as above, IV. (Text), V. (Plates). Die Zeichnungen der Deutschen Schulen bis zum Beginn des Klassizismus, by H. and E. Tietze, O. Benesch, and K. Garzarolli-Thurnlackh, Vienna, 1933.

Albertina Cat. VI — as above, VI. Die Schulen von Ferrara, Bologna, Parma und Modena, der Lombardei, Genuas, Neapels und Siziliens, by A. Stix and A. Spitzmüller, Vienna, 1941.

Exhibitions:

London 1948 — Old Master Drawings from the Albertina Collection Vienna, The Arts Council of Great Britain, London, 1948.

Paris 1950 — Cent Cinquante Chefs d'Oeuvre de l'Albertina de Vienne, Paris (1950), Bibliothèque Nationale.

Venice 1961 — Disegni veneti dell'Albertina di Vienna, Catalogo della Mostra a cura di O. Benesch, Venice 1961, Fondazione Giorgio Cini.

Basan — F. Basan, Catalogue raisonné des différens objets... qui composoient le Cabinet de feu Mr. Mariette... Paris, 1775.

O. Benesch, Die Meisterzeichnung V — O. Benesch, Österreichische Handzeichnungen des XV. und XVI. Jahrhunderts. Die Meisterzeichnung V, Freiburg i. Br., 1936.

Berenson — B. Berenson, I Disegni dei Pittori Fiorentini, Milan, 1961.

Briquet — C. M. Briquet, Les Filigranes, Dictionnaire historique des Marques du Papier, I—IV, Leipzig, 1923.

L. — F. Lugt, Les Marques de Collections de Dessins & d'Estampes, Amsterdam, 1921; Supplément, The Hague, 1956.

Charles, Prince de Ligne (Cat.) — Catalogue raisonné des desseins originaux... du Cabinet de feu Le Prince de Ligne... par Adam Bartsch, Vienna, 1794.

Schönbrunner-Meder — Handzeichnungen alter Meister aus der Albertina und anderen Sammlungen. Edited by J. Schönbrunner and J. Meder, I—XII, Vienna, 1895—1908.

Wickhoff Sc. V. — F. Wickhoff, Die italienischen Handzeichnungen der Albertina, Part I, Scuola Veneziana, Jahrbuch der Kunsthistorischen Sammlungen des Allerhöchsten Kaiserhauses 12, Vienna, 1891, p. CCXV ff.

Wickhoff Sc. L. — as above, Scuola Lombarda, op., cit., p. CCLI ff.

Wickhoff Sc. B. — as above, Scuola Bolognese, op., cit., p. CCLXXVIII ff.

Wickhoff Sc. R. — as above, Part II, Scuola Romana, Jahrbuch der Kunsthistorischen Sammlungen des Allerhöchsten Kaiserhauses 13, Vienna, 1892, p. CLXXVIII ff.

Wurzbach I, II — A. v. Wurzbach, Niederländisches Künstlerlexikon I—III, Vienna—Leipzig, 1906, 1911 (III).

Publisher's note: Otto Benesch died during the period of preparation of this English language edition. Eva Benesch has contributed additions and corrections to the bibliographical entries of the catalogue, partly from his notes. Otherwise, the bibliographical material has been left exactly as it appeared in the original edition of this book.

ITALIAN MASTERS

MICHELINO MOLINARI DA BESOZZO
Documented 1388 in Pavia, 1404 in Padua, 1418—1442 in Milan.

1 Studies for an Adoration of the Magi, a Virgin and Child, God the Father and various Figures of Saints and Prophets (St. Jerome, lower right).

Silverpoint on white prepared paper. Collection number 39; on lower right in pen and bistre by another hand: Cimabue Fiorentinus.
Verso: Two Studies of the Head of a Fallow Deer (profile turned to left, and rear view). Leadpoint and pen.
273 : 204 mm.
Inv. no. 4855 (L. 174).
Provenance: Lagoy (L. 1710); M. v. Fries (L. 2903).
Albertina Cat. I, 11; Wickhoff, Sc. R. 5 (Veronese); Schönbrunner-Meder, 857; P. Toesca, La Pittura e la Miniatura nella Lombardia, Milan, 1912, pp. 443—46; R. van Marle, Italian Schools of Painting, The Hague, 1926, VII, pp. 116—118, fig. 77; A. van Schendel, Le Dessin en Lombardie jusqu'à la fin du XVe siècle, Brussels, 1938, p. 74 and no. 67.
Exhibitions: Paris, 1950, Cat. no. 6; Arte Lombarda dai Visconti agli Sforza, Palazzo Reale, Milan, 1958, no. 162, pl. LXVIII; Kunsthistorisches Museum, Vienna, Europäische Kunst um 1400, 1962, no. 267.

Various motifs and compositional ideas are freely scattered over the surface of this sheet of paper as if on a sketchbook leaf. Most of them (monkeys, horses, and spectators) are connected with an Adoration of the Magi, whose main group, including the figures of a clerical donor and his patron saint, appear at the lower edge of the page. St. Jerome writing, God the Father with His hand raised in blessing, and the various draped figures belong to other compositions. The figures of the Epiphany are, as their lightly sketched forms in silverpoint suggest, the free invention of the artist, although they do, of course, belong to the general repertory of types of about 1400. They reveal a highly individual hand, whereas the other figures are representative of the conventional types transmitted by model books. The animal drawings on the reverse are genuine studies from nature heralding Pisanello. Michelino da Besozzo was one of the chief artists of the so-called International Style, which developed in France and Central Europe from elements of the Northern Gothic and the Italian Trecento, and brought the entire West under its spell. In Italy, it flourished mainly in the north, which was open to influences from France and Germany. Michelino was in touch with the miniaturists of Paris. Late medieval ideality and preciosity of form were essential features of the artists of this style, yet the new naturalism was already developing in Michelino's circle. We owe to Toesca the convincing attribution of this drawing to Michelino. He identified it on the basis of its stylistic affinity with a miniature by the Master of the Coronation of the Virgin in Pietro da Castelletto's funeral oration of 1403 for Gian Galeazzo Visconti (Paris, Bibliothèque Nationale, ms. lat. 5888).

STEFANO DA VERONA (Stefano da Zevio)
Born Verona about 1374, died there after 1438.

2 Three Studies of Prophets with Scrolls.

Pen and bistre; upper right corner added; later inscription, lower right: Stefano Falconeto.
296 : 181 mm.
Inv. no. 24014 (acquired 1923).
Provenance: Moscardo; Calceolari; Luigi Grassi (L. 1171 b).
Albertina Cat. I, 3; A. Stix, Handzeichnungen aus der Albertina, N. F. II, Vienna, 1925, no. 7; G. Fiocco, Proporzioni III, Florence, 1950, p. 60.
Exhibitions: Verona, Museo di Castelvecchio. Da Altichiero a Pisanello, 1958, no. 46; Kunsthistorisches Museum, Vienna, Europäische Kunst um 1400, 1962, no. 290.
According to B. Degenhart (Thieme-Becker, XXXI, 1937, p. 528), these are studies for the prophets in the fresco at the side portal of S. Eufemia in Verona. Drapery, scroll, and the arrangement of the figures form an indivisible unit characteristic of the climax of the International Style. The volume of the human body is sacrificed in favor of a decorative representation whose aim is expressiveness and spiritual meaning. Stefano was the most important representative of the International Style in Verona. In his pen drawings, he developed so individual a calligraphy that his works can easily be recognized. The finest works of this very gifted draughtsman are in the F. Lugt Collection, Paris, and in the Albertina; they come from the Moscardo Collection, an old Veronese collection.

PISANELLO (Antonio Pisano)
Born probably Pisa 1395, died Rome 1455.

3 Allegory of Luxuria.

Pen and bistre on pink-tinted paper; traces of white bodycolor.
Verso: Roebuck in Profile to Right.
Pen and bistre heightened with white bodycolor.
129 : 152 mm.
Inv. no. 24018 (acquired 1923).
Provenance: Moscardo; Calceolari; Luigi Grassi (L. 1171 b).
Albertina Cat. I, 9; A. Stix, Handzeichnungen aus der Albertina, N. F. II, Vienna, 1925, Nos. 8, 9; B. Degenhart, Antonio Pisanello, Vienna, 1941, p. 27, fig. 28.
Exhibitions: London, 1948, no. 21; Paris, 1950, no. 7; Verona, Museo di Castelvecchio, Da Altichiero a Pisanello, 1958, no. 95, pl. LXXXIX; Kunsthistorisches Museum, Vienna, Europäische Kunst um 1400, 1962, no. 279.

Drawing made to record an iconographic type or as an independent work of art.
The subject, rooted in medieval allegory, is combined with a representation of the nude which in its naturalism reveals that the artist acquired his knowledge from a direct study of the human body. Pisanello, who grew out of the local traditions of Verona, through his collaboration with Gentile da Fabriano and his numerous court commissions, would have become a typical North Italian representative of the late International Style, had his personal genius not carried him beyond its limits and made him the pioneer of descriptive naturalism in North Italy. This naturalism is as significant for the beginning of the Renaissance as the establishment of a new rational basis for the representation of body and space in Florence. This drawing thus stands in the twilight of two eras: the two-dimensional, heraldic arrangement of the figure and hair is combined with an empirical knowledge of the skeleton and the bare skin, the curves and tensions of which are rendered by small, fur-like strokes, without cross-hatching, of the "Soft" or International Style. The importance of this great empiricist, which Pisanello was, is most evident in his numerous drawings.

LORENZO GHIBERTI
Born Florence 1378, died there 1455.

4 Five Studies for a Flagellation of Christ.

Pen and bistre.
216 : 166 mm.
Inv. no. 24409 (acquired 1923).
Provenance: Luigi Grassi (L. 1171 b).
Albertina Cat. III, 8; A. Stix, Handzeichnungen aus der Albertina, N. F. II, Vienna, 1925, pl. 35; A. Stix, Kunstchronik und Kunstmarkt, 59. Jg., Leipzig, 1925, pp. 139—141; J. von Schlosser, Leben und Meinungen des florentinischen Bildners Lorenzo Ghiberti, Basel, 1941, p. 100; R. Krautheimer, Lorenzo Ghiberti, Princeton, 1956, p. 129, pl. 46.
Exhibitions: London, 1948, no. 11; Paris, 1950, no. 3; Kunsthistorisches Museum, Vienna, Europäische Kunst um 1400, 1962, no. 260.

Alfred Stix was the first to identify this drawing as a work by Ghiberti; Schlosser and Krautheimer have endorsed his attribution. Popham also considered the attribution to Ghiberti reasonable. Krautheimer proves the authenticity of the drawing by a careful analysis. He correctly connects it with the Flagellation on the north door of the Baptistery in Florence, and points out the relationship of the lower figures to one of the executioners on the reliquary of the SS. Corporale in the Cathedral of Orvieto, which also has a canopy with a coffered ceiling similar to the one sketchily indicated at the upper edge of the drawing.

As a sculptor, Ghiberti, together with Jacopo della Quercia and Donatello, was one of the "fathers" of the *ars nova* of the Renaissance. As the author of the *Commentarii,* he supplemented his artistic activity with theoretical and historical reflections, thus representing the new type of the "learned artist" in the sense of the ancients. Many elements of the International Style survive in his formal idiom. In this sheet — the only example of his drawing style which has come down to us — he combines the fur-like little strokes of the International Style with a representation of the figure, moving freely and boldly in space, and revealing the new era's feeling for the body. The graphic handling of this drawing, which produces an image of absolute clarity from a multiplicity of tentative lines, reflects the working process of the bronze sculptor who first creates his models in clay.

FRA ANGELICO (Fra Giovanni da Fiesole)
Born Florence 1387, died Rome 1455.

5 Christ on the Cross.

Pen and bistre, washed, with red bodycolor and yellowish watercolor (halo); later inscription in ink: obiit 1455.
293 : 190 mm.
Inv. no. 4863 (L. 174).
Provenance: M. v. Fries (L. 2903).
Albertina Cat. III, 9; Wickhoff, Sc. R. 30; Schönbrunner-Meder 702; J. Meder, Albertina- Facsimile, Handzeichnungen italienischer Meister des XV.—XVIII. Jahrhunderts, Vienna, 1923, pl. 1; Berenson, 178; Langton Douglas, Fra Angelico, London, 1900, p. 199; F. Schottmüller, Fra Angelico da Fiesole (Klassiker der Kunst 18), 2nd edition (1924), p. XXX; J. Pope-Hennessy, Fra Angelico, London, 1952, p. 205.
Exhibition: Paris, 1950, no. 4.

This drawing combines the delicacy of a miniature with the monumentality of a fresco. It is a perfect counterpart to Beato Angelico's paintings which combine the austere solemnity of the very beginnings of the Renaissance with the spiritual ideal of monastic withdrawal from the world. We may thus consider this drawing an authentic testimonial by the saintly monk himself, although Berenson suggested the possibility that it may be by a pupil like Domenico di Michelino. The drawing conjures up the image of the peaceful cells of S. Marco in Florence (Langton Douglas supposed it to be a study for the Christ on the Cross in the upper corridor of the monastery).

LORENZO DI CREDI
Born Florence 1456 or 1459, died there 1537.

6 Portrait of a Long-Haired Youth, Wearing a Hat; Three-Quartier Profile to Right.

Metalpoint, brush and white bodycolor on yellowish-brown prepared paper.
228 : 149 mm.
Inv. no. 24414 (acquired 1925).
Provenance: W. Mayor (L. 2799).
Albertina Cat. III, 28; A. Stix, Handzeichnungen aus der Albertina, N. F. II, Vienna, 1925, no. 39; Berenson, 732 A*.
Exhibition: Paris, 1950, no. 14.

In Verrocchio's workshop special emphasis was laid on drawing in silverpoint from the model. The works of two fellow students, Lorenzo di Credi and Leonardo, are the most outstanding examples of this technique in Florence during the second half of the Quattrocento. They are often very much alike in their handling of the tool, which models the surface of the prepared, colored paper both firmly and delicately, although Leonardo's drawings express a superior vision lacking in Lorenzo's merely technically perfect sheets. The present drawing is also a fine example of late Quattrocento Florentine portraiture which was equally important in sculpture and painting.

RAFFAELLINO DEL GARBO
(Raffaello di Bartolommeo di Giovanni Carli)
Born Florence 1466, died there 1524.

7 Study for the Head of an Angel, Inclined in Profile to the Right.

Silverpoint, heightened with the brush and white bodycolor, on pinkish-yellow prepared paper; upper corners and a small strip, 2 mm. wide, along right margin added later.
192 : 190 mm.
Inv. no. 17620 (L. 174).
Provenance: G. Vasari; P. J. Mariette (L. 2097).
Albertina Cat. III, 35; Wickhoff, Sc. R. 512; Schönbrunner-Meder, 404; J. Meder, Albertina-Facsimile, Handzeichnungen italienischer Meister des XV.—XVIII. Jahrhunderts, Vienna, 1923, pl. 7; Berenson, 656; Pantheon X, Munich, 1932, p. 301, fig. facing p. 273.
Exhibition: Paris, 1950, no. 16.

Raffaellino was a pupil of Filippino Lippi, whose style he continues in his few authentic works. As in the works of his teacher and of Botticelli, naturalistic representation recedes in favor of poetic expressiveness, so evident in the pensive features of this delicate profile of an angel. Nevertheless, importance was attached to the accurate rendering of the visible: the shadow cast on cheek and neck by the shining curls, and the veins standing in clear relief on the neck. Although documentary evidence supports the assumption of a single artistic personality, Berenson divided Raffaellino's oeuvre for reasons of style between two hands, assigning the present study to the artist known as Del Garbo.

PIERO DI COSIMO (Piero di Lorenzo)
Born Florence about 1462, died there 1521 (?).

8 The Adoration of the Child by the Virgin and Two Kneeling Angels in the Stable at Bethlehem.
Chalk, pen and bistre.
Some corrections by the artist in dark ink on the figures of the Virgin and the angels; slightly enlarged at sides in Indian ink by another hand.
146 : 164 mm (oval).
Inv. no. 78 (L. 174).
Provenance: P. J. Mariette (L. 2097); M. v. Fries (L.2903).
Albertina Cat. III, 31; Wickhoff, Sc. R. 103; Schönbrunner-Meder, 1033; Berenson, 1863.

Berenson has shown that this is a design for a painting, now in the Brooks Memorial Art Gallery, Memphis, Tennessee.
Not only the invention, but also the light, spirited manner of drawing reveals the artist as a contemporary of Leonardo. There are also reminiscences of Lorenzo di Credi, Filippino Lippi, and Piero's teacher, Cosimo Rosselli. The admirable capacity of the Florentines to abbreviate and outline the human body with a firm hand is manifest in the works of this imaginative artist. Piero was also a master of landscape, in his drawings as well as in his paintings, as is apparent in the background of this sheet.

LEONARDO DA VINCI
Born Vinci 1452, died Amboise 1519.

I St. Peter.
Silverpoint, pen and bistre on blue prepared paper.
146 : 113 mm.
Inv. no. 17614 (L. 174).
Provenance: Charles, Prince de Ligne (Cat. p. 34, no. 5).
Albertina Cat. III, 18; Wickhoff, Sc. R. 64; Schönbrunner-Meder, 590; J. Meder, Albertina Facsimile, Handzeichnungen italienischer Meister des XV.—XVIII. Jahrhunderts, Vienna, 1923, pl. 23; Berenson 1113; A. E. Popp, Leonardo da Vinci Zeichnungen, Munich, 1928, no. 33; H. Bodmer, Leonardo (Klassiker der Kunst 37), Leipzig, 1931, p. 257; A. E. Popham, The Drawings of Leonardo da Vinci, London, 1947, no. 164; Great Drawings of All Time, vol. I, Italian, New York, 1962, no. 160 (W. Ames).
Exhibitions: London, 1948, no. 13; Paris, 1950, no. 12.

This magnificent character study of an apostle, with piercing, somber gaze, undoubtedly served for the St. Peter in the Last Supper, Santa Maria delle Grazie, Milan (1495—1498).

The urgent question which Peter is asking John in the fresco seems to be anticipated by the eloquent gesture of the model. In his notebooks Leonardo included instructions to young painters on how they could find the type of figure needed for a composition by studying everyday life. "Take a small sketchbook with you and observe people in their daily activities. Watch them in the streets, squares, and fields, and record them by brief indications of form."

For the figures of the Cenacolo he chose specific models and even recorded the names of some of them in his notebooks. Giovanbatista Giraldi, whose father knew Leonardo, wrote that when Leonardo wished to paint a figure, he began by deciding on the social position and character this personage was to represent — whether noble or plebeian, whether happy or serious, worried or carefree, good or bad; and when he had come to his decision, he went where he knew such people would congregate; and when he had found what was of use to him, he put it down in a little sketchbook which he used to carry in his belt.

Leonardo frequently used pen and bistre for putting the last accents on his silverpoint drawings. By this procedure he combined, as in this drawing, atmospheric effect with utmost precision in the placement of accents.

DOMENICO GHIRLANDAIO
(Domenico di Tommaso Bigardi)
Born Florence about 1449, died there 1494.

9 The Angel Appearing to Zachariah in the Temple.

Pen and bistre, washed.

Original inscriptions in pen and bistre on two figures on the right: Giuliano, Giovanni Francesco; signed in the same medium lower margin: Ghirlandaio.

259 : 374 mm.

Inv. no. 4860 (L. 174).

Provenance: P. J. Mariette; Basan, p. 70, no. 438 (L. 2097); M. v. Fries (L. 2903).

Albertina Cat. III, 26; Wickhoff, Sc. R. 102; Schönbrunner-Meder 216; J. Meder, Die Handzeichnung, fig. 300; J. Meder, Albertina-Facsimile, Handzeichnungen italienischer Meister des XV.—XVIII. Jahrhunderts, Vienna, 1923, pl. 3; Berenson, 891.

Exhibitions: London, 1948, no. 12; Paris, 1950, no. 9.

This drawing is Ghirlandaio's design for the last fresco he carried out in the choir of Santa Maria Novella, Florence, which bears the date 1490 and Poliziano's dedication. The commission to decorate the choir with frescoes depicting the lives of the Virgin and of St. John the Baptist was given to the artist by the banker Giovanni Tornabuoni. The execution of the frescoes occupied the years from 1486 until 1490. The artist represented the sacred stories in splendid scenes of contemporary life in Florence, with numerous portraits attesting his mastery of realism; they are so plentiful, especially in this scene, that they almost obscure the real content. Although the figures in the Albertina drawing are still schematized and somewhat abstract in design — with circles for eyes and geometrical, abbreviated indications of the skulls — they were intended to be portraits, as is shown by the names inscribed on the figures to the right of the altar — (Giuliano and Gianfrancesco Tornabuoni). In the fresco the portrait groups have been further enlarged: two figures were added to the group with the donor to the left of the angel and another to the group of the leading intellectuals at the lower left — the philosopher Marsilio Ficino, the Dante commentator Cristoforo Landino, the poet Poliziano, and the tutor of Lorenzo the Magnificent, Gentile de' Becchi.

PIETRO PERUGINO (Pietro di Cristoforo Vannucci)
Born Città della Pieve about 1445, died Fontignano near Perugia 1523.

10 The Adoration of the Magi.

Chalk, pen and bistre. Later inscription in pen and bistre: Pietro Perugino.

195 : 332 mm.

A strip of paper 53 mm. wide has been added along upper margin.

Inv. no. 24410 (acquired 1922).

Provenance: Conestabile; J. P. Heseltine.

Albertina Cat. III, 38; A. Stix, Handzeichnungen aus der Albertina, N. F. II, Vienna, 1925, no. 40; O. Fischel, Jahrbuch der Preussischen Kunstsammlungen, 38, Berlin, 1917, II, p. 83, no. 89, pl. X.

Exhibition: Paris, 1950. no. 10.

Study for the fresco in the Oratory of the Brethren of the Bianchi, now Santa Maria dei Bianchi at Città della Pieve (1504). The contours of the architectural elements were first incised into the paper with a stylus and then gone over with pen and bistre. The penlines of the architecture must be ascribed to the hand of the master himself since the alterations in the contours of the hills, which were drawn with the same pen, correspond with the executed fresco. On this three-dimensional stage, the artist lightly sketched the main figures of the composition in chalk, merely as notes for his own use with no thought of developing them in detail. The drawing was thus meant to be only a tool for the artist, but this very fact gives it a particular attraction.

LIBERALE DA VERONA
Born Verona about 1445, died there 1526—1529.

11 Two Studies of a Sleeping Woman with a Child at her Breast. Pen and bistre.

On the reverse (visible through the paper) an old inscription: m° Liberale fece or Vs (Wickhoff read the fece as Vs and thought it might have been written by Vasari). Two pieces of paper joined together in the middle and slightly worked over at the line of juncture; later inscription on a cartellino at bottom: Liberale da Verona.

203 : 279 mm.

Inv. no. 17617 (L. 2903).

Provenance: G. Vasari; P. J. Mariette (L. 2097; Basan, p. 75, no. 463); C. de Tersan; Moriz von Fries (L. 2903).

Albertina Cat. I, 24; Wickhoff, Sc. V. 17; M. Dobroklonsky, Old Master Drawings, London, 1929, p. 3.

Exhibitions: Paris, 1950, no. 11; Andrea Mantegna, Mantua, Palazzo Ducale, 1961, Cat. no. 141.

The drawing technique with emphasis on sharp-edged forms and the use of diagonal hatching without cross-hatching shows the artist to be a follower of Mantegna. The marked expressiveness, deviating from the conventional, that characterizes Liberale's art as a miniaturist and a panel painter. is combined here with an astoundingly realistic motif from daily life. Thus, he produced a study from nature of a unique boldness far ahead of its time.

The catalogue of the Mantegna exhibition mentions the predella with the Birth of the Virgin in the Archbishop's Palace in Verona as related in motif.

ANTONELLO DA MESSINA (Antonello di Giovanni degli Antoni)
Probably born Messina 1430, died there 1479.

12 Portrait Bust of a Boy.

Charcoal, partly rubbed.

330 : 269 mm.

Inv. no. 17611 (L. 174).

Albertina Cat. I, 30; Wickhoff, Sc. V. 11; Schönbrunner-Meder, 594 (Bonsignori); A. Venturi, L'Arte, 1921, p. 72; D. von Hadeln, Venezianische Zeichnungen des Quattrocento, Berlin, 1925, pl. 53; H. and E. Tietze, The Drawings of the Venetian Painters, New York, 1944, no. A 51; Great Drawings of all Time, vol. I, Italian, New York, 1962, no. 96 (W. Ames).

Exhibitions: London, 1948, no. 1; Paris, 1950, no. 8; Venice 1961, no. 5.

This drawing was attributed to Gentile Bellini in the old inventory. Wickhoff suggested Francesco Bonsignori who, however, in another portrait dawing in the Albertina shows an entirely different style. The latter is authenticated as Bonsignori by its correspondence with a signed painting in the National Gallery, London. The correct attribution of the present drawing to Antonello was made by Adolfo Venturi, whose opinion was rightly followed by Hadeln and by Parker (North Italian Drawings of the Quattrocento, London, 1927, pl. 35). Tietze (see above) and Lauts (in Jahrbuch der Kunsthistorischen Sammlungen, N. F. vol. VII, p. 79) thought rather of an artist working in the manner of Alvise Vivarini.

The sheet is one of the finest Venetian portrait drawings of the Early Renaissance. The lucidity and precision of form, worthy of Ingres, could have been achieved only by a great painter. It is impossible to attribute such a drawing to a minor artist, and the relationship to Antonello's paintings is so close that the attribution to him is entirely convincing.
Here we have one of the first of the large-size portrait drawings so characteristic of the Venetian artists (compare nos. 13 and 14). It was Antonello who, profoundly influenced by the Netherlandish masters — Van Eyck and his followers — transplanted their conception of portraiture to Italy.

BARTOLOMEO (BARTOLOMMEO) VENETO
Born Cremona, active in Venice, mentioned between 1502 and 1530.

13 Portrait Bust of a Youth with a Cap.
Charcoal, heightened with white chalk.
380 : 286 mm.
Inv. no. 1452 (L. 174).
Albertina Cat. I, 35; Wickhoff, Sc. V. 9; Schönbrunner-Meder, 274; J. Meder, Albertina-Facsimile, Handzeichnungen italienischer Meister, Vienna, 1923, no. 31; D. von Hadeln, Venezianische Zeichnungen des Quattrocento, Berlin, 1925, no. 86; A. Venturi, L'Arte, 1899, p. 452 and Galleria Crespi, p. 98; H. and E. Tietze, The Drawings of the Venetian Painters, New York, 1944, no. 73.

Exhibitions: London, 1948, no. 6; Paris, 1950, no. 15; Venice, 1961, no. 11.

For comments on the new conception of portraiture in Venice, see the preceding entry. The present drawing was also at one time wrongly attributed to Gentile Bellini and Bonsignori, and its author correctly identified by A. Venturi. The softer style, aiming for a more pictorial impression, clearly reveals a later artist who already belongs to the new century. Portrait drawings of this detailed kind evidently served as preparatory studies for paintings, saving the patron wearisome sittings and leaving the artist more leisure for careful work. Indeed, portraiture was regarded as one of the foremost branches of Venetian painting.

LORENZO LOTTO
Born Venice about 1480, died Loreto 1556.

14 Portrait Bust of a Young Man with a Barret.
Charcoal on brownish paper. The sleeve at the left margin reworked by another hand; possibly the strand of hair on the left extended.
398 : 317 mm.
Inv. no. 1453 (L. 174).
Albertina Cat. I, 84; Wickhoff, Sc. V. 10; Schönbrunner-Meder, 487; D. von Hadeln, Venezianische Zeichnungen des Quattrocento, Berlin, 1925, pl. 71; A. Venturi, Studi dal vero, 1927, p. 268; R. v. Marle, Italian Schools of Painting, XVII, The Hague, 1935, p. 352; H. and E. Tietze, The Drawings of the Venetian Painters, New York, 1944, no. A 326; A. Banti-Boschetto, Lorenzo Lotto, Florence s. a. p. 119; B. Berenson, Lorenzo Lotto, London, 1956, p. 16, fig. 35; J. Byam Shaw, Old Master Drawings, II, London, March, 1928, p. 54; E. Tietze-Conrat, Critica d'Arte VIII (1949—1950), pp. 218—221; U. B. Schmitt, Francesco Bonsignori, Münchner Jahrbuch, XII, 1961, p. 89 ff.

Exhibitions: London, 1948, no. 14; Paris, 1950, no. 23; Venice, 1961, no. 10.

Like nos. 12 and 13, this drawing has been attributed to Gentile Bellini and Bonsignori. Hadeln suggested Giovanni Bellini, an opinion endorsed by Byam Shaw and Van Marle. The old attribution to Bonsignori was recently taken up again by Schmitt, who considers it a portrait of a Gonzaga since it seems to have served as a model for an idealized portrait-engraving in A. Possevino's Gonzaga Iconography of 1617. The convincing attribution to Lotto was first put forward by Giuseppe Fiocco. The stereometric clarity of the structure of the head is also found in the frescoes of the guards on the Onigo Tomb in San Niccolò, Treviso. This portrait is thus an early work, dating from the first years of the sixteenth century, when Giovanni Bellini's influence is clearly noticeable.

BERNARDINO LUINI
Born about 1481—1482, died Milan (?) 1532.

II Portrait of a Lady.
Black and colored chalks.
414 : 284 mm.
Inv. no. 59 (L. 174).
Albertina Cat. VI, 405; Wickhoff, Sc. R. 71; Schönbrunner-Meder, 352; J. Meder, Albertina-Facsimile, Handzeichnungen italienischer Meister des XV.—XVIII. Jahrhunderts, Vienna, 1923, pl. 26; L. Beltrami, Bernardino Luini, Milan, 1911, p. 360; E. Schaeffer, Rassegna d'Arte, XI, 1911, p. 144; A. Ottino della Chiesa, Bernardino Luini, Novara, 1956, p. 148, no. 41.

According to Beltrami and Schaeffer, this drawing represents Ippolita Sforza Bentivoglio and was used as a study for her portrait in the fresco in the Church of San Maurizio, Milan. Neither the alleged direct connection with the fresco nor the identification of the sitter is convincing. The narrow delicate head of the lady in the drawing, and the completely different shape of her mouth and eyebrows are at variance with the strong head and full features of Ippolita Sforza.
In contrast to the large portrait drawings of the Venetians, which, as Hadeln rightly assumed, served as preparations for paintings, this drawing was undoubtedly an independent work of art. The charm of the light and subtle black chalk lines is enhanced by the misty magic of the delicate pastels. The Lombard master was inspired not only by the pensive type of Leonardo's figures, but also by his atmospheric style of drawing. Holbein must have surely seen works of this kind during his sojourn in Lombardy since they are the historical antecedents of his own portraits in colored chalks.

FRANCESCO FRANCIA (Francesco Raibolini)
Born Bologna about 1450, died there 1517.

15 The Judgment of Paris.
Brush and bistre on vellum, with additions in pen to the outlines; upper right corner added in paper.
Numeral in white bodycolor at lower right: 30 (later collector's note).
315 : 260 mm.
Inv. no. 4859 (L. 174).
Albertina Cat. VI, 13; Wickhoff, Sc. L. 3; Schönbrunner-Meder, 10; J. Meder, Albertina-Facsimile, Handzeichnungen italienischer Meister des XV.—XVIII. Jahrhunderts, Vienna, 1923, pl. 20.

Paris is surrounded by Juno, who carries the sacred fire, Athena, who bears arms, and Venus with a lyre. The carefully "chiseled" manner of drawing with the brush on vellum makes one realize that Francia was not only a painter but also a goldsmith and engraver. Through his manner of shading the background of the scene, the artist sought to achieve the effect of a classical relief. In this he was undoubtedly inspired by Mantegna and his school, whose art had probably been transmitted to him by his teachers Ercole de' Roberti and Lorenzo Costa.

GIORGIONE (Giorgio Barbarelli)
Born Castelfranco about 1477—1478, died Venice 1510.

16 The Virgin and St. Joseph Adoring the Infant Christ.
Brush and bistre.
259 : 216 mm.
Inv. no. 1649 (L. 174).
Provenance: Charles, Prince de Ligne (Cat. p. 69, Palma Vecchio, no. 1).
Albertina Cat. I, 36; Wickhoff, Sc. V. 235; Schönbrunner-Meder, 953; H. and E. Tietze, The Drawings of the Venetian Painters, New York, 1944, no. A 718; A. Venturi, L'Arte, 25, 1922, p. 114.

Exhibitions: Venice, Palazzo Ducale, Giorgione e i Giorgioneschi, P. Zampetti, Venice, 1955, p. 290, no. 5; Venice, 1961, no. 8.

Our knowledge of Giorgione's drawing style can be reliably based on three drawings: 1) A study in Windsor Castle (Tietze, no. 719) for the Allendale Adoration of the Shepherds in the National Gallery, Washington; 2) A view of Castelfranco in the Museum Boymans-Van Beuningen (Tietze, no. 709);

3) Jupiter and Antiope in the Print Room of the museum at Darmstadt (Tietze, no. 706). The present drawing, being pure brushwork, lends itself particularly to comparison with the drawing in Windsor Castle. Such a comparison shows conclusively that both are the work of the same hand, a conclusion first drawn by Stix-Fröhlich, after the previous attributions to Palma, Savoldo, and Romanino had proved unsatisfactory. Since the Allendale Adoration is now generally recognized as Giorgione's and since the Windsor drawing gives every indication of being a preparatory study for it, the present drawing must likewise be regarded as a work by Giorgione. Its high quality certainly justifies the attribution. Simplicity and naturalness are combined with solemn calm and the poetic mood characteristic of the master of Castelfranco. Furthermore, the brushwork completely corresponds to that in Giorgione's paintings, for example, in the Madonna in the Ashmolean Museum, Oxford.

TITIAN (Tiziano Vecellio)
Born Pieve di Cadore 1477 (according to tradition), died Venice 1576.

17 Two Kneeling Boys in a Landscape.
Pen and bistre.
236 : 213 mm.
Inv. no. 24364 (acquired 1923).
Provenance: P. J. Mariette (L. 1852); W. Esdaile (L. 2617); Thomas Lawrence (L. 2445); Benjamin West (L. 419); Thomas Agnew.
Albertina Cat. I, 38; W. Constable, Burlington Magazine, XLII, London, 1923, p. 192; D. von Hadeln, Zeichnungen des Tizian, Berlin, 1924, no. 7; A. Stix, Handzeichnungen aus der Albertina, N. F. II, 1925, pl. 16; H. and E. Tietze, The Drawings of the Venetian Painters, New York, 1944, no. 1970.

This drawing was executed in two stages. Titian first drew the two figures, some vegetation, and the lower part of a forked tree. To this finished drawing, he later added the landscape, a swelling of the ground forming the transition. The figures display the same style of pen drawing as the study for the frescoes in the Scuola del Santo, Padua, 1511 (Paris, École des Beaux-Arts, Hadeln, no. 1). The work must therefore be an early one. The landscape in the background, with its picturesque old castles and wooden buildings, carries the complete stamp of Giorgione's style.
Titian's drawings always served the master as preparatory studies for his paintings or prints; no independent drawings are known to us. Nevertheless — especially in his early pen drawings — he developed a decidedly graphic style reminiscent of the engraver's work in its regular parallel curves and cross-hatchings. It is the technique which was used by the circle of Giorgionesque engravers, such as the Campagnolas. It later enabled Titian to instruct printmakers — much as Rubens did at a later date — who disseminated his compositions through engravings and woodcuts. Titian was a prolific draughtsman. More of his work has been preserved than is generally realized, especially drawings from his early period. Some of his work is still attributed to Campagnola and others. The affinity to Domenico Campagnola is so close that a clearcut distinction has not yet been possible. The landscape in this drawing, too, was attributed to Campagnola, but mistakenly, since the drawing is certainly by one and the same hand. The critical catalogue of Titian's drawings is still a desideratum. That Titian's drawings, this one included, are distinguished by an inner greatness and force beyond the scope of the other Venetians, is not surprising in a painter of such genius.
The sheet was copied by Watteau in a red chalk drawing in the Louvre (Parker-Mathey, no. 438). He probably saw Titian's drawing in the Crozat Collection.

GIOVANNI ANTONIO PORDENONE (de Lodesanis or de Sachis)
Born Pordenone about 1484, died Ferrara 1539.

18 Half-Length Figure of a Horseman, with a Pludes Hat.
Red chalk.
156 : 118 mm.
Inv. no. 2408 (L. 174).

Albertina Cat. I, 53; Wickhoff, Sc. B. 469; H. and E. Tietze, The Drawings of the Venetian Painters, New York, 1944, no. 1358.

Exhibition: Venice, 1961, no. 22.

This drawing, formerly considered as a work by Romanino, was identified by Erica Tietze as a study by Pordenone for the figure of a horseman, seen from the back, in his fresco of the Crucifixion in the Cathedral of Cremona (completed 1521), "Zwei venezianische Zeichnungen der Albertina", Die Graphischen Künste, II, 1937, p. 86.) A red chalk drawing of this horseman in full-length is in the Louvre (Hadeln, Venezianische Zeichnungen der Hochrenaissance, Berlin, 1925, pl. 41). In these powerful, broadly-drawn studies from nature in red chalk, Pordenone comes very close to his great contemporary Titian. Boldly thrown on the paper and full of atmosphere, they reveal an artist striving for breadth of conception.

FRA BARTOLOMMEO (Baccio della Porta)
Born Florence 1472, died Pian' di Mugnone 1517.

19 Monastery Built into a Rocky Hillside.
Pen and bistre.
260 : 209 mm.
Inv. no. 270 (L. 174).
Albertina Cat. III, 150; Wickhoff, Sc. R. 322; Schönbrunner-Meder, 1055; F. Knapp, Fra Bartolommeo della Porta, Halle, 1903, p. 312, no. 322, fig. 44; H. v. d. Gabelentz, Fra Bartolommeo und die Florentiner Renaissance, Leipzig, 1922, no. 860; O. Fischel, Raphaels Zeichnungen, Strasbourg, 1898, no. 637; Berenson, 511 A* (1, 2, 3).

This pioneer of a heroic and solemn style of figure composition, who ushered in the High Renaissance in drawing and painting, was also the creator of delicate and sensitive landscape studies which rank him with Dürer and the masters of the Danube School. Like them he developed an effective and highly expressive formula to suggest the tellurian forces at work in plants and stone. Direct transcriptions of nature occasionally stand side by side with free combinations of observed motifs. Thus, in the present drawing, the foreground rocks and trees, which recall Dürer's quarry studies, are combined with the distant view of a small mountain monastery and its surrounding vegetation.
A group of sixty such landscape studies, which had been gathered in one album by the collector Cavaliere Gaburri in 1730, was recently dispersed at a sale at Sotheby's, London, November 20, 1957.

MICHELANGELO BUONARROTI
Born Caprese near Sansepolcro 1475, died Rome 1564.

20 Three Standing Men in Heavy Robes, Facing Left.
Pen and bistre. Lower left old inscription: n°. 61; lower right: collector's note in pencil.
292 : 198 mm.
Verso: Kneeling Man with a Flat Round Cap and Heavy Robe, Seen from the Back.
Inv. no. 116 (L. 174).
Provenance: P. J. Mariette (L. 2097); Charles, Prince de Ligne (Cat. p. 35, no. 1).
Albertina Cat. III, 129; Wickhoff, Sc. R. 150; Schönbrunner-Meder, 195 (692); J. Meder, Albertina-Facsimile, Handzeichnungen italienischer Meister des XV.—XVIII. Jahrhunderts, Vienna, 1923, pl. 9; K. Frey, Die Handzeichnungen Michelagniolos Buonarroti, Berlin, 3 vols., 1909—1911, nos. 23, 22; Berenson, 1602; L. Dussler, Die Zeichnungen des Michelangelo, Berlin, 1959, no. 235; H. Thode, Michelangelo, vol. III, Part I, Berlin, 1912, p. 68, and Michelangelo, Kritische Untersuchungen über seine Werke, vol. I, Berlin 1908, p. 4 and vol. III, Berlin, 1913, no, 525; Ch. de Tolnay, Michelangelo, vol. I, Princeton, 1943, nos. 4 and 5; L. Goldscheider, Michelangelo Drawings, London, 1951, pl. 2 and 3; J. Wilde, Italian Drawings in the British Museum, Michelangelo and his Studio, London, 1953, p. 2; A. E. Popp, Zeitschrift für Bildende Kunst, LIX, 1925/26, p. 142; J. Wilde, Belvedere, XI, 1927, p. 147; Great Drawings of All Time, vol. I, New York 1962, no. 178 (W. Ames).

Exhibitions: A. E. Popham, Italian Drawings Exhibited at the Royal Academy, Burlington House, London, 1930; Oxford, 1931, no. 208; London, 1948, no. 15; Paris, 1950, no. 17.

In the years 1488—89, Michelangelo was a pupil of Ghirlandaio. In 1489, he joined the art school directed by Bertoldo in the Medici Gardens, and from 1490 to 1492, he lived as a guest in the palace of Lorenzo de' Medici. These years witnessed his earliest drawings, free copies of frescoes by Giotto and Masaccio, examples of which have been preserved in the Albertina, the Louvre, and the Graphische Sammlung, Munich. They follow Ghirlandaio's technique of pen drawing, but the masterly handling of the cross-hatching reveals an intensive study of German graphic art, especially of Schongauer's works. The same manner of hatching was used by Michelangelo in working stone. These drawings, which progress from mere copies to free adaptations and thus become original creations, reveal the changed spirit of the young generation of 1470. This generation turned away from the then fashionable works of late Quattrocento art and looked to the monumental style of the masters of 1300 and 1400 for their models. Berenson was the first to point out that this group of figures in ceremonial robes was probably drawn after Masaccio's no longer extant fresco of the consecration, of the church ("Sagra") in the cloister of Santa Maria del Carmine. A drawing in red chalk by another artist in the Casa Buonarroti (De Tolnay, vol. I, p. 179 and fig. 73) shows the same group; in spite of its inferior quality it seems to be more faithful to the original than is that of Michelangelo, who permitted himself many creative liberties. The robe of the main figure is less abstract in Michelangelo's drawing and treated more like cloth falling naturally over the body; the head of the man shows a sharp profile of somber and heroic expression. Michelangelo has dealt with the minor figures even more freely, which has given rise to the erroneous opinion that he added them at a later date. The figure on the right has been said to reproduce the gatekeeper with the keys, a figure in Masaccio's fresco specifically mentioned by Vasari. But in addition to the keys, this man also carries a writing case tied to his belt, so that this assumption is hardly correct. The kneeling figure on the reverse has been presumed to be a copy after Ghirlandaio or Pesellino (Meder), but most experts are agreed that it also harks back to a work of Masaccio's.

III The Dead Christ Supported by St. John, Nicodemus, Joseph of Arimathea, the Virgin, and the Holy Women.

Red chalk, some black chalk.
320 : 251 mm.
Verso: Legs of a Man; Drapery Study. Pen and bistre.
Inv. no. 102 (L. 174).
Provenance: P. J. Mariette (L. 2097); Charles, Prince de Ligne (Cat. p. 36, 10).

Albertina Cat. III, 135; Wickhoff, Sc. R. 136; Schönbrunner-Meder, 73; Berenson, 2502; P. d'Achiardi, Sebastiano del Piombo, Rome, 1908, p. 326—27; L. Dussler, Sebastiano del Piombo, Basel, 1942, no. 251; R. Pallucchini, Sebastian Viniziano, Milan, 1944, pp. 82, 180; H. Thode, Michelangelo, Kritische Untersuchungen über seine Werke, vol. II, pp. 411, 498, and vol. III, no. 521; L. Dussler, Die Zeichnungen des Michelangelo, Berlin, 1959, no. 696; E. Panofsky, Herkules am Scheidewege, Studien der Bibliothek Warburg, Leipzig, 1930, p. 114, note 3 (Circle of Marco dal Pino); H. von Einem, Jahrbuch der Preussischen Kunstsammlungen, 61, 1940, p. 83; K. T. Parker, Catalogue of the Collection of Drawings in the Ashmolean Museum, Oxford, 1956, p. 179, under no. 342; see also A. E. Popham and J. Wilde, The Italian Drawings of the XV. and XVI. Centuries in the Collection of His Majesty the King at Windsor Castle, London, 1949, no. 438; Ch. de Tolnay, Michelangelo, vol. V. Princeton, 1960, p. 216, Cat. 239.
Exhibitions: London, 1948, no. 20; Paris, 1950, no. 19.

This drawing is so close to Michelangelo's mature style that it was always considered to be by him. Berenson was the first to suggest that it might be by Sebastiano del Piombo. This opinion was endorsed by D'Achiardi, and Pallucchini in their monographs, but rejected by Dussler.

The drawing so closely resembles another one of the same subject and in the same technique in the Ashmolean Museum,

Oxford, that it is difficult to distinguish two hands. It is true that there is a difference in the plastic conception of the composition, but from the technical and stylistic point of view there is hardly any discrepancy. The Oxford drawing shows a powerful block of figures with bulky, cubic shapes dramatically developed in depth. This led Parker and Wilde (Catalogue of the Michelangelo Exhibition in the British Museum, 1953, no. 95) to date the sheet in the fifties.
The Albertina drawing, on the other hand, develops the composition more in the manner of a relief, in which the slender, manneristically-elongated figures are fused in flowing curves. For this reason Berenson dated it about 1514—17, but he also dated the Oxford drawing, likewise attributed by him to Sebastiano, 1515—18. Von Einem stresses the stylistic differences between the two sheets and maintains that neither of them is by Michelangelo.
Both drawings were claimed for Michelangelo by Thode and Brinckmann (Michelangelo-Zeichnungen, Munich, 1925, pl. 76) as well as by the Albertina Catalogue (Stix-Fröhlich). Wilde and Parker retain the Michelangelo attribution of the Oxford sheet.
Panofsky, however (Repertorium für Kunstwissenschaft, 1927, p. 50, note 1), rejects Michelangelo's authorship of the Oxford drawing, and is inclined to give the Albertina drawing to the circle of Marco dal Pino or Daniele da Volterra (Herkules am Scheideweg, p. 114, note 3).
Parker stresses the close connection of the Oxford drawing and the one in Vienna ("the most nearly related drawing is a Pietà in Vienna").
De Tolnay calls the attribution of the Vienna drawing to Michelangelo "doubtful". As for the Oxford drawing, he mentions a certain affinity with the drawings of Rosso, but prefers to leave the question of attribution open. Thode associates the cartoon of a Pietà with nine figures, mentioned in the inventory of Michelangelo's property, to the Oxford drawing; De Tolnay relates it to the Albertina drawing. De Tolnay points out quite properly, that the structure of the slender figures in the Albertina drawing is close to the style of the Florentine Mannerists of 1525—35, and that its sfumato corresponds to Michelangelo's drawings of the same period. This dating is probably correct.
The difficulty in attributing the Oxford drawing to Sebastiano is due to the fact that it embodies a style of Michelangelo that goes beyond the time of Sebastiano's death. For this reason Dussler also rejected the attribution to Sebastiano. The drawings in Oxford and Vienna are so closely related in technique that the rejection of one would automatically lead to the rejection of the other. The Oxford drawing has lately found strong supporters, and we must therefore — notwithstanding all doubts and reservations — endorse the attribution of the Albertina drawing to Michelangelo and explain the difference in style of these two important drawings by their difference in date.
The pen studies on the reverse were recognized by J. Wilde — according to a note in his handwriting on the mount — as a drawing by a disciple after a sheet of studies at Chantilly (Berenson, no. 1397).

21 Standing Male Nude, Seen from the Back.

Pen and bistre over light preparatory drawing in chalk. Upper left in another hand: 3; chalk inscription lower right: Buonarota. The sheet's several folds, breaks, and losses have been repaired. Wherever the old drawing was destroyed by the damage to the paper, it has been restored.
Verso: Virgin and Child. Pen and bistre, light preparatory drawing in chalk.
381 : 189 mm.
Inv. no. 118 (L. 174).
Provenance: P. J. Mariette (L. 2097).

Albertina Cat. III, 132; Wickhoff, Sc. R. 152; Schönbrunner-Meder, 419 (360); J. Meder, Albertina-Facsimile, Handzeichnungen italienischer Meister des XV.—XVIII. Jahrhunderts, Vienna, 1923, pl. 11; Berenson, 1603; L. Dussler, Die Zeichnungen des Michelangelo, no. 700; H. Thode, Michelangelo, Kritische Untersuchungen über seine Werke, vol. III, Berlin, 1913, no. 526; A. E. Brinckmann, Michelangelo-Zeichnungen, Munich, 1925, no. 16; Ch. de Tolnay, Michelangelo, I, Princeton, 1943, fig. 285; J. Wilde, The Italian Drawings of the XV. and XVI. Centuries in the Collection of His Majesty the King at Windsor Castle, London, 1949, p. 262; J. Wilde, Italian Drawings in the Department of Prints and Drawings in the British Museum, Michelangelo and his Studio, 1953, p. 14; Great Drawings of All Time, vol. I, Italian, New York, 1962, no. 184 (W. Ames).

Exhibitions: London, 1948, no. 16; Paris, 1950, no. 17 a.

The drawing, a study from the model, was intended for the cartoon of the Battle of Cascina, which Michelangelo was commissioned to paint in 1504. It is an example of the detachment of the plastic form, layer by layer, from the white ground of the paper by means of Michelangelo's masterly manipulation of the hatching. This procedure is analogous to the working method of the sculptor chiseling a figure out of a block of white marble. The arms, which are not executed much beyond the shoulders, still seem "enclosed in the block", if such a metaphor is permissible.

The Albertina owns another study (Cat. III, no. 130) for the fresco in the Sala del Consiglio of the Palazzo Vecchio, which was to depict Florentine warriors of the Battle of Cascina, hurrying to arms after having been surprised by the enemy while bathing. The project never progressed beyond the stage of the cartoon, which became the most famous and most influential work of art in early sixteenth century Florence. Both studies were mistakenly regarded as copies by some scholars. In addition to their artistic quality, a technical peculiarity proves them to be authentic: the delicate preparatory outlines in black chalk or leadpoint. The same technique was used for the study of the Virgin on the reverse of the present drawing, which is considered an original by nearly all the experts. J. Wilde connects it with the Madonna of Taddeo Taddei (London, Royal Academy); this seems all the more plausible as it would bring the date of the recto and the verso very close to each other (i. e., respectively about 1504—05 and 1506).

J. Wilde has pointed out that the same nude reappears, though in reverse, in a studio drawing in the Louvre (Berenson, 1597, recto) and that details of it appear as écorchés in red chalk drawings at Windsor Castle (Cat. 439—441), which are pages from an anatomical sketchbook used in Michelangelo's studio. Although Wilde does not make any definitive decision as to the authenticity of the drawing, he nevertheless emphatically stresses its Michelangelesque character and the authenticity of the Virgin on the reverse.

The allegedly bad state of preservation of the Albertina drawing has also been emphasized on occasion. It is actually better than that of the other drawing for the Battle of Cascina in the Albertina (Cat. III, 130) which has perceptibly suffered from moisture and abrasion.

The present drawing, which has been horizontally folded several times, has broken along the folds; it was later repaired in these areas, and the interrupted pen lines restored. A bigger loss between the upper thighs also seems to have been mended. Otherwise the structure of the drawing is faultlessly preserved, a fact which greatly facilitates its judgment. The outlines have been partly gone over in bistre of a slightly lighter shade. This is most obvious in the area of the torso, but it is also apparent in the lower parts of the thighs, particularly on the inner side of the right knee, on the legs, and in the horizontal line within the bend of the right knee. As these corrections, above all in the area of the knee, are highly meaningful, the present author considers them to have been made by Michelangelo himself.

RAPHAEL (Raffaello Santi)
Born Urbino 1483, died Rome 1520.

22 Madonna with the Pomegranate.

Black chalk; traces of horizontal breaks at the shoulder level of the Virgin.
411 : 295 mm.
Inv. no. 4879 (L. 174).
Provenance: Julien de Parme; Charles, Prince de Ligne (Cat. p. 6, no. 16).

Albertina Cat. III, 49; Wickhoff, Sc. R. 238; Schönbrunner-Meder, 21; J. Meder, Albertina-Facsimile, Handzeichnungen italienischer Meister des XV.—XVIII. Jahrhunderts, Vienna, 1923, pl. 12; O. Fischel, Raphaels Zeichnungen, Strasbourg, 1898, no. 9; O. Fischel, Raphaels Zeichnungen, Berlin, 1913, vol. I, no. 53; O. Fischel, Raphael, London, 1948, vol. I, p. 47; O. Fischel, Raphael, Berlin, 1962, p. 34.

Exhibitions: London, 1948, no. 24; Paris, 1950, no. 25.

The Madonna with the Pomegranate is perhaps the finest extant drawing of Raphael's early Umbrian period. It presents in simple clarity the feminine ideal developed by the young artist under the influence of his teacher Perugino (see no. 10), an ideal combining loveliness with nobility. His technique of drawing in chalk also follows Perugino's, but goes beyond it in the vigorous system of cross-hatching. It shows that the art of the northern engravers was not unknown to the younger members of Perugino's workshop.

Fischel sees a close connection between this drawing and the feminine types in the Marriage of the Virgin (Milan, Brera), which Raphael painted in 1504, prior to his first visit to Florence. Furthermore, he places the drawing at about the same time as the Ansidei Madonna of 1505 (London, National Gallery), and the altarpiece, Madonna and Saints from the Convent of Sant'Antonio, Perugia (New York, The Metropolitan Museum of Art, formerly J. Pierpont Morgan Collection), both of which date from the time of Raphael's first visit to Florence. To the present author, however, the religious lyricism of this drawing appears to be more closely related to the mood of the Madonna Conestabile della Staffa (Leningrad, Hermitage) and of the Madonna from the Solly Collection (Berlin, Staatliche Museen), so that a date of origin before 1504 seems more likely.

23 Four Studies for the "Madonna in the Meadow".

Pen and bistre.
246 : 363 mm.
Verso: Studies for the Same Painting.
Inv. no. 207 (L. 174).

Albertina Cat. III, 50; Wickhoff, Sc. R. 248; Schönbrunner-Meder, 213 (55); J. Meder, Albertina-Facsimile, Handzeichnungen italienischer Meister des XV.—XVIII. Jahrhunderts, Vienna, 1923, pl. 14; O. Fischel, Raphaels Zeichnungen, Strasbourg, 1898, no. 56; O. Fischel, Raphaels Zeichnungen, Berlin, 1913, III, no. 115 (116); O. Fischel, Raphael, London, 1948, I, p. 50; O. Fischel, Raphael, Berlin, 1962, p. 36.

Studies for the painting the "Madonna in the Meadow", Vienna, Kunsthistorisches Museum.

The years 1504 to 1508 are referred to as Raphael's "Florentine period". During this period he visited Florence several times and made a close study of the new Florentine art. His plain Umbrian way of composing and his Umbrian ideal of the Madonna were transformed under the powerful influence of Leonardo, especially through Leonardo's cartoon, the Virgin and Child with St. Anne, which strongly impressed not only Raphael but also his Florentine contemporaries. The group of mother and child shows more movement and, at the same time, is more compact in its outline, integrating itself within the triangular form that Leonardo and Fra Bartolommeo had developed in their Madonna compositions. The purest and finest result of this synthesis of Umbria and Florence is the Madonna in the Meadow of 1505, in the Kunsthistorisches Museum, Vienna. The present sheet is covered on both sides with compositional ideas for this painting. Raphael seems to have followed Leonardo's example also in that he let his compositional idea unfold like a living organism in a series of ever new variations. His main problem was the relationship of the two children, the Infant Christ and the little St. John. In the painting the Infant Christ, lightly held by His mother, tries to take His first steps toward His playmate and, seeking either support or a toy, seizes John's little cross. The motif of the "first step" is explored on the recto of the drawing, where the artist, after a preliminary attempt in the lower part of the sheet, seems to have continued in the upper left-hand corner. The reverse is mainly devoted to the two children. There is a wealth of impressions from everyday life, illustrating the plainly human in Raphael's otherwise exalted art.

There is an old copy of this drawing in the Uffizi (Fischel, 1898, no. 57).

24   Study for the Muse Euterpe.
     Pen and bistre; the two lower corners added.
     244 : 217 mm.
     Inv. no. 219 (L. 174).
     Provenance: Timoteo Viti; Crozat; Gouvernet; Julien de
     Parme; Charles, Prince de Ligne (L. 592 and no. 35), Cat.,
     p. 6, no. 13.
     Study for the Muse to the left of Apollo in the fresco Par-
     nassus, Stanza della Segnatura.
     Verso: Drapery study for the muse standing to the right
     of Apollo, seen from the back. Upper right corner patched up
     with paper almost to the middle of the sheet; later inscrip-
     tion, lower left: raphael d'urbino.
     Albertina Cat. III, 65; Wickhoff, Sc. R. 262; Schönbrunner-
     Meder, 374 (786); J. Meder, Albertina-Facsimile, Handzeich-
     nungen italienischer Meister des XV.—XVIII. Jahrhunderts,
     Vienna, 1923, pl. 17; O. Fischel, Raphaels Zeichnungen, Stras-
     bourg, 1898, no. 111; O. Fischel, Raphaels Zeichnungen,
     Berlin, 1922, V, no. 250 (252 erroneously indicated as re-
     verse of Fischel 251, The Muse Erato, Albertina Cat. III, 66).
     Exhibitions: London, 1948, no. 28; Paris, 1950, no. 32.
     Between June, 1509, and November, 1511, Raphael painted
     his most important frescoes, those decorating the walls of the
     Stanza della Segnatura in the Vatican. In addition to designs
     for the complete compositions or for various groups within
     the compositions, there have also been preserved studies for
     individual figures in which we can admire the range and
     wealth of Raphael's invention. His familiarity with the world
     of antiquity, demonstrated in the Parnassus, led him to seek
     his models among antique statues. While the head, the arms,
     and the torso of Euterpe are drawn from life, the drapery
     is copied with few alterations from the so-called Sleeping
     Ariadne in the Vatican. Living model and antique prototype
     are so skillfully fused into an organic whole that the trans-
     ition from one to the other is not noticeable. Euterpe's
     counterpart, the Muse Erato, is represented in another pre-
     paratory drawing in the Albertina which is closely related
     to the present one.

ANDREA DEL SARTO (Andrea di Agnolo)
Born Florence 1486, died there 1530.

25   Head of a Woman with Lowered Gaze.
     Red chalk; remainder of an old inscription in bistre: Di...;
     frame drawn in brush and bistre by a later hand.
     197 : 139 mm.
     Inv. no. 4867.
     Albertina Cat. III, 162; Schönbrunner-Meder, 562; Beren-
     son, 160; S. J. Freedberg, Andrea del Sarto, Cambridge, Mass.,
     1963, p. 127.
     Berenson has shown that this slightly lowered head served as
     a preparatory study for the Madonna in the Lamentation for
     S. Pietro in Luco Mugello (now in the Palazzo Pitti, Florence).
     Andrea painted the panel for this convent in 1523—24, when
     he took refuge there from the plague.
     Most of Andrea's drawings, invariably executed in red or
     black chalk, are masterly studies, after the model, for his
     paintings. There is a clarity and precision in his rendering of
     forms that is marble-like and suggests the cleavage of stone,
     despite the fluidity of line and the sfumato of modeling. Un-
     doubtedly, this serious style of drawing, like the style of all
     other Florentine artists active in the first decades of the
     sixteenth century, was overshadowed by Michelangelo's spirit.
     Andrea's art of drawing continued to exert an influence in
     Florence well into the seventeenth century.

FRANCIABIGIO (Francesco di Cristofano)
Born Florence 1482 (1483?), died there 1525.

26   Head of a Young Woman, Three-Quarter Profile to the Left.
     Black chalk, heightened with white chalk on reddish-yellow
     prepared paper; early nineteenth century inscription:
     Raphaël d'Urbino 72 (?).
     183 : 178 mm.
     Verso: Three Studies of the Belvedere Torso.
     Pen and bistre. 18th century inscription in ink: Raphaello da
     Urbino / fec:ᵗ da il Torso / di Belvedere. NB: Verso, Tête p : r
     Une Madonna: / p̃r Raphaël d'Urbino.

19th century inscription in pencil: Winkler Cabinet; also, 1352.
Rafael d'Urbino. / Cat. de Rutgers.
Inv. no. 27472 (acquired 1937).
Provenance: A. Rutgers; Winkler; H. W. Campe (L. 1391).
Albertina Cat. VI, 717.

This fine portrait study, which the present author discovered
on the art market in 1937, was attributed to Raphael in previous collections. For all its quality, however, it obviously
fails to justify this attribution. On the basis of its style, it is
the work of a Florentine artist from the circle of Andrea del
Sarto, an artist who was susceptible also to Raphael's influence and distinguished as a portraitist. These qualifications
fit Franciabigio, whom the author suggests as the draughtsman of this charming sheet. This attribution is confirmed by
a comparison with the authentic study at Oxford for St. John
in the fresco of the Last Supper in the refectory of the
Convento della Scalza in Florence (Parker, Catalogue II, 232).
The pen sketches on the reverse after Apollonius' torso in the
Belvedere are by another hand.

JACOPO PONTORMO (Jacopo Carrucci)
Born Pontormo 1494, died Florence 1557.

27   Portrait of a Seated Woman, Turned to the Left, with her
     Left Arm Resting on the Arm of the Chair, Half-Length.
     Black and red chalk. Later inscription in pen and bistre, upper
     left: Andrea del Sarto; pencil inscription, upper right: 22;
     upper left corner added.
     389 : 243 mm.
     Inv. no. 164 (L. 174).
     Albertina Cat. III, 220; Wickhoff, Sc. R. 202; Waagen, II,
     p. 136; Berenson, 2368 C*; Pantheon, X, Munich, 1932, p. 301.
     Pontormo, who as a painter was one of the earliest founders
     of Florentine Mannerism, was the most outstanding draughts-
     man among Andrea del Sarto's followers. Like Andrea, he drew
     a great many lively and expressive studies from life that
     served in the realization of his bold, abstract, and spiritualized
     compositions. It was only in his last period that he fell under
     the spell of Michelangelo's overpowering draughtsmanship.
     Pontormo's portraits are all reality, though an intensified
     reality. They demonstrate that wherever the development of
     Mannerism can be observed, the increase in the abstract ele-
     ment did not preclude a more intense, even if only partial,
     comprehension of reality. The present drawing was identified
     by Berenson as a work of Pontormo (Waagen, who rightly
     appreciated its quality, deemed it a work by Andrea del Sarto,
     Wickhoff only a copy thereof). It is equal to Pontormo's
     finest portraits, whether painted or drawn, which proclaim
     a new human ideal formed by spiritual nobility.

GIULIO ROMANO (Giulio Pippi)
Born Rome 1499, died Mantua 1546.

28   Apollo and the Nine Muses.
     Pen and bistre.
     254 : 401 mm.
     Inv. no. 323.
     Albertina Cat. III, 96; Wickhoff, Sc. R. 390; H. Dollmayr,
     Jahrbuch der Kunsthistorischen Sammlungen des Allerhöch-
     sten Kaiserhauses, 16, Vienna, 1895, p. 262, fig. 9; F. Hartt,
     Giulio Romano, New Haven, 1958, vol. I, p. 298, no. 184.
     Design for the fifth scene in the cycle of frescoes in the
     Loggia della Grotta in the garden of the Palazzo del Té,
     Mantua.
     Raphael's pupil Giulio Romano was active in the service of
     Duke Federigo Gonzaga at Mantua from the end of 1524 until
     his death. His main work there was the summer residence,
     the Palazzo del Tè, for which he was given a free hand in the
     architecture and the fresco decoration. Between the principal
     periods of construction, 1527—29 and 1530—35, the Casino
     della Grotta, a miniature palace standing isolated in the gar-
     den, was built. Giulio decorated its loggia with a cycle of
     frescoes called "An Allegory of Life", which is probably based
     on some unidentified literary source. The present drawing is
     a study for the representation of the "Dance". The player of
     the lyre probably represents Apollo. The nine figures var-
     iously playing musical instruments, dancing, and looking on,
     are characterized as feminine in the drawing and may repre-
     sent the Muses.

POLIDORO DA CARAVAGGIO (Polidoro Caldara)
Born Caravaggio 1496—1500, died Rome 1543.

29   Amor, Eyes Bandaged and Carrying a Big Heart, Runs towards a Seated Girl, Stretching out her Arms to him; on the Left, Several Studies of Hands.

Red chalk. Lower right, old inscription in pen and bistre: polidoro. Watermark: hand with flower, Briquet 10790.
183 : 298 mm.
Recto: Marriage of the Virgin.
Inv. no. 380 (reverse).
Albertina Cat. III, 172 (reverse); Wickhoff, Sc. R. 452; see H. Voss, Die Malerei der Spätrenaissance in Rom und Florenz, vol. I, 1920, p. 82, note 1; A. E. Popham, Catalogue of the Fenwick Collection, 1935, p. 35, no. 4; P. Pouncey and J. A. Gere, Italian Drawings ... in the British Museum, Raphael and his Circle, London, 1962, no. 204.
Old attribution: Domenichino. Morelli: Polidoro.

The artist, a native of Upper Italy, came to Rome where he participated in the decoration of the Logge in the Vatican which was proceeding after Raphael's design under the direction of Giulio Romano and Giovanni da Udine. It was here that Polidoro developed his talent for decoration which, later on, manifested itself in numerous fresco paintings, mainly in the decoration of house façades in grisaille.
The present drawing bears on its recto a Marriage of the Virgin, a composition with many figures. It is part of a series of drawings in red chalk preserved in the Albertina, the Louvre, and the British Museum, which obviously come from the same sketchbook. The sheets combine free compositions with drawings from ancient models and studies from life. In this drawing the group of Eros and the young girl is a free invention typical of that aspect of Mannerism developed by Raphael's School: Raphael's style enhanced by Michelangelo's heroic manner. In contrast, the masterly studies of hands and arms are the result of direct observation.

PIERINO (PERINO) DEL VAGA (Pietro Buonaccorsi)
Born Florence 1500—1501, died Rome 1547.

30   The Martyrdom of the Ten Thousand under King Sapor in **Persia.**

Pen and brush and bistre, washed, heightened with white bodycolor on brown paper; lower left corner missing, cut in upper part.
364 : 339 mm.
Inv. no. 2933 (L. 174).
Provenance: P. J. Mariette, Basan p. 38, no. 223.
Wickhoff Sc. L. 384 (Giovanni Battista Sassi).
A copy in the Fogg Museum of Art, A. Mongan — Paul J. Sachs, Drawings in the Fogg Museum of Art, Cambridge, Mass., 1946, no. 191; Bernice Davidson, Master Drawings I. no. 4, Winter 1963, pp. 20, 25, no. 6, Pl. 16.

Pierino, a Florentine by birth, was, along with Giulio Romano, the most important artist of Raphael's workshop. Like Polidoro, he started his career in Rome by taking part in the decoration of the Logge in the Vatican under the direction of Giovanni da Udine. Of all the members of Raphael's studio he had the greatest gift for decoration, and so was predestined for the execution of numerous fresco commissions. When he fled Rome for Florence in 1523 because of the plague, the Compagnia dei Martiri commissioned him to paint a fresco representing the Martyrdom of the Ten Thousand for the church of the monastery of Camaldoli. Vasari in his "Vita" of the artist accorded the preparatory drawing and the cartoon great praise, but the fresco was never executed. Until now a drawing from the Loeser Collection in the Fogg Museum of Art in Cambridge, Mass., U.S.A., has been regarded as the study mentioned by Vasari (P. J. Sachs and A. Mongan, Drawings in the Fogg Museum of Art, no. 191). The authors of the Albertina catalogue considered the present drawing a copy. Walter Vitzthum correctly observed that the relationship is just the reverse.
The artist has very cleverly fitted the composition into the Gothic arch at his disposal, the latent Gothic element in Mannerism facilitating his task. The scenes of the background were inspired by Dürer's woodcut of the same subject (Bartsch 117).

CORREGGIO (Antonio Allegri)
Born Modena 1489—1494, died there 1534.

31   Young Man Holding up a Basin.
Red chalk.
282 : 205 mm.
Inv. no 26042 (acquired 1930).
Provenance: W. Rudinoff.
Albertina Cat. VI, 354; O. Benesch, Old Master Drawings, VI, London, March 1932, p. 64 and Pl. 60; A. E. Popham, Correggio's Drawings, London, 1957, p. 195, no. A 125.

Exhibition: Paris, 1950, no. 43.

In 1522 Correggio signed the contract for the decoration of the cupola of Parma Cathedral with an Assumption of the Virgin. He started work in 1526 and received payments until 1530; but at his death the decoration was still not entirely finished.
Correggio was a prolific draughtsman, and the number of his existing drawings — always studies and sketches for paintings — is surprisingly large. The present drawing is a study for one of the youths on the parapet carrying incense burners and censers. It is undoubtedly by the same hand as a long-famous drawing in the Albertina which bore Correggio's name in the collections of Crozat, Julien de Parme and Prince de Ligne: the study for one of the apostles (Cat. VI, 353) standing in front of the parapet who protects himself from the brilliant light. Both figure studies reveal this artist's typical loose chalk strokes with open parallel hatching. The author cannot agree with A. E. Popham's attribution of the study of the apostle to Annibale Carracci (loc. cit. no. A 124), since the origin of this drawing in the first half of the sixteenth century can hardly be queried.

PARMIGIANINO (Francesco Mazzola)
Born Parma 1503, died Casal Maggiore 1540.

32   The Virgin with the Infant Christ and an Angel.
Pen and bistre, washed, on reddish tinted paper.
Collector's number: 16.
201 : 161 mm.
Inv. no. 2630 (L. 174).
Wickhoff Sc. L. 60.

Exhibition: Vienna, Albertina. Parmigianino und sein Kreis (K. Oberhuber), Vienna, 1963, no. 23.

On the mount confirmation of the old attribution by Morelli ("Vero Mo").

Analogous to the Mannerism developed by a younger generation of artists from the premises provided by the works of Michelangelo, Raphael and Andrea del Sarto in Rome and Florence, there also originated a mannerist movement in Northern Italy based on the heritage of the great masters of the classical High Renaissance. Thus in Parma where Correggio had been active since 1518, the art of Parmigianino grew out of the precedents created by this artist. A Roman sojourn from 1523 to 1527 left the impress of the art of Michelangelo and Raphael, and their followers. His style evolves as a quintessence of the cult of form, refined and spiritualized to the utmost. Parmigianino was a painter a slow and extremely self-critical artist who carefully prepared his paintings by numerous drawings. These rank among the highest achievements of Italian draughtsmanship.
A. E. Popham identified the present drawing as a preparatory study for an unfinished painting in an English private collection. In the painting the figure of the angel is omitted. The work dates from the artist's mature period, perhaps from his years in Bologna, like the "Holy Family in a Landscape" of the Museo di Capodimonte in Naples. While the latter betrays the influence of Sebastiano del Piombo, the present sheet in the classical fullness of the figure recalls Raphael. The elongated limbs of the Madonna with their "radiating" tapering fingers and toes, and the delicate brittleness of the draperies, are entirely Parmigianino's own stylistic properties.

FRANCESCO PRIMATICCIO
Born Bologna 1504, died Paris 1570.

33 Women at a Game of Draughts, with a Girl Playing the Lute, and a Faun, the Cymbals.

Red chalk, heightened with brush and white bodycolor, on yellowish paper. Right half of a lunette. Lower right, seventeenth century inscription: Bologne F.

272 : 238 mm.

Inv. no. 1989 (L. 174).

Albertina Cat. VI, 30; Wickhoff Sc. B. 31; L. Dimier, Le Primatice, Paris, 1900, p. 454, no. 159.

Preparatory drawing for the right wing of "The Concert", the fresco above the balcony of the ballroom of Fontainebleau. The preparatory drawing for the left wing was in the collection of the Marquis de Chennevières, Paris (Dimier 226). The most original monument of the Late Renaissance style known as "Mannerism" is the Palace of Fontainebleau and its decoration. Francis I and Henry II summoned leading mannerist artists from Italy to France and entrusted them with the decoration of the palace: Rosso, Primaticcio, Vignola, Serlio, Benvenuto Cellini and Niccolò dell'Abbate. A kind of academy, consisting of Frenchmen, Italians and Netherlanders, thus developed at Fontainebleau, blending the Late Renaissance art of the South and of the North and making the palace an artistic center whose influence radiated throughout Europe. The "Style of Fontainebleau" consequently has become a concept of art history.

Primaticcio, who in his youth worked for six years on the decoration of the Palazzo del Tè in Mantua under the direction of Giulio Romano, was eminently gifted for the task of executing large decorative frescoes. He was called to Fontainebleau in 1532. He first worked together with Rosso, who influenced the formation of his style, as did the art of Parmigianino which must have been familiar to him as a native of Bologna. Reminiscent of Parmigianino above all are the slender female figures with elongated limbs. The Albertina is rich in Primaticcio studies for Fontainebleau. The present design was intended for a spandrel of the ballroom decorated by Primaticcio between 1550 and 1556.

It demonstrates the artist's superior ability at balancing a rich and complicated composition, and adapting it to the semicircle available to him. Primaticcio's favorite technique — red chalk and white bodycolor — permits careful modeling and a clear accentuation of the plastic values, within the richness of invention.

NICCOLÒ DELL' ABBATE
Born Modena about 1506, died Fontainebleau 1571.

34 Coriolanus Receiving his Wife and his Mother with the Women of Rome in the Volscian Camp.

Pen and bistre, washed, brush and white bodycolor on brown paper. Inscription by another hand: Nicolas labadj.

394 : 528 mm.

Inv. no. 14396 (L. 174).

Wickhoff Sc. B. 47.

Exhibition: Vienna, Albertina. Parmigianino und sein Kreis (K. Oberhuber)), Vienna, 1963, no. 182.

Virgilia, Coriolanus' wife, points admonishingly to Rome, which is seen in the distance and is "symbolically" represented by the Arch of Titus, the Temple of Vesta, the Pyramid of Cestius, an early Christian column from the tomb of St. Peter in St. Peter's, and the statue of Marcus Aurelius. The women are summoning Coriolanus' mother Volumnia to act as their spokesman.

The artist, who had already done a series of interesting frescoes in the tradition of Emilian and Ferrarese art in Bologna during the forties, was called to Fontainebleau in 1552. As a collaborator of Primaticcio's in murals and decorative projects, he was extensively influenced by the latter's style. In his attitude and silhouette, Coriolanus is a typical Primaticcio figure. The modeling with high lights brushed in white bodycolor on tinted paper corresponds also to Primaticcio's manner of drawing. The half-length

figures at the lower edge are a characteristic feature of the mannerist way of building up a composition in stages, which originated in Michelangelo's Crucifixion of St. Peter in the Capella Paolina.

The artist found more scope for his individuality in his panel paintings, where he could display his mastery of landscape painting.

MASTER OF FLORA

35 The Annunciation.

Pen and bistre, washed, heightened with white bodycolor.

317 : 241 mm.

Inv. no. 2592 (L. 174).

Albertina Cat. VI, 363 (School of Parma, middle of the 16th century); Wickhoff, Sc. L. 18 (Camillo Boccaccino).

Anonymous artist, probably Italian, active in the School of Fontainebleau, called after his main work, the painting of "Flora", formerly collection of Baron d'Albenas, Montpellier. Sylvie Béguin, L'Ecole de Fontainebleau, Paris, 1960, p. 73 ff; see also the catalogue of the exhibition: Charles Sterling, Le Triomphe du Maniérisme Européen, Amsterdam, 1955, nos. 78, 79; (Sylvie Béguin) Art de France, no. I, Paris, 1961, pp. 301—304.

The identity of the hand responsible for this drawing and the "Cephalus and Procris", Germain Seligman, New York (Exhibition: Van Clouet tot Matisse, Museum Boymans, Rotterdam 1958, Cat. no. 11, fig. 8) is evident.

The attribution of the present author is based on the correspondence of style with the known works of the master. The drawing combines grace and liveliness of invention with a subtle technique derived from the drawings of Primaticcio and Niccolò dell'Abbate. The typical graceful figures are in complete accord with those of the artist's paintings. This highly gifted anonymous master, whose rare works embody the courtly atmosphere of Fontainebleau in its purest form, was a younger artist among the followers of Primaticcio and Niccolò dell'Abbate. It is significant of the international character of this powerful mannerist movement that it is not easy to decide whether the artist was of Italian or French origin. The former is more probable.

As there is a copy by his hand of Primaticcio's "Concert" in the ballroom of Fontainebleau, his works, which are fairly similar in style, cannot be dated before the middle of the century. They show a preference for the precious and jewel-like, for ornament which finds expression in the hair styles and garments of the figures as well as in the furniture of the rooms. He seems to have been known to French artists of the Empire period like Prud'hon and Girodet-Trioson.

LELIO ORSI
Born Novellara 1511, died there 1587.

36 Young Woman, Sewing, Seated in an Open Doorway.

Pen and brush and bistre on brownish paper, heightened with white bodycolor. Squared for transfer in leadpoint. Old inscription, perhaps by the artist's own hand: lelio da nivelara.

288 : 161 mm, silhouetted along the frame of the door.

Inv. no. 2728 (L. 174).

Wickhoff Sc. L. 160.

Exhibition: Reggio Emilia, Mostra di Lelio Orsi, 1950, p. 138, no. 30.

Design for a decorative wall fresco.

Lelio Orsi was one of the most individual artists of the Late Renaissance in North Italy. His art derived essentially from a synthesis of the inspirations he received from Correggio and Michelangelo, and a strong Nordic element, probably going back to Dürer and the German masters. The style of the contemporary North Italian mannerists had no significant effect on him. He thus developed in provincial seclusion, so to speak, a highly expressive art, a kind of expressionism which led to splendid achievements in draughtsmanship. Even Rembrandt valued him highly as a draughtsman and collected his works.

The present drawing is probably a project for an illusionistic wall-painting, of which Orsi produced a series of examples. In spite of the effort to achieve a correct perspective construction (in accordance with the problem posed), the result is a work of genuine feeling, full of poetry and intimate charm.

JACOPO BASSANO (Jacopo da Ponte)
Born Bassano about 1517—1518, died there 1592.

37 Portrait of an Elderly Woman.

Brush and oil, in various colors on brownish paper; contemporary inscription: La Matre di Mr. Galeasso Gallassi fu lasciato Nella Re / di dto galeasso et Anibal fratelli et figli di d. tta Madona. Lower right: the numeral 64.
353 : 249 mm.
Inv. no. 17656 (L. 174).
Provenance: Charles, Prince de Ligne (Cat. p. 63, no. 1).
Albertina Cat. I, 71; Wickhoff, Sc. V. 137; Schönbrunner-Meder, 651; H. and E. Tietze, The Drawings of the Venetian Painters, New York, 1944, no. A 199; W. Arslan, I Bassano, Milan, 1960, p. 380; R. Pallucchini, "Commento alla Mostra di Jacopo Bassano", Arte Veneta, 1957, p. 118, fig. 116.
Exhibitions: London, 1948, no. 7; Venice, Jacopo Bassano, 1957, p. 254, no. 26; Venice, 1961, no. 39.

The technique of drawing in oil with the brush, although unusual with Jacopo Bassano, is frequently found in Venetian art of this period (as for instance with Jacopo and Domenico Tintoretto). There is consequently no reason to question the old attribution in favor of a seventeenth century artist as do the Tietzes and Arslan, who prefer to attribute this drawing to Domenico Fetti or to some other Seicento artist from Emilia. The ductus of the brush stroke is completely sixteenth century and corresponds to the underpainting of Venetian Cinquecento pictures. Pallucchini has correctly attributed the drawing to Jacopo Bassano's last period. In its simplicity and human directness it fully conforms to the bourgeois, but psychologically penetrating character of Jacopo's portrait painting. It is one of the most magnificent and forward-looking accomplishments of Venetian Cinquecento draughtsmanship.

JACOPO TINTORETTO (Jacopo Robusti)
Born Venice 1518, died there 1594.

38 Male Nude.

Charcoal; eighteenth or early nineteenth century inscription in bistre, lower right: G. Tintoretto.
328 : 227 mm.
Inv. no. 24475 (acquired 1923).
Provenance: Sir Joshua Reynolds (L. 2364).
Albertina Cat. I, 90; A. Stix, Handzeichnungen aus der Albertina, Vienna, 1925, N. F. II, plate 23; H. and E. Tietze, The Drawings of the Venetian Painters, New York, 1944, no. 1752; E. Tietze-Conrat, Die Graphischen Künste N. F. I, Vienna, 1936, p. 91.
Exhibitions: London, 1948, no. 34; Paris, 1950, no. 44.

Tintoretto's drawings are mostly studies in chalk or charcoal for individual figures in his compositions or studies after sculpture. The male nudes follow the mannerist principle of form of the "sacco di noci" (bag of nuts), with an over-emphasis on the muscular parts of the naked body. Also mannerist is a certain abstraction in the representation of the body, where movement is the artist's only concern; this makes it hard to decide whether a drawing is a study after a live model or after some small plastic model the artist had made for this purpose. In the present drawing it is probably a case of the former. The attitude of the seated man is that of a live model holding on to a rope with one arm. Erica Tietze-Conrat thought the figure had been used in reverse for the executioner in the center of the Martyrs' Altar in S. Giorgio Maggiore, a late work of Tintoretto's. But the ponderation of the figure in the painting is completely different: the man is not sitting, he is standing; he does not hang on the rope, he pulls it up. Tintoretto strove, by his own avowal, to make his art a synthesis of Titian and Michelangelo, of color and drawing (disegno). Hence drawing played a prominent role in his creative activity.

PAOLO VERONESE (Paolo Caliari)
Born Verona 1528, died Venice 1588.

39 Sheet of Compositional Designs.

Most of these sketches are preparatory for the composition "The Doge Sebastiano Ziani Receiving Pope Alexander III Disguised as a Pilgrim near the Scuola della Carità". At the upper left are three studies, one on top of the other, for the composition "Pope and Doge Sending Envoys with Peace Proposals to Frederick Barbarossa".
Pen and bistre, washed. Various inscriptions in the artist's hand in which the word "Capitanio" is repeated; this, as proved by the inscription at the upper left, refers to the doge: Capitanio gradicente il Papa a Venezia; lower right, in ink: Paolo (?).
298 : 216 mm.
Verso: Studies of Boats for the Same Composition. Pen and bistre, washed.
Inv. no. 24476 (acquired 1923).
Provenance: Luigi Grassi (L. 1171b).
Albertina Cat. I, 108; A. Stix, Handzeichnungen aus der Albertina, N. F. II, Vienna, 1925, plate 28; D. v. Hadeln, Venezianische Zeichnungen der Spätrenaissance, 1926, p. 27; G. Fiocco, Paolo Veronese, Bologna, 1928, p. 210, no. 3; H. and E. Tietze, The Drawings of the Venetian Painters, New York, 1944, no. 2152; B. Degenhart in Halm, Degenhart, Wegener, Hundert Meisterzeichnungen aus der Staatlichen Graphischen Sammlung München, Munich, 1958, p. 50.
Exhibitions: Paris, 1950, no. 45; Venice, 1961, no. 42.

These studies were intended for two historical paintings in the Sala del Maggior Consiglio for which Veronese was given the commission after the fires in the Ducal Palace in 1574 and 1577. He was no longer able to execute them personally, and they were executed after his death by the "Heredes Paoli" (Benedetto and Carletto Caliari) who continued his workshop. They belong to the series representing episodes of the conflict between Pope Alexander III and the Emperor Frederick Barbarossa on the north wall of the room. The present drawing was part of a sketchbook, another leaf of which with designs for the same scenes is in the Graphische Sammlung in Munich (Inv. no. 1951: 63). Veronese shared with Tintoretto, the other leading painter of the Late Renaissance in Venice, the gift of creating large compositions with many figures, but with him they do not appear in a dramatic chiaroscuro, but in brilliant daylight and in gay, frequently refracted and iridescent colors. The majority of his drawings are thus devoted to collective compositions, always in pen or brush. The many variations on such a sheet of studies testify to the care with which the artist pondered his creations. In spite of their looseness, these drawings originate from a solid cubic body structure as distinguished from the drawings of artists who are closer to the Baroque, as for instance Palma Giovane. Veronese's individual studies from nature are always done in black and white chalk, and in contrast to Tintoretto's sombre austerity and sinister anonymity convey an impression of colorful, breathing life as do the chalk drawings of Titian.

FRANCESCO SALVIATI (Francesco de'Rossi)
Born Florence 1510, died Rome 1563.

40 The Birth of the Virgin.

Pen and bistre, washed, heightened with white bodycolor on blue paper; squared in leadpoint for transfer; inscription in pencil lower right: Francesco Salviati; and numeral 9 in upper left corner.
348 : 264 mm.
Inv. no. 478 (L. 174).
Wickhoff Sc. R. 569.

Study for an Altarpiece. The composition obviously derives from Andrea del Sarto's fresco in S. Maria dell'Annunziata in Florence, which, in its turn, was inspired by Dürer's woodcut from the Life of the Virgin. The group of women in the foreground has been transposed from Andrea's classical High Renaissance style into Pierino del Vaga's Raphaelesque mannerism which strongly affected Salviati. Joachim follows the model of Michelangelo's Moses. Several of the ideas found in this drawing recur in Salviati's fresco of the "Birth of St. John the Baptist" painted in 1551 in the Oratory of S. Giovanni Decollato in Rome.

The drawing was probably made between 1544 and 1548, when the artist, who traveled extensively, was active in Florence. As a fellow-student with Vasari in Baccio Bandinelli's studio and as a pupil of Andrea del Sarto, Salviati belonged to the middle generation of Mannerists who effected a synthesis of the styles of Florence and Rome. By reason of his sojourn in Venice and the residence of his pupil Giuseppe Salviati in this city, he played an important role in transmitting the style of Florence and Rome to the Venetian painters, particularly to Tintoretto.

FEDERICO BAROCCI
Born Urbino 1526, died there 1612.

41 Edge of a Forest.

Charcoal, brush and bistre and white bodycolor.

323 : 283 mm.

Inv. no 567 (L. 174).

Provenance: P. J. Mariette, Basan p. 28, no. 169 (L. 2097). Albertina Cat. III, 396; Wickhoff Sc. R. 663; A. Schmarsow, Federigo Baroccis Zeichnungen III, Die Zeichnungen in den Sammlungen ausserhalb Italiens, Abhandlungen der philologisch-historischen Klasse der kgl. sächsischen Gesellschaft der Wissenschaften XXX, Leipzig, 1914, p. 36; H. Olsen, Federico Barocci, Figura 6, Stockholm (Uppsala), 1955, p. 182; the same, Copenhagen, 1962, p. 235.

This great artist was, apart from Pontormo, Parmigianino, and Tintoretto, the only outstanding painter and draughtsman of genius produced by Mannerism in Italy. He belonged to the third and last generation of mannerist painters (his date of birth is sometimes given as 1535). Like El Greco, he outgrew the movement with which he was connected more by his unrealistic, iridescent color and certain principles of composition than by the molding of forms which consciously conform to Correggio's late classical style. In contrast to the formalism of Florence and Rome where only the works of Raphael attracted him, the Umbrian artist, faithful to his native tradition, emphasized the emotional fervor which, as with El Greco, assumes visionary intensity. It was, if any, this purely religious painter who gave adequate expression to the spirituality of the Counter-Reformation in Italy. Accordingly, assiduous drawing from nature, not only of the human figure but also of the human face as the mirror of the soul, played a major role in his art. Along with his drawings from life, he made landscape studies of such surprising modernism that they seem to anticipate those of Rubens. They are not imaginary compositions like the landscape drawings of the Bolognese, but direct observations of nature, which capture the full magic of light and atmosphere with a delicate touch of the brush. The present drawing is one of the finest.

GIORGIO VASARI
Born Arezzo 1511, died Florence 1574.

42 The Forge of Vulcan.

Pen and bistre, washed; old inscriptions in pen and bistre; Vasari; asta . . . 12 Bt (apparently an indication of scale).

229 : 411 mm.

Inv. no. 517 (L. 174).

Provenance: P. J. Mariette (L. 2097). Old attribution. Wickhoff Sc. R. 612.

In 1555, Vasari painted the frescoes in the Sala degli Elementi of the Palazzo Vecchio as a courtly allegory on Francesco de' Medici. On the side of the chimney-piece he depicted the element of Fire, symbolized by Vulcan's Forge. In his "Ragionamenti sopra le invenzioni da lui dipinte", an imaginary dialogue between the "Principe" (Ferdinando de' Medici) and "Giorgio" (Vasari), he described the scenes in detail. Vulcan forges the arrows for Venus, whose Erotes

give them the final polish. The three Cyclopes, Sterope, Bronte, and Piragmone, forge Jupiter's thunderbolts which other Erotes put into the glowing fire.

The present drawing is Vasari's careful original design for the Element of Fire. His assistant in the execution of these frescoes was Cristofano Gherardi, called Doceno, in whose biography Vasari reports that Doceno painted the group of the Cyclopes and the decorative framework. For this purpose Doceno made an outline sketch of the present sheet for his own use (Uffizi, Gabinetto Disegni e Stampe, No. 760; Carlo Gamba, I disegni della Galleria degli Uffizi, vol. 17, plate 13), which, in its hasty execution, is easily recognized as such.

Vasari acquired more fame by his lives of Italian artists than by his numerous works, which are mostly decorative frescoes. As a busy "virtuoso" of painting and architecture, he traveled a great deal and left an enormous number of works, especially in Florence and Rome. These follow the particular models he admired at the time. Salviati, a friend of his youth, greatly influenced his decorative imagination. Michelangelo, with whom he was on friendly terms, gave him cartoons for execution. Vasari was more original as an architect (he built the Uffizi) and as a draughtsman. He was the first to assemble a collection of drawings according to historical principles.

FEDERICO ZUCCARI
Born Sant'Angelo in Vado, probably 1540 (1542 or 1543), died Ancona 1609.

43 Taddeo Zuccari Painting the Frescoes on the Façade of the Palazzo Mattei in Rome, with the Graces Guiding his Brush; Michelangelo, Riding on a Mule, Watches him at Work.

Pen and bistre, washed, over preparatory drawing in black chalk; several original inscriptions in pen and bistre, below the painter on the wall of the house: Thaddeo Zuccaro, on the mule's saddlecloth: Michelangelo. B. Rota; on the awning: gratie ...; on the cornice underneath: Taddeo Zuccaro fece (illegible date).

262 : 410 mm.

Inv. no. 575 (L. 174).

Albertina Cat. III, 273; Wickhoff Sc. R. 673; H. Voss, Die Malerei der Spätrenaissance in Florenz und Rom, Berlin, 1920, p. 467.

Exhibition: London, 1948, no. 36.

This drawing was part of a series of pen drawings illustrating the story of the life of Federico's brother Taddeo; the series formerly belonged to Mariette (see his Abecedario) and is now dispersed among the collections of the Louvre, the Albertina, London and Munich. Taddeo painted the frescoes on the Palazzo Mattei in 1548 at the age of eighteen. A painting made after the present drawing — probably not by Federico's hand — is in the Museo del Palazzo Venezia (Mostra Le Case Romane con facciate graffite e dipinte, Rome, Palazzo Braschi, 1960, p. 80).

The brothers Taddeo and Federico Zuccaro were the leading artists of Mannerism in Rome during the second half of the sixteenth century. As extremely prolific fresco painters, their decorative skill was evident in practically every monumental project of importance. Their compositional gift found clearer and more original expression in their numerous drawings than in their paintings. Federico was also important as theoretician of the Mannerist movement. A widely traveled and busy "virtuoso", he made his art known not only all over Italy, but in the North as well. Engravers disseminated his inventions. His sketchbooks also contain attractive studies from nature like the landscape studies made on a journey to Cividale with Palladio.

LUCA CAMBIASO
Born Moneglia near Genoa 1527, died Escorial 1585.

44 The Flight into Egypt.

Pen and bistre, washed, over light preparatory drawing in black chalk; lower right, inscriptiton (partly cut off) in red chalk: L. Cangiasi.

283 : 217 mm.

Inv. no. 2744 (L. 174).

Wickhoff Sc. L. 176.

Luca Cambiaso, the most important painter of Late Mannerism in Genoa, was an enormously prolific draughtsman. Almost all great collections have drawings by his hand. He made drawings either for their own sake or for practice; only a few can be connected with his altarpieces or frescoes in Genoa and elsewhere. The art historical significance of his drawings surpasses that of his paintings although among the latter there are some important achievements, particularly the night scenes. In his drawings Cambiaso developed — far ahead of his time — an astounding cubism which sometimes assumes experimental forms corresponding in their abstraction to twentieth-century cubism. Through the wide circulation of his drawings, he influenced the artists of Late Mannerism in the North (Bartholomaeus Spranger).

LODOVICO CARRACCI
Born Bologna 1555, died there 1619.

45 Allegorical Subject, with the Coat of Arms of Mantua.

Pen and bistre, washed.
280 : 207 mm.
Inv. no. 2090.
Provenance: Lempereur (L. 1740); M. v. Fries (L. 2903).
Engraved by Olivier Gatti (A. Bartsch, Le Peintre-Graveur, Vienna, XIX, 18, 46).
Albertina Cat. VI, 77; Wickhoff Sc. B. 134; H. Bodmer, Lodovico Carracci, Burg b. M. 1939, p. 154, no. 171, fig. 134.
Another design of the same allegorical subject is to be found in the Ambrosiana in Milan, in the Padre Resta album (no. 184).

While in Mannerism it is the ability of the artist as a draughtsman which is foremost, in the Baroque, as in the High Renaissance, the emphasis shifts again to the pictorial. The Carracci, who ushered in the Baroque, excelled in both. Their drawings reveal a new naturalness and directness, qualities which can be enjoyed in this drawing by Lodovico, the eldest of the three Carracci. The little grove rises most attractively amidst the assembly of the gods (Pallas Athena, Apollo, Neptune, Jupiter, Venus and Hercules) in the center of which is a figure in armor (Mars?), with closed visor, a scene romantic in mood and blending antiquity and the Middle Ages in the dream-like fashion of an opera by Monteverdi. The light stroke of the pen attests a mastery in rendering the nude acquired in assiduous study of the model, a skill enabling the draughtsman to dispense with the abstract schemes of Mannerism.

ANNIBALE CARRACCI
Born Bologna 1560, died Rome 1609.

46 Portrait of the Lute-Player Mascheroni.

Red chalk, heightened with white chalk on yellowish paper; later inscription in pencil: Annibale Carracci del.
409 : 282 mm.
Inv. no. 25606 (acquired 1929).
Provenance: Lempereur (L. 1740); Friedrich Amerling; Archduke Frederick.
Albertina Cat. VI, 109; L. Baldass, Die Graphischen Künste XLI, Vienna, 1918, pp. 1-2.
Exhibition: Mostra dei Carracci, Disegni, Bologna, 1956, Cat. no. 103, fig. 35.
Preparatory drawing for the painting in the Dresden Gallery, executed about 1593—1594. The painting comes from the Duke of Modena's collection, where Malvasia (Felsina Pittrice, 1678, I, p. 502) saw it and called it "il sonatore Mascheroni", a friend of Annibale's. About 1599 Agostino Carracci made an engraved portrait of the actor Giovanni Gabrielli, whose identity with Mascheroni ("the big masked man") was later surmised. The resemblance, however, is not convincing. Moreover, Gabrielli was portrayed — true to his profession — with a mask in his hand, while the lute, the music, and the pen in the Dresden portrait point to a professional musician. Denis Mahon therefore termed as uncertain the identity with Gabrielli (Catalogue of the exhibition in Bologna and Studies in Seicento Art and Theory, Warburg Institute XVI, 1947, pp. 226-27, note 50), and it is preferable to retain the old title of "Mascheroni". The

Dresden portrait represents the half-length figure of a man playing the lute. There is a pen and ink sketch for the same portrait at Windsor Castle (R. Wittkower, The Drawings of the Carracci, London, 1952, p. 133), and another study in the Uffizi (No. 12405). A copy of the present drawing is preserved in the Louvre (Inv. no. 7625).

Although Mannerism created a great deal which is of importance in portrait painting, it never attained the spontaneity, the directness, and the grasp of the totality of body and mind which distinguish the Baroque portrait. Caravaggio, the Carracci, and Rubens at about the same time paved the way for this new art of portraiture, which is the result of a new conception of Man.

GIOVANNI LANFRANCO
Born Parma 1582, died Rome 1647.

47 Christ Walking on the Water, with Peter.

Pen and bistre, washed, with some white bodycolor over preliminary indications in red and black chalk; squared for transfer in red and black chalk; lower left, a wide strip of paper added. Later inscription in leadpoint: Lanfranco; lower right, old inscription in pen and bistre: h. 141.
311 : 267 mm.
Inv. no. 2798 (L. 174).
Provenance: J. Richardson (L. 2169 recto).
Wickhoff Sc. L. 235 ("eigenhändig"); see Dessins Romains du XVIIe Siècle, XXIIIe Exposition du Cabinet des Dessins, Musée du Louvre, Paris, 1959, Catalogue, mentioned at no. 14; J. Bean-W. Vitzthum, Bolletino d'arte XLVI, series IV, 1961, p. 107, fig. 2.
Design for the altarpiece in St. Peter's in Rome. An earlier, more cursory sketch for the same composition is in the Louvre, Paris (W. Vitzthum, The Burlington Magazine, CII, London, 1960, p. 75, fig. 33).

The text from Giovanni Pietro Bellori, Le Vite de Pittori, Scultori et Architetti, Paris, 1675, p. 374, referring to the painting, has been transferred to the back of the mount; to the left of this text is the beginning of the English translation. These texts were probably copied from inscriptions which were originally noted down by Richardson on the reverse of the drawing, but are now invisible as the drawing has since been pasted down.

This is one of the most brilliant designs of the Baroque period, demonstrating that it is no longer the effect of the unbroken line, but a correctly placed accent and shadow that matter. The impression of extreme dynamism of the forms bathed in light is thus conveyed. The sketch in the Louvre for this composition limits itself almost entirely to the effect of the brushwork on the paper, producing a whirlpool of light and shade. Such a style of drawing results in a greater unity of effect than had been achieved in any previous century — with emphasis on the essential and disregard of the secondary. The squaring of the present drawing demonstrates that it is here already in its final stage and about to be transferred to the cartoon.

The altarpiece was one of the last Roman works of Lanfranco, who was a pupil of Agostino and Annibale Carracci, the latter having made him his assistant in the fresco decoration of the Palazzo Farnese. The altarpiece for St. Peter was painted shortly before Lanfranco's move to Naples in 1633 or 1634.

GUIDO RENI
Born Bologna 1575, died there 1642.

48 Apollo in the Sun Chariot, Led by Aurora and Accompanied by the Hours.

Preparatory drawing in red chalk, pen and ink; collector's number in pencil: 110.
125 : 256 mm.
Inv. no. 24550 (acquired 1925).
Albertina Cat. VI, 151; J. Meder, Die Vorzeichnung zu Guido Renis Aurora, Die Graphischen Künste XLVIII, Vienna, 1925, Mitteilungen pp. 40, 41, figs. 1, 2; O. Kurz, Jahrbuch der Kunsthistorischen Sammlungen in Wien, N. F. XI, 1937, p. 200.
Exhibition: Mostra di Guido Reni, Bologna, 1954, Cat. p. 136, no. 16.

Design for the fresco of 1613-14 in the Casino dell'Aurora of the palace of Cardinal Scipione Borghese (now Palazzo Rospigliosi Pallavicini) in Rome. Another and more detailed study for the same fresco (a fragment with Apollo's chariot and part of the team of horses) is in the Cabinet des Dessins of the Louvre (G. Rouchès, Dessins Italiens du XVIIe Siècle, Paris, plate 8).

The artist, who came from the studio of the Carracci, spent much time in Rome, where, together with Annibale Carracci, he was considered the main representative of Bolognese neo-classical art. He entered the service of Cardinal Scipione Borghese in 1608. In addition to ecclesiastical commissions for the cardinal, he painted in 1613-14 the secular ceiling decoration of the Casino in the park of the Palazzo Borghese, the famous "Aurora", Reni's principal work in fresco. In accordance with Reni's classicism the composition is executed in the manner of a frieze in relief. But even the preparatory sketches reveal how strongly the artist, in accordance with his time, was governed by the idea of light, color, and space.

GUERCINO (Giovanni Francesco Barbieri)
Born Cento 1591, died Bologna 1666.

49   The Return of the Prodigal Son.
Pen and bistre, washed.
201 : 268 mm.
Inv. no. 2325 (L. 174).
Albertina Cat. VI, 217; Wickhoff Sc. B. 383.

The artist, who grew up under the influence of the pictorial accomplishments of the Carracci and their Bolognese contemporaries, and was lastingly impressed by a stay in Venice, was in his youth the most original and lively artist in Bologna. He was an extremely prolific draughtsman who also was active as a teacher. The present sheet is a masterpiece of expressive movement and colorful light effects. As they are reunited, father and son are overcome with joy. Servants bring clothes for the naked. The vibrant play of line is supported by the brush, which creates an atmosphere of airiness and space through half-shadows filled with light. Only the most important carriers of expression — heads and hands — are marked by darker accents. All the rest appears saturated with light — a magnificent achievement of Baroque plein-air. Guercino was, as we know from his own words, an admirer of Rembrandt. The connection with the painting in Turin assumed in the Albertina catalogue (Stix-Spitzmüller) does not go beyond the identity of subject.

PIETRO DA CORTONA (Pietro Berrettini)
Born Cortona 1596, died Rome 1669.

50   Figures of the Old Testament on Clouds (Adam and Eve, Noah, King David, and others).
Black chalk.
384 : 730 mm.
Inv. no. 14217 (L. 174).
Provenance: Charles, Prince de Ligne (Cat. p. 52, no. 11).
Albertina Cat. III, 712; Wickhoff Sc. R. 996; Giuliano Briganti, Pietro da Cortona, Florence, 1962, p. 326.

Study for a group of figures in the fresco of the cupola of the Chiesa Nuova (S. Maria in Vallicella) in Rome, painted by the artist during his second Roman period in 1648-51; he was a native of Tuscany and created his main works in Florence and Rome.

Pietro da Cortona was the outstanding master of the Roman High Baroque, a contemporary of the great architects Bernini and Borromini. Like them he made use of illusionist perspective. With his ceiling frescoes, he opened up the closed spaces of architecture, his visionary ideal spaces creating the basis for the illusionist ceiling paintings of the High and Late Baroque. In the shaping of his celestial spaces, peopled by powerful figures, he was inspired by the masters of the High Renaissance — Correggio, Michelangelo, and Raphael — but he also had something new and independent to set against the art of the sixteenth century.

BALDASSARE FRANCESCHINI (Il Volterrano)
Born Volterra 1611, died Florence 1689.

51   The Coronation of the Virgin with a Concert of Angels.
Red chalk, pen and gall nut ink; monogramm BF and indications of the instruments in the artist's own hand: Liuto / Traverso / Violino / Tromba / G(ran) Tromb(on)e / Fagotto.
215 : 346 mm.
Inv. no. 23897 (acquired 1924).
Albertina Cat. III, 669.

Sketch for the main group of the fresco in the cupola of the Presbytery of SS. Annunziata in Florence, designed in 1676 and executed in 1680—83. The Albertina possesses another design for the main group and several sketches for angel musicians. The artist was so interested in the composition of the celestial orchestra that he made a note of the individual instruments on the sheet. In the upper right corner an organ has been added.

The cupola of SS. Annunziata was the last large fresco painted by the artist, who suffered a stroke following its completion. He prepared his numerous religious and secular frescoes in spirited, expressive drawings in red chalk, which he liked to accent with the pen. They are full of sparkling life, in artistic effect often superior to the finished paintings.

STEFANO DELLA BELLA
Born Florence 1610, died there 1664.

52   Death Riding across a Battlefield.
Black chalk, pen and bistre, red chalk, washed with Indian ink. Original numeral: 195.
194 : 220 mm.
Inv. no. 961 (L. 174).
Provenance: Moriz von Fries (L. 2903).
Albertina Cat. III, 538; Wickhoff Sc. R. 1071 and plate X. Etching in the reverse direction by the artist's own hand, A. de Vesme, Le Peintre-Graveur Italien, 1906, no. 93.

The subject of this drawing is a revival in contemporary form of the Late Gothic and German Renaissance Dances of Death, particularly Holbein's. (See Della Bella's sketchbook, Albertina Cat. III, 608—614.) Masterly control of the natural form and a grandiose fantasy combine to create a drawing of unique force of expression. In an almost playful manner Death lets go of the reins of his horse, which is as full of weird life as its rider. The profiles of the horses are repeated with a fine pen in the upper right corner. Turmoil, clouds of dust, and powder smoke fill the field over which Death dispatches his emissaries.

Della Bella was Italy's most important seventeenth-century etcher, who developed his style under the influence of Callot's etchings. During an extended stay in Paris he worked for Callot's publisher. A visit to Amsterdam in 1647 may have brought him in touch with Rembrandt, who certainly had a decisive influence on his way of drawing and etching.

GIOVANNI BENEDETTO CASTIGLIONE (Il Grechetto)
Born Genoa 1616, died there 1670.

IV   Rachel with her Children and the Flocks of the Returning Jacob, in a Landscape.
Brush and turpentine and oil on paper.
375 : 532 mm.
Inv. no. 14419 (L. 174).
Provenance: P. J. Mariette, Basan p. 57, no. 349.
Albertina Cat. VI, 514; Wickhoff Sc. L. 283; J. Meder, Die Handzeichnung, Vienna, 1919, p. 158, note 1.

In Castiglione's art genre plays such an outstanding part that even biblical subjects appear to be scenes of everyday rural life. As an eminent depictor of landscape and animals, he mainly chose subjects which gave him an opportunity to represent them. His numerous brush drawings are mostly independent works of art as are the monotypes which this successful etcher carried out as artistic experiments. With a small color scale of ochre, terra di Siena, and some accents in oil he produced drawings of the greatest coloristic richness which were famous into the eighteenth century; they were widely reproduced, and exerted an international influence (on Fragonard for instance). Although there was no pupil relationship with Van Dyck during his Genoese years as has been asserted — Castiglione was only a child at the time — Van Dyck's lively handwriting evidently influenced his studies and drawings.

SIMONE CANTARINI (Il Pesarese)
Born Oropezza near Pesaro 1612, died Verona 1648.

53 The Virgin and Child in the Clouds, Surrounded by Angels Making Music, Looking down on Saints in Adoration.

Red chalk; later inscription in ink: Del Cantarini.
415 : 265 mm.
Inv. no. 2466 (L. 174).
Wickhoff Sc. B. 527.

An orchestra of angels, conducted by St. Cecilia, is grouped in a semi-circle behind the Madonna. Four half-length figures of saints appear at her feet.
The graceful composition has something of the sweetness of Umbrian Late Mannerism. Cantarini was influenced not only by the Venetians, but also by Barocci before becoming Reni's pupil. The delicate draughtsmanship of this sheet recalls the fact that Cantarini, like his teacher, was an excellent etcher.

FRANCESCO SOLIMENA (L'Abate Ciccio)
Born Canale di Serino 1657, died Barra near Naples 1747.

54 San Gennaro in Bishop's Robes, Holding the Ampulla Containing the Sacred Blood.

Black chalk, brush and bistre, washed; signed on the open missal in bistre: Solimena fecit.
400 : 236 mm.
Inv. no. 23730 (acquired 1924, together with a lot of Neapolitan drawings which supposedly go back to the art critic Bernardo de Dominici, 1684—1750).
Albertina Cat. VI, 628; Ferdinando Bologna, F. Solimena. Naples, 1958, p. 278.

Solimena painted an altarpiece in the Cathedral of Salerno, a donation of the Mazza family, in honor of Naples' principal saint, whose blood miraculously liquefies every year on the 19th of September. F. Bologna sees certain relationship to the painting in the Eller Collection in Naples.
By virtue of the international dissemination of his works, Solimena, the leading artist of the Neapolitan Late Baroque, influenced the whole of Europe. Together with the Venetians, he became the most important factor in the development of Austrian Baroque painting. Prince Eugene of Savoy and the family of the Counts of Harrach entrusted him with commissions. His atmospheric loose drawings, which attain a high degree of pictorial illusion, carry on the style of Giovanni Lanfranco, Mattia Preti, and Luca Giordano.

GIOVANNI BATTISTA PIAZZETTA
Born Venice 1682, died there 1754.

55 Self-Portrait.

Charcoal, heightened with white chalk on greenish Venetian paper. Signed and dated; below at left in pen and bistre: Io Gio': Batta. Piazzetta disegnai di propà: mano / in età d'Anni 52; at lower right: A di 10 Dece / 1735.
350 : 241 mm.
Inv. no. 1771 (L. 174).
Albertina Cat. I, 253; Wickhoff Sc. V. 365; A. Ravà, G. B. Piazzetta, Florence, 1921, frontispiece; R. Pallucchini, L'Arte di Giovanni Battista Piazzetta, Bologna, 1934, p. 100; ibid. 1956, p. 53, plate 133.
Exhibition: Venice, 1961, no. 88.

As a self-testimonial of the artist, who, with Tiepolo, was the greatest master of the Late Venetian Baroque, the present drawing assumes particular significance. The careful inscription testifies to the importance that the artist himself attached to it. The broad countenance reveals a consciousness of his own worth, and at the same time a seriousness and devotion to his high artistic mission. In spite of the comparatively small number of his works, Piazzetta laid the foundation not only for Venetian Settecento painting, but far beyond this for western painting of the Late Baroque. His drawings manifest the same mastery as his paintings. A high degree of realistic representation is achieved by the most subtle graphic means, the equivalent of the glowing colors in the interplay of atmosphere and chiaroscuro. Shining skin, fluffy hair, and the texture of fabrics are conjured up with a maximum of illusion by loosely-knit strokes in combination with patches and spots of the black and white chalk on the unrefined Venetian paper. Piazzetta's famous large studies of heads were widely copied inside and outside his workshop.

GIOVANNI BATTISTA TIEPOLO
Born Venice 1696, died Madrid 1770.

56 St. Fidelis of Sigmaringen Exorcising a Possessed Man.

Pen and bistre, washed, brush and white bodycolor, over preliminary drawing in black chalk.
502 : 352 mm.
Inv. no. 1813 (L. 174).
Albertina Cat. I, 304; Wickhoff Sc. V. 408; P. Molmenti, G. B. Tiepolo, Milan (1909), p. 237, note 11, no. 6; E. Sack, Giambattista und Domenico Tiepolo, Hamburg, 1910, p. 270, no. 977.
Exhibition: Paris, 1950, no. 47.

In the 1750's Tiepolo painted for the church of the Capuchin order in Parma an altarpiece, dedicated to the saints of the order, St. Fidelis of Sigmaringen and St. Joseph of Leonessa. The painting is now in the Gallery of Parma (A. Morassi, A Complete Catalogue of the Paintings of G. B. Tiepolo, London 1962, p. 44, fig. 120). Two drawings, in the Albertina, of St. Fidelis as exorcist (Cat. 303 and 304) are presumably ideas for the altar-painting. The present drawing in particular shows Tiepolo at the height of his mature mastery, acquired in the execution of his large commissions for the frescoes and altar-paintings of his Würzburg period (1752—53). They are distinguished by strongly dramatic spatial effects. The bold and free pen strokes reduce figures and scenery to the simplest and most effective formula. Shadow accents and heightenings in white applied with the brush blend figures and vegetation into the atmosphere and achieve a sense of unity by means of an aura of silvery light for which the painter Tiepolo is famous.

57 Study for St. Charles Borromeo Kneeling.
Red and white chalk on blue Venetian paper.
291 : 290 mm.
Inv. no. 32968 (acquired 1960).
Provenance: Prince Liechtenstein (Sales catalogue Klipstein & Kornfeld, Auction no. 98, Berne, June 16th, 1960, no. 322, plate 56).
Exhibition: Venice, 1961, no. 104.

Study for the altarpiece painted by Tiepolo for the monastery church of S. Pasquale at Aranjuez, now in the Art Museum of Cincinnati. The modello for the altarpiece is in London, the Count Antoine Seilern Collection, 56 Princes Gate, Italian Paintings and Drawings, London, 1959, no. 175, plate CXXXVIII.

Tiepolo, who worked in Madrid from 1762 until his death, was commissioned towards the end of his life to paint seven altarpieces for the newly built monastery church of S. Pasquale at Aranjuez. They were completed and installed in their respective places in 1769 (with the exception of St. Charles), but were taken down after the artist's death on the instigation of the King's confessor Giovacchino de Electa. The intrigues against Tiepolo contributed a great deal to the embitterment of the master's last days. He died in 1770. Some of the paintings have survived only as fragments, but five of the modelli have been preserved. They show that these altarpieces — legends of saints of a moving simplicity and narrative fervor — were Tiepolo's last word in painting. The present study for St. Charles Borromeo had not been identified prior to its acquisition for the Albertina by the author. It demonstrates the old master's unimpaired sureness of touch in the handling of his medium. All substance begins to vibrate, it is permeated by light and loses all physical weight, leading to a spiritualization of matter that relates the great Venetian draughtsman, painter, and etcher to his model Rembrandt.

CANALETTO (Antonio Canale)
Born Venice 1697, died there 1768.

58 The Porta Portello with the Brenta Canal in Padua.

Pen and bistre, washed in bistre and sepia, guide lines in lead-point and red chalk.
334 : 530 mm.
Inv. no. 1856 (L. 174).
Provenance: P. J. Mariette, Basan p. 46, no. 274.
Albertina Cat. I, 358; Wickhoff Sc. V., 451; D. v. Hadeln, Die Zeichnungen von Antonio Canal, genannt Canaletto, Vienna 1930, p. 30; see also a drawing of the same motif in K. T. Parker, The Drawings of Antonio Canaletto in the Collection of His Majesty the King at Windsor Castle, 1948, no. 82, plate 56; W. G. Constable, Canaletto, Oxford, 1962, vol. II, no. 676.

Exhibitions: Il Settecento Italiano, Venice, 1929, sala 8, no. 4; Venice, 1961, no. 115.

A drawing in Windsor Castle (Constable no. 675) represents the same locality, but seen from a point farther to the right. The church of the Carmini appears in the background. Constable mentions a painting by Canaletto of the same motif and a replica (previously Agnew; Philip Hofer Collection), which he is inclined to attribute to Bellotto.
As in Dutch art, the veduta was especially cultivated in Venetian art of the seventeenth and eighteenth centuries; it reached its zenith in the work of Canaletto and Guardi. Canaletto's conception of space is already scientifically correct in the sense of nineteenth-century optics. He probably also used the expedient of the camera obscura. Nevertheless the delightful curl and crispness of the pen line reveal the Rococo artist's inclination toward ornament. An additional wash with the brush creates a wonderful impression of airiness and space; in his pure pen drawings this effect is produced by oblique hatchings.

FRANCESCO GUARDI
Born Venice 1712, died there 1793.

59 The Piazzetta in Venice.

Pen and bistre, washed, over preliminary indications in lead-point; lower right in leadpoint: Guardi.
541 : 387 mm.
Inv. no. 24367 (acquired 1925).
Provenance: Guido von Rho.
Albertina Cat. I, 377; J. Byam Shaw, The Drawings of Francesco Guardi, London, 1949, p. 66, no. 32.
Exhibition: Venice, 1961, no. 118.

Sketch for the painting in the Academy of Fine Arts in Vienna, R. Eigenberger, Die Gemäldegalerie der Akademie, Vienna, 1927, text volume no. 504, plate volume 31.
In contrast to Canaletto's topographical correctness in the veduta, Francesco Guardi embodies the expressive, the personal, the fantastically intuitive element. Beginning as the painter of ecclesiastic figure compositions which his father, the founder of the studio, had cultivated, he transferred the expressive style of his religious paintings to secular work. When he in turn directed the studio together with his brother Gianantonio, he became increasingly interested in the veduta, mainly for economic reasons, as there was a growing demand for this kind of painting. He became a master of this genre; his ability as a painter and draughtsman ranks him with Piazzetta and Tiepolo. The present drawing is a preparatory study for one of his latest paintings. All solid form has dissolved into a flickering play of capricious stenographic symbols of expression. In an ingenious shorthand the draughtsman paraphrases what he actually observes: the Piazzetta teeming with people in the hazy atmosphere of the city of the lagoons. The crease in the middle of the drawing indicates that it was a double page in a sketchbook.

GIOVANNI DOMENICO TIEPOLO
Born Venice 1727, died there 1804.

60 Study of the Head of a Bearded Oriental with a Fur Cap.

Brush and brown oil. Inscription below: Gio Batt Tiepolo no 16 (9), in a different hand: the two first names and the numeral 169 crossed out, after Tiepolo "Dom. co" and at the end the numeral 7 added. Left and right, two vertical lines.
424 : 289 mm.
Inv. no. 1819 (L. 174).
Albertina Cat. I, 288; Wickhoff Sc. V. 414; J. Meder, Albertina-Facsimile, Handzeichnungen italienischer Meister des XV.—XVIII. Jahrhunderts, Vienna, 1923, plate 37; P. Molmenti, G. B. Tiepolo, Milan (1909), p. 237, note 11, no. 1; E. Sack, Giambattista und Domenico Tiepolo, Hamburg, 1910, p. 270, no. 974; O. Benesch, Alte und neue Kunst I, Vienna 1952, p. 68.

Exhibitions: Paris, 1950, no. 48; Mostra del Tiepolo, Venice, 1951, no. 87; Venice, 1961, no. 112.

This splendid study of a head in "Rembrandt's manner" was always considered by experts to be a work of the father, in spite of the old correction in the inscription. But the contributions of father and son have by no means been critically separated in either the paintings or the drawings devoted to heads of this type. The present drawing is executed in brush and oil, a technique never used by Giambattista, whereas Giandomenico used it repeatedly. A head of an apostle or saint in profile, in the Albertina, executed in the same technique (Inv. no. 30387 — shown as no. 111 in the exhibition of the Fondazione Cini, Venice, 1961, with the present drawing as no. 112), is recognizable at first sight as work of Giandomenico's. This necessarily leads to the restoration of this "Rembrandt Oriental" to Giandomenico, in spite of its extraordinarily high quality.

GERMAN, AUSTRIAN AND SWISS MASTERS

VIENNESE MASTER
About 1425—1430.

61 The Annunciation.

Pen and brush and Indian ink, touches of watercolor.
402 : 276 mm.
Inv. no. 25447 (acquired 1927).
Provenance: Rumohr.
Albertina Cat. IV, 7; O. Benesch, Die Meisterzeichnung V, 21; O. Benesch, Jahrbuch der Kunsthistorischen Sammlungen, Vienna, 1928, N. F. II, p. 70; Great Drawings of all Time, New York, 1962, II, no. 310 (O. Benesch).

The "International Style" — also called the "soft style" in German-speaking countries (see nos. 1 and 2) — developed in the decades around 1400, flourishing particularly on the Upper and Lower Rhine, in Westphalia and Lower Saxony, in Bohemia and in Austria. Vienna with its court was one of its most brilliant centers. The present drawing, which is among the finest and most typical examples of this style, a style which is remarkable for its representation of architecture and landscape, originates from the Vienna circle. The room of the Virgin has the appearance of a richly decorated chapel, thrown open in front like a stage. Its roof is crowned by two curious cupolas recalling Melchior Broederlam's Dijon altar of 1392—99. The artist was guided by western models (French-Burgundian and Upper Rhenish). The mountain scenery with its monasteries and castles corresponds to that in pictures from the Upper Rhine and Lake Constance. The loveliness of the Madonna, however, is specifically Austrian and recurs in paintings by the Vienna successors of the Master of the Votive Panel of St. Lambrecht, as for instance in the works of the Master of the Vienna Presentation.

The representation of the Angelic Salutation is unusual. The angel knocks at the door or pushes it gently open while his words appear in Hebrew letters on the gable of the projecting roof; its front column has been simply omitted by the draughtsman in order to avoid overlapping with the figure of the angel. Some watercolor has been added to the gray Indian ink: e. g., a bright red in the mandorla of God the Father, some golden ochre in the beams of light emanating from it, and in the sea of stars. The woodwork of the chapel, too, was given touches of color.

VIENNESE MASTER
About 1440.

62 Christ Carrying the Cross.
Pen and Indian ink on paper mended in various places.
324 : 238 mm.
Inv. no. 25889 (acquired 1930).
Verso: Architectural stage of a town with harbor and land-scape in the background; in an enclosure in the foreground to the left, the Crowning with Thorns. Modern inscription in pencil: Hans Multscher.
Provenance: R. Weigel; C. Rodrigues (L. 897) Sale, Amsterdam, Fr. Muller, 12th and 13th July 1921, no. 82.
Albertina Cat. IV, 12; F. Kieslinger, Die mittelalterliche Plastik in Österreich, Vienna, 1926, text for plates 21/22; O. Benesch, Die Meisterzeichnung V, 39.
Exhibition: Österreichische Malerei und Graphik der Gotik, Vienna, Kunsthistorisches Museum, 1934, Cat. no. 37.

The oeuvre of this artist as a draughtsman was first assembled by the present author. The convincing identification with the woodcarver of the so-called Znaim Altar in the Öster-reichische Galerie was made by F. Kieslinger. To the group of individual drawings of this master must be added a related work, the Biblia Pauperum from the Weigel Collection, now in the Pierpont Morgan Library, New York (P. Heitz–W. L. Schreiber, Biblia Pauperum, Strasbourg, 1903, MS no. 20).
The composition, executed in fine outlines, embodies the vigorous, heavy, crowded figure style of the late 1430's and 1440's, of which the "Wurzach Altar" by Hans Multscher is the best-known example. The tentative strokes of the pen, frequently swinging out in delicate parallels, indicate that this is an original sketch and not a copy. The woodcarver is interested first and foremost in the cubic outlining of the figures. In spite of its strong plastic quality, the relation of the present drawing to panel painting is evident. The woodcarver of the Znaim Altar derives his style from that of the Master of Christ Carrying the Cross in the Worcester Collection in Chicago, known to us not only by this small painting, but also by a series of drawings (Benesch, op. cit., 41 ff.). Both artists embody a dramatic trend in Viennese art of the 1440's. The executioner on the lower margin, seen from the back, was taken over from the Worcester Carrying of the Cross. He frequently occurs in other works of the Viennese School, for example, in the choir stalls of St. Stephen's Cathedral, which were destroyed by fire in 1945.
The influence of this Viennese style radiated as far as Hungary. M. Csánky (Az Országos Magyar Szépmüv. Múzeum Évkönyvei X, p. 70) ascertained that some of its motifs were used on the wings of the high altar of St. Elisabeth at Kassa (Košice). E. Gombrich has discovered three reliefs of the Passion in Esztergom, which are related to the Znaim Altar and to the Master of Laufen (Magyar Müvészet XI, Budapest, 1935, p. 223 ff.).
In spite of their importance and influence, comparatively few examples of this trend in Viennese art have survived. Among these are two carved reliefs from an altar in the parish church of Sievering, representing the Nativity and the Adoration of the Magi, as well as a piece of goldsmith's art, a gilt copper relief of the Crucifixion in the Walters Art Gallery in Baltimore. In all the sculptural works of this artistic trend the relationship with panel painting, noted above, is clearly discernible.

UPPER GERMAN SCHOOL
About 1445.

63 St. George Fighting the Dragon.
Chiaroscuro drawing with brush and white bodycolor on black prepared paper; lower right corner cut off.
181 : 128 mm.
Inv. no. 3053 (L. 174).
Albertina Cat. IV, 9; Schönbrunner-Meder 1158; J. Meder, Die Handzeichnung, Vienna, 1919, p. 50, note 2; O. Benesch, Die Meisterzeichnung, V, at no. 42; F. Winzinger, Deutsche Meisterzeichnungen der Gotik, Munich, 1949, no. 9.

The technical execution of this drawing in short little strokes and dots of white bodycolor on a black ground recalls the "stippled manner" of the engravings mainly used in nielli at this early period. (There is a technically related drawing with ornamental birds, at Frankfort, Frankfurter Zeichnungen, XV, 2.) The connection with early German engraving is clear in any case. The composition in its main features resembles St. George and the Dragon by the Master of the Nuremberg Passion (Lehrs I, p. 161, 14; Geisberg 35). The rich landscape, steeply built up in terraces, is found in painting of the Upper Rhine, Lake Constance, and the old Austrian Alpine Foreland. This was also the locale of Konrad Witz' art, to whose sphere of influence the present drawing definitely belongs, as is attested by the heavy, angular forms of the drapery and the armor. A certain roundness in the formal articulation — one should speak of "bends" rather than "breaks" — and the use of trecento landscape props makes this drawing appear archaic as compared to the work of Witz, and links it with various aspects of the Bavarian-Austrian school (for example, with the so-called Master of Weilheim).
At the upper margin an angel is rescuing the princess. Another at the lower left corner watches the struggle with the dragon. The royal parents observe the scene from a balcony of the castle.

NICOLAUS MAIR VON LANDSHUT
Born Munich 1490, mentioned at Landshut 1492, 1499 and 1514, died Landshut 1520.

64 Christ Enthroned with Two Angels, in Front of an Architectural Niche.

Brush and white bodycolor on black prepared paper; signed MAIR, inscribed in niche: MCZS.
212 : 157 mm.
Inv. no. 4847 (L. 174).
Albertina Cat. IV, 213; Schönbrunner-Meder 146; J. Meder, Die Handzeichnung, Vienna, 1919, p. 353; J. Meder, Albertina-Facsimile, Handzeichnungen deutscher Meister des XV. und XVI. Jahrhunderts, Vienna, 1922, plate 3.

The artist, who is repeatedly mentioned in documents as court painter to the Dukes of Bavaria, is the last offspring of Bavarian Late Gothic art, of which the greatest exponent was Jan Pollak. His paintings and drawings can be clearly identified on the basis of his signed engravings. Mair was regarded as a precursor of the Danube School, especially because of his chiaroscuro drawings. The flickering lights and the elaborate, involved settings lend his works a mysterious and fantastic quality. Meder supposed this sheet to be a model for a graphic work because Christ's left hand is raised in benediction and not His right.

STYRIAN, BEGINNING OF FIFTEENTH CENTURY
65 The Apostle Thomas.

Pen and gray Indian ink, washed. Upper right corner and upper left margin of the paper repaired. Later inscription in pen and Indian ink, above: Sanctus Thomas Aplus, below: ·1451·.
118 : 76 mm (edges irregularly cut).
Inv. no. 24998 (acquired 1930).
Provenance: Abbey of Vorau, Styria.
Albertina Cat. IV, 6; O. Benesch, Die Meisterzeichnung V, 4; K. Rathe, Die Graphischen Künste, Mitteilungen der Gesellschaft für vervielfältigende Kunst, Vienna, 1932, pp. 20, 21, fig. 1.

Exhibitions: Österreichische Malerei und Graphik der Gotik, Vienna, Kunsthistorisches Museum, 1934, no. 34; Europäische Kunst um 1400, Vienna, Kunsthistorisches Museum, 1962, no. 272.

The Austrian origin of this drawing would be established by its provenance alone, even if the evidence of its style did not attest to it. The drawing decorated the inside of the cover of a codex in the Monastery of Vorau in Styria, whose patron is the saint represented here. The relation to other Austrian drawings of the "soft style" is obvious: to a St. Margaret in the Print Room at Budapest, and to a St. Magdalen, dated 1410, in the Cabinet des Dessins of the Louvre (L. Demonts, Inventaire général, Écoles Allemande et Suisse, Paris, 1938, no. 387).

Drawings of this kind were created not only as preparations for panel paintings, but also for works of applied art. The church of S. Tomà in Venice owns a reliquary in the shape of a little altarpiece in gilt bronze with wings in enamel, the origin of which the present author was able to establish as Austrian at the exhibition of Artigianato Liturgico, Venice, 1950, on the basis of its connection with the above drawings. The enamels of the wings show rows of male and female saints very closely related to those drawings. The figure of St. Thomas in the upper row of the left wing displays a particularly close affinity to the present drawing.

AUSTRIAN ALPINE FORELAND
About 1440.

66 Christ as Gardener and St. Mary Magdalen.

Pen and Indian ink, washed in gray, watercolor and bodycolor. 139 : 100 mm (cut along the margins).
Inv. no. 26031 (acquired 1930).

Provenance: Grahl (L. 1199); Licht; Czeczowiczka.

Albertina Cat. IV, 8; O. Benesch, Die Meisterzeichnung V, 40. The coloring in green bodycolor was not done by the draughtsman.

The present drawing is probably a small devotional picture, an independent work of art, which, in the manner of a single woodcut, was colored later. Although it dates from the time of Konrad Witz, it still retains many reminiscences of the "soft style." This relates it to the panels of an altarpiece from the convent of the Dominican nuns at Adelhausen near Freiburg im Breisgau (now in the Augustiner-Museum at Freiburg).

MARTIN SCHONGAUER
Born Colmar about 1430, died Breisach 1491.

67 The Martyrdom of St. Ursula and her Companions.

Pen and bistre, partly retraced in black ink (by another hand); the corners cut off and restored.
176 : 283 mm.
Inv. no. 3026 (L. 174).

Albertina Cat. IV, 27; Schönbrunner-Meder 671; J. Rosenberg, Martin Schongauer, Handzeichnungen, Munich, 1925, p. 37, fig. 50; E. Buchner, Martin Schongauer, Berlin, 1941, pp. 123-127, fig. 71; F. Winzinger, Die Zeichnungen Martin Schongauers, Berlin, 1962, no. 34.

This significant drawing was for a long time mistaken by the experts as a work of one of Schongauer's followers. Credit is due to E. Buchner for having pointed out its high quality and for recognizing it as a work from Schongauer's last period when he was working on the frescoes at Breisach. In spite of the wealth of minute detail and the agitation of its Late Gothic design, the composition is permeated by an almost classical grandeur and quietness of invention as befits the mature late art of a great master. Its tragic subject thus gains solemnity and significance. The drawing reveals the strong systematization of graphic technique common to Schongauer's late engravings and drawings. It exemplifies the art which Dürer, in his eagerness to learn, was searching for when he left his home town in 1490 and set out on his travels.

The drawing exerted influence on Schongauer's circle. The composition was used in a predella panel by the Zurich Master of the Pink (Zurich Nelkenmeister) in a Basle private collection and in the panel of an altarpiece from Isenheim in the Unterlinden Museum at Colmar (Cat. 1959, no. 748).

ALBRECHT DÜRER
Born Nuremberg 1471, died there 1528.

68 Self-Portrait at the Age of Thirteen.

Silverpoint on white prepared paper; inscribed by the artist's own hand at a later date: Dz hab Ich aws eim spigell nach mir selbs kunterfet Im 1484 Jar do ich noch ein kint was Albrecht Dürer. (This I portrayed after myself from a mirror in the year 1484 when I was still a child Albrecht Dürer.)
275 : 196 mm.
Inv. no. 4839 (L. 174).
Provenance: Imhoff.

Albertina Cat. IV, 30; F. Winkler, Die Zeichnungen Albrecht Dürers, Berlin, 1936 ff., no. 1; Schönbrunnner-Meder 94; F. Lippmann, Zeichnungen von Albrecht Dürer, Berlin, 1883, vol. I ff., 448; H. Wölfflin, Albrecht Dürer Handzeichnungen, Munich, 1914, plate 1; J. Meder, Die Handzeichnung, Vienna, 1919, p. 95, fig. 37; J. Meder, Albertina-Facsimile, Handzeichnungen deutscher Meister des XV. und XVI. Jahrhunderts, Vienna, 1922, plate 4; H. and E. Tietze, Der junge Dürer, Augsburg, 1928, no. 1; E. Panofsky, Albrecht Dürer, Princeton, 1948, II, no. 996; Great Drawings of All Time, New York, 1962, II, no. 330 (O. Benesch).

Exhibitions: London, 1948, no. 83; Paris, 1950, no. 52.

This drawing represents a phenomenon as unusual in the history of art as in the history of ideas. That a child in the closing years of the Middle Ages, which were so restrained in the matter of self-representation, should, at an age when he would normally be playing, create his own likeness, is something new and completely unexpected. With eyes aglow with the wonderment of beholding, he drew himself from the mirror, burning with an inner urge. The small Mozart was, it is true, also an important composer and virtuoso at this age, but this was largely the result of training from earliest youth by an enterprising father. The young Dürer, however, had to carry his point against the will of a restraining father who wanted him trained only in his own craft as a competent goldsmith. This proof of his talent may have helped to tip the balance in favor of the permission to enter a painter's workshop as so ardently desired by the young boy.
That young Dürer had learned his father's craft well is attested by his later mastery as an engraver. Moreover, he was thoroughly grounded in the use of the silverpoint in the goldsmith's workshop; the present drawing reveals that the style of the Netherlandish silverpoint drawings was not unknown to him. His father, who "lang in Niederland gewest bej den grossen künstern," probably had acquainted him with it. The drawing shows him as a young goldsmith's apprentice; it was not until two years later that he entered Wolgemut's workshop. The figure was outlined in light, sketchy strokes; a pentiment is visible in the outstretched forefinger. The cap with a tassel is the same as that worn by the small boy in a portrait in the Pommersche Landesmuseum at Stettin, which may possibly be an Augsburg copy of a lost self-portrait of the same year.
The absence of the left hand is due to the fact that in the mirror it was the draughtsman's right hand. But it is noteworthy that the gaze does not meet the viewer as it usually does in self-portraits drawn from the model. Perhaps the draughtsman made use of two mirrors as Burgkmair did later in the portrait he drew of himself.

V The Hare.

Brush and watercolor and bodycolor; monogram, and dated 1502.
251 : 225 mm.
Inv. no. 3073 (L. 174).
Provenance: Imhoff (Heller p. 82, no. 57).

Albertina Cat. IV, 49; Winkler op. cit. 248; Schönbrunner-Meder 70; Lippmann, op. cit. 468; H. Wölfflin, Albrecht Dürer Handzeichnungen, plate 16; H. and E. Tietze, Der junge Dürer, no. 197; E. Panofsky, Albrecht Dürer, Princeton, 1948, II, no. 1322.

Exhibitions: London, 1948, no. 87; Paris, 1950, no. 64.

A copy in the Walter Gay Collection, Louvre.

Dürer's unbounded urge to investigate and comprehend artistically the world of living creatures led him at the beginning of the sixteenth century to paint a series of the most delightful watercolor studies of plants and animals. Of these, the "Hare" is the most famous and the most popular. Dürer kept the tame animal in his studio as a model, as is apparent from the reflection of the window bars in the pupils of its eyes. The feeling for the color values, and the texture of the animal's body, for the soft fur and the delicate bone structure are rendered with unsurpassed perfection. At the same time the diffidence and reverence with which man seeks to enter the closed door of the animal world are moving and admirable. They would be quite incompatible with the aims of an Italian artist, solely intent on great form.

For Dürer the world of animals and plants was God's creation, and as such took an active part in the story of the Creation and the Redemption. The hare is one of the animal companions of the first human couple in the engraving of the Fall of Man of 1504 ("Adam and Eve"), just as little hares romp about as playmates of the Infant Christ in the earlier woodcut of the "Holy Family with Three Hares" (B. 102), and in the later drawing of a Holy Family in Basle (1509, Winkler 466). That the hare in the famous engraving should represent the sanguine temperament, in accordance with Renaissance theory, as stated by E. Panofsky on p. 85 of his book on Dürer, does not convince the present author.

69 Hands Raised in Prayer.

Brush and Indian ink and white bodycolor on blue prepared paper.
291 : 197 mm.
Inv. no. 3113 (L. 174).

Albertina Cat. IV, 95; Winkler op. cit. 461; Schönbrunner-Meder 188; Lippmann op. cit. 507; H. Wölfflin, Albrecht Dürer Handzeichnungen, plate 31; J. Meder, Die Handzeichnung, p. 49, fig. 19; J. Meder, Albertina-Facsimile, Handzeichnungen deutscher Meister des XV. und XVI. Jahrhunderts, Vienna, 1922, plate 15; H. and E. Tietze, Kritisches Verzeichnis der Werke Albrecht Dürers, II, Basle, 1937, W 57; E. Panofsky, Albrecht Dürer, Princeton, 1948, II, no. 493.

Exhibitions: London, 1948, no. 95; Paris, 1950, no. 71.

Dürer, who until now had cultivated religious painting only in the form of devotional pictures, small altarpieces, and the "pala" in the Italian manner, was commissioned in 1508 and 1509 by the Frankfort citizen Jakob Heller to paint a monumental altarpiece, with the Assumption of the Virgin as its central panel, for the local church of the Dominicans. The Elector Maximilian acquired it later for his collection in the Residenz at Munich, where it was a victim of the fire which destroyed the palace. But Dürer's drawings for this extraordinary painting, on which he expended the utmost effort and devotion, are still preserved. There is a series of them in the Albertina. They are executed in brush, Indian ink, and white bodycolor on prepared paper in various colors — so-called "chiaroscuro drawings". They are preparatory studies of individual figures, heads, hands, and draperies for the painting. Dürer followed the method of masters of the Italian High Renaissance in assembling a monumental composition from details carefully studied from the model. But the expressiveness with which he invested these details of the drawing goes far beyond the possibilities of the Italians. The powerful heads of the apostles as well as these hands, which belonged to a praying apostle at the right edge of the painting, encompass a whole world of strong faith and religious fervor even without consideration of their relationship to the completed altarpiece.

70 Christ on the Mount of Olives.

Pen and bistre. Monogram and date 1515 in the artist's own hand; lower right corner restored.
296 : 221 mm.
Inv. no. 3141 (L. 174).

Preparatory drawing, in the opposite direction, for the etching on iron, Bartsch 19, J. Meder, Dürer-Katalog, Vienna, 1932, no. 19.

Albertina Cat. IV, 118; Winkler op. cit. 585; Schönbrunner-Meder 292; Lippmann op. cit. 536; J. Meder, Albertina-Facsimile, Handzeichnungen deutscher Meister des XV. und XVI. Jahrhunderts, Vienna, 1922, plate 18; H. and E. Tietze,

Kritisches Verzeichnis der Werke Albrecht Dürers, II, Basle, 1937, no. 646; E. Panofsky, Albrecht Dürer, Princeton, 1948, II, no. 558.

Exhibitions: Albrecht Dürer im Germanischen Museum, Nuremberg, 1928, Cat. no. 186; Paris, 1950, no. 75.

Dürer made a few attempts at etching on hammered iron plates, a technique introduced into the history of graphic art by an Augsburg family of armorers called Hopfer in the course of the production of plates for intaglio. Dürer realized the importance of this graphic technique for the development of dramatic light and dark contrasts and, at the same time, its ability to convey a direct impression of a loose, spontaneous pen drawing. There thus originated the etching "Christ on the Mount of Olives" of 1515, for which this sheet is the preparatory drawing. Dürer repeatedly depicted Christ's suffering on the Mount of Olives, rendering His agony in the face of His terrible fate in a deeply moving manner. But here Christ accepts the cup calmly, and from His head there already radiates the glory of the victor over death, who rises from the tomb. A radiant strength flows from the hatchings of this drawing, not only in bright areas like Christ's halo, but also in dark areas like the shadows of the night laid over the landscape. Indeed the rays of light pass directly into those of darkness, and from both streams the same vital energy.

VI The Large Piece of Turf.

Watercolor and bodycolor. Dated on right, below plantain: 1503; lower right corner and a similar piece in the center of the lower margin are missing.
411 : 315 mm.
Inv. no. 3075 (L. 174).

Albertina Cat. IV, 54; Winkler, op. cit. 346; Schönbrunner-Meder 351; Lippmann op. cit. 472; J. Meder, Albertina-Facsimile, Handzeichnungen deutscher Meister des XV. und XVI. Jahrhunderts, plate 12; H. and E. Tietze, Der junge Dürer, Augsburg, 1928, no. 238; E. Panofsky, Albrecht Dürer, Princeton, 1948, II, no. 1422; L. Behling, Die Pflanze in der mittelalterlichen Tafelmalerei, Weimar, 1957, p. 111.

Exhibitions: London, 1948, no. 92; Paris, 1950, no. 65.

See note to colorplate V. Just as "The Hare" is Dürer's most famous animal piece, so the present watercolor is his most famous plant study. It is the primus inter pares in a series of similar studies of flowers and plants, all of them dated by Winkler in the years 1503—1505, although some of them bear the dates 1508 and 1526 added by different hands. Dürer himself dug up this "Large Piece of Turf" as well as the "Small Piece of Turf" (also in the Albertina), and a series of individual flowers, including a "Cowslip" which recently turned up on the English art market, dug them up with the soil so as to be able to study the delicate growth of the plants as closely as possible and in the last detail. This black garden soil unquestionably reveals in both "Pieces of Turf," in the "Big Buttercup" (Providence, Rhode Island), in the "Cowslip" (London), in the "Columbine," the "Celandine," and the "Three Medicinal Herbs" (all in the Albertina) the hand of the same artist. Yarrow, plantain, and dandelion are the plants which can definitely be distinguished in the "Large Piece of Turf".

Books on plants illustrated with drawings or woodcuts already existed in German art of the late fifteenth century. Like them, Dürer's watercolors are testimonials of the awakening interest in the natural sciences. But he invested this small microcosm with the greatness of the macrocosm, with the feeling for the active and creative forces of the universe, as was possible only through his privileged artist's eye.

71 Study of a Ninety-Three Year Old Man.

Brush and Indian ink and white bodycolor on gray-violet prepared paper. Monogram, the date 1521, and inscription in the artist's hand: Der man was alt 93 jor und noch gesunt und fermuglich zw antorff (The man was 93 years old and still healthy and vigorous, at Antwerp); corners diagonally trimmed and replaced. Watermark (?); coat of arms with

three lilies and Gothic "e" (mentioned by Meder in Lippmann's Albertina volume under no. 568).
416 : 282 mm.
Inv. no. 3167 (L. 174).
Albertina Cat. IV, 144; Winkler, op. cit. 788; Schönbrunner-Meder 156; Lippmann, op. cit. 568; J. Veth - S. Muller, Albrecht Dürers Niederländische Reise, Berlin-Utrecht, 1918, I, p. 37 f., plate XXXVIII; J. Meder, Die Handzeichnung, Vienna, 1919, p. 279, fig. 94b; H. Wölfflin, Albrecht Dürer, 5th edition, 1920, p. 312; J. Meder, Albertina-Facsimile, Handzeichnungen deutscher Meister des XV. und XVI. Jahrhunderts, plate 23; H. and E. Tietze, Kritisches Verzeichnis der Werke Albrecht Dürers, II, Basle, 1938, no. 804; E. Panofsky, Albrecht Dürer, Princeton, 1948, II, no. 817; Great Drawings of All Time, New York, 1962, II, no. 361 (O. Benesch).

Exhibitions: London, 1948, no. 101; Paris, 1950, no. 79.

On the occasion of his visit to the Netherlands, Dürer in 1521 painted a half-length figure of St. Jerome (now in the National Museum, Lisbon) for Rodrigo d'Almada, an art lover from Portugal. In preparation of the panel, he made large detailed brush drawings, four of which are in the Albertina and one in the Print Room in Berlin: they are studies for the head, the left hand, the skull, and the lectern. The most imposing of these drawings is the pensive head, which attracted Dürer by the wealth of its expressive features. The result is a masterpiece among his representations of men, a portrayal full of moral gravity and spiritual greatness. The mood of meditation is fully caught. There is ornamental beauty not only in the play of line on the picture plane but in the plastic accentuation of the body in space as well. The representation becomes thereby, in spite of all its human warmth, removed from reality, somehow transmuted, like an exquisite piece of the silversmith's art. It prompted Winkler to suggest that the present drawing was not made from the model, but was " a transformation of the first sketch, worked with the utmost perfection by the brush." This opinion, however, is contradicted by the artist's own inscription, which testifies to the amazement of an eye-witness before an unusual phenomenon of life and is comprehensible only as a statement based on reality. The Berlin drawing (Winkler, 789) corresponds more closely to the painting in the direction of the gaze and the position of the head and must have probably been made — if it is by Dürer — immediately before the execution of the panel. Winkler's suggestion that Dürer used the present drawing for the head of St. Peter in the "Four Apostles" in the Pinakothek in Munich is not convincing to the present author as Dürer undoubtedly used a younger model whom he portrayed in 1526 in a leadpoint drawing, now in the Musée Bonnat at Bayonne (Winkler, 871).
Four copies — in Budapest, Oxford, the Albertina, and in an English private collection — attest the drawing's fame in former times.

HANS SUESS VON KULMBACH
Born Kulmbach about 1480, died Nuremberg 1522.

72 The Adoration of the Child with St. Catherine and St. Barbara. On the wings: St. John the Baptist and St. John the Evangelist.
Design for a triptych.

VII Detail: Center section (enlarged).
Pen and bistre and Indian ink, the center section in watercolor.
Dürer's monogram and date 1508 in pen and bistre.
195 : 384 mm.
Inv. no. 3120 (L. 174).
Albertina Cat. IV, 180; Schönbrunner-Meder 471; F. Winkler, Die Zeichnungen Hans Suess von Kulmbachs und Hans Leonhard Schäufeleins, Berlin, 1942, no. 83; J. Meder, Die Handzeichnung, p. 334; F. Winkler, "Verkannte und unbeachtete Zeichnungen des Hans von Kulmbach", Jahrbuch der Preussischen Kunstsammlungen, 50, Berlin, 1929, p. 26 ff; F. Winkler, Die Zeichnungen Albrecht Dürers, II, 1937, Appendix, text to plates XXVIII and XXIX.

This study for an altarpiece is closely related to a similar and only slightly larger one in the Albertina (Cat. 181, Winkler, Kulmbach, no. 84) which shows the Coronation of the Virgin in the center section and is dated 1511. Both studies were drawn with light strokes of the pen in bistre and then the center section was gone over in pen and Indian ink, and watercolor. In the course of this process a few angels behind St. Catherine and the Virgin, and above the manger, were discarded in the present drawing, but they are still clearly visible through the brickwork of the wall.
Both drawings were previously thought to be by Dürer. Winkler, too, in his Dürer corpus, attributed the finishing of both the center sections to Dürer, but in his book on Kulmbach's drawings he changed his opinion. Meder was the first who convincingly proposed Kulmbach's name. Actually, Kulmbach painted a triptych for the Tucher family in 1513 which was set up in St. Sebald's Church in Nuremberg; in its design Dürer had an essential part. Much in demand at the time and deeply absorbed in engraving, the master left the completion of this large painting to his disciple.
Winkler later was inclined to consider the two watercolor designs as earlier projects for the Tucher altar and to date the collaboration of the two artists back to 1508. He accordingly attributed documentary value to both dates and to the Dürer monogram. That the two center pieces with their soft, gay coloring seem closer to Kulmbach than to Dürer cannot be disputed. Winkler finally assumed that both sheets were executed at the same time, i. e., in 1511, but supposed that the idea for the present drawing goes back to 1508.

HANS SEBALD BEHAM
Born Nuremberg 1500, died Frankfort-on-Main 1550.

73 Portrait Bust of a Bearded Warrior.
Black chalk. Monogram: HSP and inscription in the artist's own hand: ·AETATIS SVAE XIXV· (55).
306 : 203 mm.
Inv. no. 17551 (L. 174).
Albertina Cat. IV, 192; Schönbrunner-Meder 412; M. J. Friedländer - E. Bock, Handzeichnungen deutscher Meister des XV. und XVI. Jahrhunderts, Berlin, p. 52 and plate 48; A. Rosenberg, Sebald u. Barthel Beham, Leipzig, 1875, p. 92, no. 14.

The brothers Beham belonged to the youngest generation of Dürer's disciples. They were prolific engravers and their numerous, finely-worked small engravings earned them the name of "the Little Nuremberg Masters." Hans Sebald's most important works artistically are his powerful portraits which represent the model in a clear and objective manner. The present drawing is a good example of his portraiture which, in its plain, almost dry manner, differs noticeably from the inner pathos and the high tension of Dürer's drawing style. Here we are approaching the objective, balanced, and controlled rendering of the human character typical of the German Late Renaissance.

HANS BALDUNG GRIEN
Born Weyersheim near Strasbourg 1484-85, died Strasbourg 1545.

74 Head of "Saturn".
Black chalk. Monogram and date [1] 516 in the artist's own hand; inscription in pen and bistre by a later hand, SATVRNO ·L·, and by yet another hand in red ink: Grien.
332 : 255 mm.
Inv. no. 17549 (L. 174).
Provenance: Charles, Prince de Ligne, Cat. p. 141, no. 1.
Albertina Cat. IV, 302; J. Meder, Albertina-Facsimile, Handzeichnungen deutscher Meister des XV. und XVI. Jahrhunderts, Vienna, 1922, plate 27; C. Koch, Die Zeichnungen Hans Baldung Griens, Berlin, 1941, no. 48; G. v. Térey, Die Handzeichnungen des Hans Baldung gen. Grien, Strasbourg 1894—96, no. 245; Great Drawings of All Time, New York, 1962, II, no. 377 (O. Benesch).

Exhibitions: (O. Benesch) Hans Baldung Grien, Exhibition in honor of the 450th anniversary of the master's birth, Albertina, Vienna, 1935, no. 24; London, 1948, no. 79; Paris, 1950, no. 86; Hans Baldung Grien Ausstellung, Kunsthalle, Karlsruhe, 1959, no. 150.

Although the inscription "SATVRNO" is by a later hand, it undoubtedly renders a correct iconographic tradition. The Roman god, in association with his planet, played an important role in the philosophical and astrological speculation of the Renaissance. In alchemy it was lead which was associated with him, in medicine, it was black gall. He appears as an uncouth, sombre fellow in representations of the planets in the fifteenth century, like Chronos devouring his own children and ruling over a wild race of warriors, poor peasants, and men of "dishonest" pursuits.

"Mein Kind sind siech, bleich, dürr und kalt / Grob, träg, neidig, traurig und ungestalt" (My children are sickly, pale, thin and cold / Rough, lazy, envious, sad and misshapen) says the "Wolfegg Hausbuch". In the theory of the humors he is associated with the melancholic temperament. But, as its master, he also displays a positive quality: the creative genius of the thinker and artist, their depth of thought and their wealth of invention, just as Dürer represented them in his engraving "Melancholia."

The manner in which Dürer's most important and independent pupil has combined all these associations in one head is one of the greatest achievements of old German draughtsmanship. In one face, he concentrated all that is ugly, choleric, and unkempt, savage even to the point of madness, but there is also spiritual fire flashing in the piercing gaze. As C. Koch has said, the question whether this is a study or a poetic invention must remain open. Probably it is both: a strange-looking man may have struck the artist as the embodiment of the Renaissance idea of the antique god, and in his rendering the type was expressively and fantastically intensified. The sheet, probably Baldung's most important work as a draughtsman, originated at the end of his Freiburg period and is probably an echo of the powerful impression that the art of Master Mathis in nearby Isenheim made upon him.

MATTHIAS GRÜNEWALD (Mathis Gothardt-Neithardt)
Native of Franconia, probably born in Würzburg about 1475, died Halle 1528.

75 A Saint with a Staff, Standing in a Forest.
Black chalk heightened with white bodycolor on yellowish paper; watermark, head of an ox with a cross and a serpent.
362 : 293 mm.
Verso: unfinished study of a saint, related to St. Anthony in the left stationary wing of the Isenheim Altar.
Inv. no. 3047.

Albertina Cat. IV, 296; M. J. Friedländer, Die Zeichnungen von Matthias Grünewald, Berlin, 1927, no. 26; L. Behling, Die Handzeichnungen des Mathis Gothart Nithart genannt Grünewald, Weimar, 1955, no. 22; G. Schönberger, The Drawings of Mathis Gothart Nithart, called Grünewald, New York, 1948, no. 19; F. Winkler, Die Meisterzeichnung, IV, no. 52; A. Burkhard, Matthias Grünewald, Cambridge, Massachusetts, 1936, plate 94; J. Meder, Albertina-Facsimile, Handzeichnungen deutscher Meister des XV. und XVI. Jahrhunderts, plate 40; Great Drawings of All Time, New York, 1962, II, no. 75 (O. Benesch).

Exhibitions: London, 1948, no. 106; Paris, 1950, no. 86.

The present drawing is one of the finest by Dürer's great counterpart in the German Renaissance. All the drawings of Master Mathis give the impression of being complete and independent works of art, yet for most of them, whether they be pure studies from nature or imaginary scenes (usually they are both), connections with paintings can be established. The reverse of this drawing indicates that it was made about the time of the Isenheim Altar (dated 1515). It has been assumed that this figure represents a St. Joseph in a Rest on the Flight into Egypt or in a Holy Family in the Wood. The splintered old oak trees twining their branches around the saint reveal a feeling for nature which links Master Mathis with the masters of the Danube School. The same cosmic feeling for nature is found in a drawing of "Christ the King in a Forest" (perhaps intended for the altar of Oberissigheim) and in the study for the Stuppach Madonna (both in Berlin).

In contrast to the firm stance of Dürer's figures this saint rather floats in a medieval manner, yet the way he blends with the natural beauty of his surroundings in a mild silvery light is so tremendously modern in vision that this artistic conquest of reality is fully equal to Dürer's. In some places chalk and brush work with miniature-like precision, but there are also large optical surfaces and light and dark flecks intensely suggestive of color. It would be a mistake to regard this manner of drawing as that of an artist who was solely a painter — it is of the same graphic significance and has the same linear eloquence as Dürer's. But its aim is different: the creation of a visionary world of mystic expression and religious fantasy.

LUCAS CRANACH THE YOUNGER
Born Wittenberg 1515, died Weimar 1586.

76 Portrait of Prince Alexander of Saxony, about 1564.
Brush and oil over light preparatory drawing in chalk on prepared paper; both corners on the left repaired.
327 : 240 mm.
Inv. no. 3202.

Albertina Cat. IV, 371; M. J. Friedländer-E. Bock, Handzeichnungen deutscher Meister des XV. und XVI. Jahrhunderts, Berlin, p. 55, plate 71; E. Bock, Amtliche Berichte, Berlin, XXXII, p. 137.

The present portrait of Prince Alexander (born 1554) is related to that of Princess Elisabeth of Saxony, perhaps as its companion piece, M. J. Friedländer-E. Bock, Staatliche Museen zu Berlin, Die deutschen Meister, Kupferstichkabinett, Berlin, 1921, I, p. 21, Inv. no. 4452, plate 27.
The date 1564 was arrived at by Bock through an estimate of the age of the prince who was born in 1554. Lucas Cranach the Younger followed his father's method of portraiture in making brush studies in the presence of the sitter, which then served as models for working out the panels. There is an attractive contrast between the loosely-sketched outlines of the drawing and the careful modeling of the head which in large part anticipates the appearance of the painting to follow.

LUCAS CRANACH THE ELDER (Family Name: Müller)
Born Kronach 1472, died Weimar 1553.

VIII Portrait of Hans Luther, Father of Martin Luther.
Brush and bodycolor on oiled paper.
218 : 183 mm (silhouetted along the outline of the head; measurements of original paper: 196 : 183 mm).
Inv. no. 26156 (acquired 1931).
Provenance: Count Salm.

Albertina Cat. IV, 365; O. Benesch, Die Graphischen Künste, Mitteilungen der Gesellschaft für vervielfältigende Kunst, Vienna, 1932, p. 15, fig. 12; J. Rosenberg, Die Zeichnungen Lucas Cranachs d. Ä., Berlin, 1960, no. 76; O. Benesch, The Art of the Renaissance in Northern Europe, Cambridge, Massachusetts, 1947, p. 61, fig. 35 and London, 1965, p. 69, fig. 37.

Exhibition: London, 1948, no. 82.

Portraiture was the only sphere of artistic production in which the Elder Cranach preserved the vigor of his youth in Vienna into his last period. In his works the figures of the religious reformers and their contemporaries pass before our eyes like a living gallery of history. As models for his carefully executed panels, he made direct life studies in bodycolor on paper, which in liveliness and immediacy far surpass the paintings. This drawing, which was identified by the present author at an earlier date, was produced at Wittenberg in 1527, on the occasion of a visit by Luther's parents to their son. The painting, together with the companion portrait of Luther's mother, is at the Wartburg near Eisenach. The brush drawing is imbued with a greatness and an inner life that place it far above the panel, which is hard and tight by comparison. Luther's father was a miner. The primitive strength of the man speaks to us quite differently in the drawing and the painting.

BERNHARD STRIGEL
Born Memmingen, about 1460; died there 1528.

77 Christ and the Twelve Apostles.
Pen and bistre, brush and Indian ink and white bodycolor, the flesh color a reddish shade, on grayish-yellow prepared

paper. Left side: Simon, Judas Thaddaeus, Bartholomew, Philip: 121 : 126 mm; center: Peter, James the Younger, Christ, Thomas, Andrew: 119 : 124 mm; right side: James the Elder, John, Paul, Matthew: 120 : 126 mm.

Inv. nos. 31329, 31330, 31331 (acquired 1952).

Provenance: Abbey of Seitenstetten, Lower Austria.
Schönbrunner-Meder 1433; K. T. Parker und W. Hugelshofer, Bernhardin Strigel als Zeichner, Belvedere 8, Vienna, 1925, Heft 8, p. 39 and fig. 16.

Exhibition: Neuerwerbungen alter Meister 1950—58, Vienna, 1958, Albertina, Cat. no. 6.

Strigel, like the Elder Holbein, was a master of transition: formal elements of the Late German Gothic still assert themselves strongly in his early works, as, for instance, in the present drawing, the correct attribution of which is owed to E. Buchner. It is the design for a predella, the base of an altarpiece, for which the subject of Christ with His apostles was frequently used in wood carvings of the fifteenth century. The style of the modeling likewise seeks to create the impression of figures in the round. Nevertheless its almost tangible smoothness is different from the linear brittleness of a Schongauer, a difference explainable in terms of the whole generation separating the artists, even if the difference between the dates of the two drawings (nos. 67 and 77) is not so great.

HANS BURGKMAIR THE ELDER
Born Augsburg, 1473; died there 1531.

78 Self-Portrait of the Artist at the Time of his Betrothal.
Pen and Indian ink, watercolor (coat, chestnut-brown; leggings and doublet, gray-blue and crimson; cap and shoes, dark gray).

Above the figure, an inscription by the artist's own hand: In solcher gestalt nam ich mein weyb / ana allerlayin dar bey was der stat / fogt und her hanns graber Docktor / konrady beutinger und es geschach in / seinem hauss in dem hauss das des minerss ist gewösen an sant thomans abent des / zwölf boten ann ainer miwoch um / das ain im jar 1497. (This is the way I looked when I was betrothed to Anna Allerlayin in the presence of the Stadtvogt and Herr Hanns Graber, Doctor Konrad Peutinger, and it took place in his house, which once belonged to Mynner, on the evening of St. Thomas on a Wednesday in the year 1497.)
Below on the right the numeral 41 in another hand.
Inv. no. 31327 (acquired 1952).
Provenance: Abbey of Seitenstetten, Lower Austria.

79 Self-Portrait of the Artist as a Bridegroom.
Pen and Indian ink, watercolor (coat, light brown; leggings, deep purplish brown; cap and shoes, gray). Above the figure, an inscription in the artist's own hand: also bin ich gen kirchen gangen auf / meiner hochzeyt an sannt ulrichs / abend im jar 1498 (Like this I went to church on the occasion of my wedding on the evening of St. Ulrich in the year 1498.)
158 : 73 mm.
Inv. no. 31328.

Provenance: Abbey of Seitenstetten.
H. Röttinger, Münchner Jahrbuch der bildenden Kunst, 1908, II. Halbband, p. 48, illus.; A. Burkhard, Hans Burgkmair d. Ä., Leipzig, 1934, fig. 2; P. Halm, Münchner Jahrbuch der bildenden Kunst, Dritte Folge, XIII, 1962, p. 116, figs. 48, 49.

Exhibitions: Grosse Kunst aus Österreichs Klöstern, Österreichisches Museum für angewandte Kunst, Vienna, 1950, Cat. no. 95; Neuerwerbungen alter Meister, 1950—1958, Vienna, 1958, Albertina, Cat. nos. 7, 8.

Hans Burgkmair the Elder was the pupil of his father, Thoman Burgkmair, and of Martin Schongauer. His early works prior to 1500 — mostly drawings and some panels and woodcuts — show this pioneer of southern Renaissance art still under the spell of the late Gothic style. Both these small watercolor studies had value for the artist as personal souvenirs. They perhaps were once part of a family chronicle or album like those started by Dürer. In any case they reveal

the charm and freshness inherent in such direct testimonials of the life of the past. One of the persons mentioned in the text was the classical scholar Peutinger, who also was Dürer's friend. The great men in art and in the intellectual life of this classical period of German art stood in close personal relationship.

HANS HOLBEIN THE ELDER
Born Augsburg, about 1465; died Isenheim, 1524.

80 Head of a Young Man with Hunting Hat.
Silverpoint on white prepared paper.
134 : 100 mm.
Inv. no. 7825 (L. 174).

Albertina Cat. IV, 205; O. Benesch, Zeitschrift für bildende Kunst, 64, Vienna, 1930-31, pp. 39, 40 (illustrated).

Exhibitions: Paris, 1950, no. 51; Die Malerfamilie Holbein in Basel, Kunstmuseum, Basle, 1960, Cat. no. 73; Hans Holbein der Ältere und die Kunst der Spätgotik, Augsburg-Rathaus, 1965, Cat. no. 84.

Old inventory: Aert Claessens van Leyden.
Apart from a small group of important panel paintings, the skill of the Elder Holbein as a portraitist is primarily manifested in his silverpoint sketchbooks. These contain a profusion of representations of men of his time and surroundings, not solemnly posing for a portrait, but in the naturalness of their everyday life, as the draughtsman caught it. The father thus laid the foundation for the portraiture of the son. Some of these heads appear in the master's religious paintings, thus contributing to their aliveness and humanization. Although there was always an idea of eventual utilization behind this spontaneous portraiture, it owed its origin first and foremost to an artistic impulse.
The present drawing, once attributed to a Dutch artist and first claimed for the Elder Holbein by the present author, was certainly part of one such silverpoint sketchbook.

AMBROSIUS HOLBEIN
Born Augsburg, probably 1494; died Basle, about 1519.

81 Half-Length Portrait of a Young Boy Looking Left.
Silverpoint, red chalk (lips), heightened with white bodycolor on white prepared paper.
142 : 109 mm.
Inv. no. 4832 (L. 174).
Preparatory drawing for the portrait of the fair-haired boy in Basle, Kunstmuseum (Inv. no. 294).

Albertina Cat. IV, 340; A. Woltmann, Holbein und seine Zeit, Leipzig, 1874, II, p. 95, no. 24; W. Hes, Ambrosius Holbein, Studien zur deutschen Kunstgeschichte, Heft 145, Strasbourg, 1911, pp. 116—117, plate XXIX.

Exhibition: Die Malerfamilie Holbein in Basel, Kunstmuseum, Basle, 1960, Cat. no. 93.

Old inventory: Lorenzo di Credi.
Ambrosius, son of Hans Holbein the Elder and brother of the Younger, was at his best in his portraiture, which is clearly based on the achievements of his father. The connection with his father is evident in this careful silverpoint drawing. It is the preparatory drawing for a painting in the Kunstmuseum in Basle which has its companion piece in the portrait of the dark-haired little brother of this boy, also prepared in a silverpoint drawing (Print Room, Basle, Inv. 1921, 44). Both paintings came from the Amerbach collection; in its inventory of 1586 they bear the name of Ambrosius Holbein.

JÖRG BREU THE ELDER
Born Augsburg, about 1475—1480; died there 1537.

82 Portrait of a Young Man with Red Cap.
Black, reddish and yellow chalk, slight heightening in white; the eyes and the outline of the ear gone over in black with the pen, the background covered with light brownish-gray bodycolor, probably at a later date; water-stains on cheek and neck; upper right corner replaced.
222 : 157 mm.
Inv. no. 6660 (L. 174).

Provenance: Charles, Prince de Ligne (Cat. p. 139, no. 1).
Albertina Cat. IV, 209 (Augsburg Master); Schönbrunner-Meder 3 (Lucas Cranach the Elder); J. Meder, Albertina-Facsimile, Handzeichnungen deutscher Meister des XV. und XVI. Jahrhunderts, plate 39 (Lucas Cranach the Elder); E. Buchner, Beiträge zur Geschichte der deutschen Kunst II, Munich, 1928, p. 336 and fig. 243.

Exhibition: London, 1948, no. 80.

This portrait, previously attributed to Cranach, was recognized by E. Buchner as the work of the powerful Augsburg artist who worked in Austria at the same time as Cranach, in the early years of the century. The attribution is confirmed by comparison with the Head of a Woman of 1519 in Berlin (Cat. 803). The tense modeling of the skin by curved parallel lines, the sketchy treatment of the garment's neckline are the same in both. Portraiture was especially cultivated in Augsburg (see the notes to nos. 80, 81 and 83). Breu, next to Burgkmair the most important artist of the High Renaissance in Augsburg, liked, as did the Elder Holbein, to introduce heads of a portraitlike character into his religious paintings.

DANIEL HOPFER I
Born Kaufbeuren, about 1470; died Augsburg, 1536.

83 Half-Length Figure of a Young Girl with a Plumed Hat. Pen and brush, and Indian ink and white bodycolor. Inscription in the shape of a neckband: NIT·AN·VR (interpreted as: Ursula do not touch me).
433 : 320 mm.
Inv. no. 17595 (L. 174).
Albertina Cat. IV, no. 211; E. Eyssen, Daniel Hopfer, Thesis, Heidelberg, 1904, p. 42, no. 5; Schönbrunner-Meder 5; J. Meder, Albertina-Facsimile, Handzeichnungen deutscher Meister des XV. und XVI. Jahrhunderts, Vienna, 1922, plate 34; M. J. Friedländer — E. Bock, Handzeichnungen deutscher Meister des XV. und XVI. Jahrhunderts, Berlin, n. d., plate 91.

Exhibition: London, 1948, no. 107.

Daniel Hopfer played an important role in the history of the graphic arts. He was an etcher of armor by profession. His familiarity with the technique of etching on iron plates which were parts of suits of armor led him to make etched intaglio plates. The way was thereby free for the development of etching (see note to no. 70). Hopfer was the author of a large graphic oeuvre, particularly of ornamental pattern sheets which were intended to be used for all kinds of decorative arts. Growing out of the Late Gothic tradition, he was among the earliest disseminators of Italian Renaissance ornament in the North, taking as his models the works of the Mantegnesque engravers of Upper Italy. His graphic oeuvre also included decorative architecture, figure composition, and portraiture. His figures are ornamental in character. This applies in a high degree to the present drawing which is distinguished by its precious, jewel-like character, its charm of line, and ornamental contours within the picture plane. Costume, jewelry, and flower (probably a columbine) are enjoyed to the full in all their decorative details.
Meder regarded the interlaced ornament worn by the sitter in a small version on her necklace, and in a larger embroidered version on her hat and stomacher, as a love-knot and assumed her to be an Augsburg lady of easy virtue. The neckband with its ironically provocative inscription seems to confirm this assumption. If this is correct, the Venetian courtesan portrait — to which Dürer also made a valuable contribution — has found a Northern successor here.

ALBRECHT ALTDORFER
Born Regensburg, shortly before 1480; died there 1538.

84 Abraham Sacrificing Isaac (?).
Pen and Indian ink, and white bodycolor on grayish-green prepared paper. Date cut off on upper margin.
190 : 156 mm.
Inv. no. 3212 (L. 174).
Provenance: Charles, Prince de Ligne (Cat. p. 140, no. 4).

Albertina Cat. IV, 217; H. L. Becker, Die Handzeichnungen Albrecht Altdorfers, Munich, 1938, no. 73; Schönbrunner-Meder 514; J. Meder, Albertina-Facsimile, Handzeichnungen deutscher Meister des XV. und XVI. Jahrhunderts, Vienna, 1922, plate 35; M. J. Friedländer, Albrecht Altdorfer, Leipzig, 1891, p. 155, no. 30 (1514, "Martyrdom of a Female Saint by Decapitation"); H. Tietze, Albrecht Altdorfer, Leipzig, 1923, p. 80; L. v. Baldass, Albrecht Altdorfer, Vienna, 1941, p. 80; A. Winzinger, Albrecht Altdorfer, Zeichnungen, Munich, 1952, no. 25.

Exhibition: Albrecht Altdorfer, Munich, 1938, Cat. no. 80.

About the turn of the century there originated in the Danube region of Austria a new style in painting and the graphic arts based on the creative achievements of Cranach, Breu, and the younger Frueauf, — who at that time worked in Vienna and its surroundings — and also soon bringing sculpture under its spell. This was the "Danube style" and the "Danube School." It reached its climax in the works of Altdorfer and Huber. A characteristic feature of the style is the close fusion of the event — whether religious, mythological, or historical — with the landscape. In Altdorfer's works cosmic forces seem to shape the representation of landscape and man alike, rendering them integral parts of the same whole. In 1511 Altdorfer undertook a journey down the Danube to Austria as a drawing of the Danube narrows near Sarmingstein (Budapest, Museum) bears witness. The present sheet was probably made about the same time, as the wooded mountain slopes are very similar in their structure to those in the view of Sarmingstein. It is a picturesque Danube landscape in which the biblical scene unfolds.
Altdorfer developed the technique of drawing in Indian ink and white bodycolor on tinted prepared paper to exceptional heights. Nearly all his drawings in this manner are independent works of art. They were frequently copied both in and outside his studio, evidence that they were already sought after by collectors and amateurs at the time of their origin. The curly line of the pen creates a delightfully effervescent, almost Baroque, ornamentalism that effects the reciprocal assimilation of all forms.
The meaning of the scene is somewhat obscure. It has also been called the "Martyrdom of a Saint," as the executioner is not an old patriarch, but a young man. But the interceding angel and the ram on his right — in spite of the indistinct drawing recognizable by its horns — make it seem probable that the subject is Abraham's Sacrifice of Isaac.

IX The Adoration of the Magi.
Pen and Indian ink, and white bodycolor on blue prepared paper.
188 : 138 mm.
Inv. no. 30959 (acquired 1950).

Provenance: Prince Liechtenstein, formerly Vienna.
Schönbrunner-Meder 279; H. L. Becker, op. cit., Cat. no. 183; F. Winzinger, Albrecht Altdorfer, Zeichnungen, Munich, 1952, Cat. and fig. no. 32; H. Tietze, op. cit., p. 78; L. Baldass, op. cit., p. 130.

Exhibition: Neuerwerbungen alter Meister, 1950—1958, Albertina, Vienna, 1958, Cat. no. 9.

A copy by the monogrammist H R 1531 is in Berlin, M. J. Friedländer — E. Bock, Zeichnungen deutscher Meister, Berlin, 1921, Kupferstichkabinett I, p. 69, Inv. no. 84; there is a copy, dated 1513, in the Kunsthalle, Karlsruhe (Becker 142), and another, with monogram C W and dated 1548, in the École des Beaux-Arts, Paris, Masson collection (Becker 171).
Altdorfer introduced into his religious representations not only the magic charm of landscape (see the note to no. 84), but also the enchanted mood of the setting, chosen for the most part from his own surroundings. The Adoration of the Magi thus takes place here within old walls overgrown with vines, that might be part of a vaulted chamber in the ruins of a castle or of the gate of some small medieval town. The radiating arrangement of the thin, slate-like stone slabs can still today be found in old archways in Austria. It enabled the draughtsman to make the architecture appear as if it

had organically developed like natural rocks or the face of a mountain. Altdorfer must certainly have seen Michael Pacher's altarpiece at St. Wolfgang on one of his journeys to Austria. Its impact upon him is noticeable in a number of his works, including this drawing, in the strong three-dimensional effect of the composition. The spatial arrangement draws the eye irresistibly into depth. The Virgin looms large in the foreground, while the figures of the background diminish rapidly in size. Such means of spatial suggestion Altdorfer derived from Pacher.

Experts agree that this excellent drawing is a work by Altdorfer's own hand; only H. Becker regards it as a studio replica. A superior version, which would justify this assumption, is not known. Various copies testify to the fame of the drawing in the past; they are far inferior in quality to the original. The earliest of these copies is dated 1513; the original must therefore have been made in 1512 at the latest.

ERHARD ALTDORFER
Born Regensburg, about 1485; died Schwerin, 1562.

85   Mountain Landscape with Sailing Vessels on a Bay.
Pen and bistre.
206 : 311 mm.
Inv. no. 17546 (L. 174).
Albertina Cat. IV, 221; Schönbrunner-Meder 867; K. T. Parker, Drawings of the Early German Schools, London, 1926, no. 62 (closely related to the etching, Bartsch VIII, pp. 67, 71); W. Jürgens, Erhard Altdorfer, Lübeck, 1931, p. 67, fig. 11; O. Benesch and Erwin M. Auer, Die Historia Friderici et Maximiliani, Berlin, 1957, p. 93.

Exhibitions: Albrecht Altdorfer, Munich, 1938, Cat. no. 351; Die Kunst der Donauschule 1490—1540, St. Florian—Schlossmuseum Linz, 1965, Cat. no. 165.

Albrecht Altdorfer's younger brother Erhard was also a product of their father's workshop, but fell at once under the influence of the more important Albrecht, whose style was clearly defined at an early date. Erhard's drawings and engravings, made in Regensburg about 1506, show him as a close follower of his brother. He probably left Regensburg early and turned up in Austria, where he painted altarpieces for the abbeys of Lambach and Klosterneuburg. Erhard's early Austrian works reveal close contact with the author of the illustrations of a manuscript in the Vienna State Archives: the so-called "Meister der Historia Friderici et Maximiliani." This important anonymous artist was Albrecht Altdorfer's earliest follower among Austrian artists. In 1512 Erhard Altdorfer was called to Schwerin as court painter to Duke Henry the Peace-Lover. But he retained the "Danube Style" acquired from his brother and developed in Austria, although his later works are quieter and neater than his vigorous and spirited early ones from his Austrian period. The present landscape drawing belongs to the former category and was identified by J. Meder as Erhard's work on the basis of comparison with the artist's only authentic landscape etching.

MONOGRAMMIST F H (Veit Hirschvogel?)

86   Mountain Landscape with St. Eustace.
Pen and bistre; monogram F H.
276 : 413 mm.
Inv. no. 24660 (acquired 1925).
Albertina Cat. IV, 198.

This drawing is a synthesis of the style of the Nuremberg and the Danube Schools. The group of dogs in the lower left corner shows that the draughtsman had Dürer's engraving of St. Eustace in mind, but the effervescent pen stroke in the depiction of the luxuriant landscape also reveals the influence of Albrecht and Erhard Altdorfer. Such a synthesis of the Nuremberg and Danube styles is in keeping with the art of the glass painter, etcher, and cartographer Augustin Hirschvogel, who was born in Nuremberg and died in Vienna. Actually the drawing so closely resembles Augustin Hirschvogel's style that it was ascribed to him. The Tietzes (Albertina Cat.) therefore supposed that the monogram was originally an A H and that the first letter was later changed

to an F. This opinion does not stand up under close examination of the original. The present author therefore suggests the possibility of reading the monogram as "Feit Hirsfogel." Veit Hirschvogel the Younger was Augustin's elder brother, born in Nuremberg in 1485 and, like Augustin, a pupil of his father, the glass painter Veit Hirschvogel the Elder. According to J. Neudörfer's report he was also an engraver. Only one drawing by his hand is known: a view of Aschaffenburg in the Heller Collection of the Bamberg Library (Studien zur deutschen Kunstgeschichte, Heft 65, plate III); it can without difficulty be regarded as a work by the same hand as the present drawing.

MASTER OF THE MATER DOLOROSA FROM SEITENSTETTEN.

87   Mater Dolorosa.
Pen and brush and Indian ink, heightened with white on reddish tinted paper. Dated 1518.
153 : 100 mm.
Inv. no. 31326 (acquired 1952).
Provenance: Abbey of Seitenstetten.
Schönbrunner-Meder 1357; E. Bock, Die Zeichnungen in der Universitätsbibliothek Erlangen, Frankfort-on-Main, 1929, at no. 739, fig. XIX; O. Benesch, Die Meisterzeichnung, V, 63.

Exhibitions: Albrecht Altdorfer, Munich, 1938, no. 667; Grosse Kunst aus Österreichs Klöstern, Vienna, 1950, Cat. no. 108; Neuerwerbungen alter Meister, 1950—1958, Vienna, Albertina 1958, Cat. no. 10.

The anonymous artist, probably active in the Austrian Danube region and named after the present drawing, is known by a series of drawings which the author connected with a Danube School panel representing the shoemaker's workshop of St. Crispin and St. Crispinian (now in the Österreichische Galerie; formerly Figdor Collection). His finest drawing is a Virgin from the Ehlers Collection, now in the Print Room in Berlin. A characteristic feature of his work is the technique of flashing white lights applied with the brush on colored paper. His drapery with its rounded, rumpled folds brings him very close to Wolf Huber, to whose wider circle he probably belonged.

88   St. Jerome.
Pen and brush, and Indian ink and white bodycolor, washed, on reddish-brown prepared paper.
144 : 98 mm.
Inv. no. 30747 (acquired 1948).
Provenance: Prince Liechtenstein, formerly Vienna.
Schönbrunner-Meder 993; O. Benesch, Die Meisterzeichnung, V, p. 54 f.

Exhibitions: Von der Gotik bis zur Gegenwart, Neuerwerbungen, 1947—1949, Albertina, Vienna, 1949-50, Cat. no. 4; Die Kunst der Donauschule, St. Florian—Schlossmuseum Linz, 1965, Cat. no. 209.

The present drawing was identified by J. Meder as a work by the same hand as the Mater Dolorosa from Seitenstetten (see no. 87). Charming and typical of the Danube School is the manner in which the ornamental tree-tops of the pinewood invade the saint's study; man and landscape form an indissoluble unity.

JÖRG KÖLDERER AND HIS WORKSHOP
Descended from a peasant family from Hof near Inzing, mentioned in Innsbruck since 1497; died there 1540.

89   The Triumphal Car of Emperor Maximilian I.

X   Detail
Pen and brush, watercolor and bodycolor, heightened with gold on vellum.
448 : 938 mm.
Inv. no. 25246 (transferred from the National Library, 1927). Page no. 93 from the Triumphal Procession of Emperor Maximilian I.
Provenance: Abbey of St. Florian; Imperial Library, Vienna.

Albertina Cat. IV, 270; F. Schestag, Jahrbuch der kunsthistorischen Sammlungen des Allerhöchsten Kaiserhauses, I, 1883, pp. 154 ff.; K. Giehlow, ibid., 29, 1910, pp. 23—27; L. Baldass, Der Künstlerkreis Kaiser Maximilians, Vienna, 1923, p. 39; L. Baldass, Albrecht Altdorfer, Kunstgeschichtliche Einzeldarstellungen, II, Vienna, 1923, pp. 13 ff.; O. Benesch, Beiträge zur Geschichte der deutschen Kunst, II, Augsburg, 1928, pp. 268 ff.; L. Baldass, Jahrbuch der kunsthistorischen Sammlungen in Wien, N. F. 12, p. 140; L. Baldass, Albrecht Altdorfer, Vienna, 1941, p. 27 ff.; O. Benesch und E. M. Auer, Die Historia Friderici et Maximiliani, Berlin, 1957, pp. 110 ff.

Exhibitions: Albrecht Altdorfer, Munich, 1938, Cat. no. 564; Maximilian I, Vienna, 1959, Cat. p. 88, no. 258, fig. 46.

The two largest woodcut publications undertaken by the Emperor Maximilian I were the "Triumphal Arch" and the "Triumphal Procession", for which he commissioned the very best artists in the field of graphic art in Upper Germany. The idea of these genealogical and historical glorifications of his person and his house came from the Emperor himself. At Mantua in the palace of Francesco Gonzaga II, his personal friend, he certainly had seen Mantegna's triumphal procession. The program was devised by Stabius, the drawings for the project were prepared by the court painter Jörg Kölderer in Innsbruck. Kölderer, the son of a Tyrolese peasant family from the hamlet Hof near Inzing in the Upper Inn valley, was active in various capacities as architect, sculptor, painter, miniaturist and draughtsman. He did not belong to any particular school, rather he was more of a kind of self-taught artist, whose versatility made him most acceptable to the Emperor with all his various projects. He died at an advanced age in 1540. His authentic works which have come down to us are mainly the watercolor illustrations of the imperial inventories of armories, of the hunting preserves, and fishing grounds. They show Kölderer as a somewhat clumsy draughtsman closely dependent upon fifteenth century forms. The first documentary report concerning the work on the "Triumphal Procession" dates from 1507. In 1512 Kölderer dispatched the finished work in two copies. In the same year Dürer began his work on the "Triumphal Car".

The miniature series is regarded as one of these two copies. It was intended as an especially luxurious version for the Emperor's personal use. The copy which Dürer, Schäufelein, Springinklee, Burgkmair, and Altdorfer used as a model must have consisted of plain pen drawings which were completely re-edited in the woodcut version.

The complete miniature series numbered 109 sheets, 62 of which have been preserved and are in the Albertina. The miniatures differ completely in style and manner of drawing from Kölderer's authentic watercolors. They show the style of the then modern Danube School. Kölderer was a capable organizer who knew how to engage young artists for the execution of the extensive commissions. In 1510-11 Altdorfer was in Austria. About the same time Wolf Huber of Vorarlberg set out on his first journey — historically confirmed — to the countries of the Eastern Alps and to the Danube region. Nothing is more probable than that they visited Kölderer's shop in Innsbruck and drew the young artists under their spell, perhaps even collaborated in the work. Several hands can be distinguished among the miniatures, two of which are strikingly close to Altdorfer and Huber.

The heart of the "Triumphal Procession" is the Car of the Emperor drawn by twelve white horses. In front of the Emperor are seated his wife Mary of Burgundy, his daughter-in-law Joanna of Castile, his son Philip the Handsome, and his daughter Margaret, regent of the Netherlands, and finally Philip's children, Charles V, Ferdinand I, Eleanor, Isabel, Mary, and Catherine.

CIRCLE OF WOLF HUBER

90   The Story of the Prophet Daniel.
Pen and Indian ink, washed.
269 : 375 mm, at the right a strip of paper, 126 mm wide, was added.
Inv. no. 26712 (acquired 1935).

This drawing was part of a series of designs for frescoes depicting scenes from the Book of Daniel. It actually consists of the larger right half and the smaller left half of two fragmentary sheets which have been pasted together. The scenes are enclosed in a semi-circle and were apparently intended to cover the arched segments of a vault. Hanging from garlands are shields which were meant to carry inscriptions taken from the text of the Bible. The frescoes were more likely designed for the decoration of a secular building than an ecclesiastical one. (Holbein's town hall frescoes at Basle also represented scenes from the Old Testament.)
The left arch shows Daniel's rescue from the lions' den (Daniel, chapter 6), the right one, the vision of the four animals (Daniel, chapter 7). In the Museum Boymans-Van Beuningen there is another drawing from the same cycle (Collection Koenigs, D I 242) which tells the story of Belshazzar (Daniel, chapter 5).
These drawings, with their unpretentious narrative style and their direct manner of representation, are probably by an artist from Passau, thoroughly trained in the style of Wolf Huber.

WOLF HUBER
Born Feldkirch about 1485, died Passau 1553.

91   View of Vienna.
Pen and bistre; dated 1530.
146 : 132 mm.
Inv. no. 26159 (acquired 1931).
Provenance: Count Salm.

Albertina Cat. IV, 288; J. Meder, Die Graphischen Künste, Mitteilungen der Gesellschaft für vervielfältigende Kunst, Vienna, 1931, Heft 1, p. 10, fig. 1; E. Heinzle, Wolf Huber, Innsbruck, n. d., fig. 53.

Exhibition: Albrecht Altdorfer, Munich, 1938, no. 486.

Wolf Huber, a native of Feldkirch in Vorarlberg, was, together with Albrecht Altdorfer, the most important artist of the Danube School. The work of Huber the draughtsman even surpasses that of the painter. The conquest of landscape by drawing is owed, above all, to him, not in the form of a fantastically intensified apotheosis of nature as with Altdorfer, but in the form of a plain pictorial record that was of the utmost importance for the origin and development of the veduta. From 1510 onward, views of his journeys to Austria begin to appear in his sketchbooks. During the reign of the Prince Bishop Wiguleus Fröschl (1500—1516) he settled at Passau. His special patrons were the counts Niklas of Salm III and IV, who employed him as architect at Neuburg Castle on the Inn. When Count Niklas of Salm III died in 1530 of wounds received during the defense of Vienna against the Turks, Huber went to Vienna for the exequies in the suite of his sons Niklas and Wolfgang (later Prince Bishop). He probably also designed the tumba of his patron (now in the Votivkirche in Vienna). During this visit Huber made the present drawing, which is a view of war-damaged Vienna from the south. In the foreground can be seen the deserted Turkish emplacements in the suburb of Wieden. In the middle of the riddled walls is the Kärntnertor with its tower; and on its left the Mehlmarkt (now Neuer Markt), the Church of St. Augustine, and, in the distance, the Church of Maria am Gestade. St. Stephen's Cathedral dominates the view of the city. The same view of Vienna appears in the background of a portrait of Count Palatine Philip the Valiant, dated 1530, in the Bayerisches Nationalmuseum, Munich.
Without the use of hatching or wash, by a pure linearism varying only in intensity of stroke, Huber knew how to evoke the magic of light and air in his landscapes and vedute.

92   Portrait Bust of a Young Woman.
Red chalk; the background left, in brush and Indian ink, by a later hand. Monogram and date of 1544 in the artist's own hand.
Inv. no. 3016 (L. 174).

Albertina Cat. IV, 289; J. Meder, Die Handzeichnung, p. 127; J. Meder, Albertina-Facsimile, Handzeichnungen deutscher Meister des XV. und XVI. Jahrhunderts, plate 36; R. Riggenbach, Der Maler und Zeichner Wolfgang Huber, Basle, 1907, p. 69, no. 16; M. Weinberger, Wolf Huber, Leipzig, 1930, p. 203; E. Heinzle, Wolf Huber, Innsbruck, n. d., fig. 67.

Exhibition: Albrecht Altdorfer, Munich, 1938, Cat. no. 495.

A monumental drawing from the master's late period in which the portrait character is emphasized, as it is in the portrait of a man, drawn in 1522, in the former Oppenheimer Collection (now Collection Dr. Robert von Hirsch, Basle). In comparison with the earlier pictorial looseness, forms have gained in plastic clarity. The head, which deliberately does not show the same detailed execution as the drapery of the bust, is isolated within the picture space in an almost sculptural effect. Nevertheless the mastery of modeling by means of the light lends it an atmospheric softness. The work has much in common with the portraits of Dürer's second Venetian period. Huber knew the Venetian art of Antonello's and Giovanni Bellini's time which he evidently studied at its source.

URS GRAF
Born Solothurn about 1485, died 1527, presumably in Basle.

93 Lansquenet's Lass Wading through a Brook.
Pen and Indian ink. Monogram with dagger and Basle staff, and date (partly cut off): 152. by the artist's own hand.
199 : 145 mm.
Inv. no. 3051 (L. 174).

Albertina Cat. IV, 334; Schönbrunner-Meder 250; K. T. Parker, Anzeiger für schweizerische Altertumskunde, N. F., XXIII, 1921, no. 36; K. T. Parker, Zwanzig Federzeichnungen des Urs Graf, plate 5; H. Koegler, Beschreibendes Verzeichnis der Baseler Handzeichnungen des Urs Graf, Basle, 1926, p. 91, no. 134.

Urs Graf, who was active as goldsmith, graphic artist, and draughtsman, knew at first hand the wild, adventurous life of the lansquenets, which he rendered in numerous masterful pen drawings. He repeatedly took part in the campaigns of the Swiss lansquenets in Italy and France out of sheer love of adventure. Not without good reason did he change the left stroke of the letter U in his monogram into a dagger. The soldiers' lass is equally provocative in finery and pose. In spite of some similarities with the art of his Swiss contemporary Niklaus Manuel Deutsch, like him a mercenary soldier, the draughtsman Urs Graf was essentially an individualist. His drawings show the hand of the trained engraver, particularly in the later years (the 1520's), from which the present drawing dates. Man and landscape blend in his works as they did in those of the Danube School, a feature which he shares with his Swiss contemporaries.

HANS HOLBEIN THE YOUNGER
Born Augsburg 1497, died London 1543.

94 Two Angels Holding an Escutcheon, before Renaissance Architecture.
Pen and brush and Indian ink over preparatory drawing in chalk; inscribed in pen and Indian ink by a later hand: H Holbein (ligature); watermark: grape (similar to Briquet 13017, Switzerland, beginning of the sixteenth century).
438 : 325 mm.
Inv. no. 31705 (acquired 1955).

Provenance: Sir Peter Lely (L. 1753); Richardson (both collectors' marks in pen and Indian ink); George le Hunte, Artramont, Wexford, Ireland; P. & C. Colnaghi, London. Design for stained glass.
Colnaghi's 1760—1960, London, 1960, no. 73.

Exhibitions: Neuerwerbungen Alter Meister 1950—1958, Albertina, Vienna, 1958, Cat. no. 11; Die Malerfamilie Holbein in Basel, Kunstmuseum, Basle, 1960, Cat. no. 257, fig. 88.

A companion piece to this drawing, slightly smaller in size, inscribed in the same way and coming from the same collections, is in the Barber Institute of Fine Arts in Birmingham. It represents two angels with an escutcheon, crowned by a mitre and a pedum, and likewise with Renaissance architecture as background. Both drawings came from the same English private collection and appeared on the art market in 1955. So for the first time a drawing by the Younger Holbein found its way to the Albertina.
Both drawings are designs for armorial panes whose shields were left blank. They were executed during the master's first Basle period (1519—1526) and are related particularly to the designs for the stained glass of St. Richardis (Woltmann 50, Ganz 157) and of the coat of arms of Andlau (Ganz 188) in the Print Room at Basle. These were intended for the

refectory of the Convent of St. Mary Magdalene "an den Steinen" in Basle.
Holbein's activity as a designer for stained glass was most intensive following his return from Lucerne and Italy. He made mostly designs for small panes of stained glass destined not so much for church decoration as for the profane rooms of ecclesiastical and secular buildings. Within this modest frame the master's decorative genius unfolded superbly. In the Albertina drawing the Late Gothic forms are definitely abandoned in favor of pure Renaissance forms. Yet something of the high tension and the dramatic pathos of the period of the great altarpieces makes itself felt. The austere beauty of the boldly conceived male angels recalls Master Mathis' Isenheim Altar, which must have been well known to the young Holbein as it was located at Isenheim where his father, Hans Holbein the Elder, lived and died.

HANS MIELICH
Born Munich 1516, died there 1573.

95 The Resurrection of Lazarus, with the Kneeling Family of the Donor.
Pen and bistre, washed; lower left, later inscription: I. N. 117.12 v.; watermark: crown.
213 : 285 mm.
Inv. no. 32916 (L. 5e); acquired from L'Art Ancien, Zurich, 1959.
Provenance: Manteau (L. 1851).

Verso: Coat of arms of alliance, with two warriors as supporters, and scrollwork below. Black chalk, pen in bistre.

Mielich received his most significant training in Regensburg where he worked with Altdorfer during the last years of the latter's life (Buchner presumes him to be the "apprentice and dear servant Hans" whom Altdorfer remembered in his will). While his works of the 1530's still show him to be a close follower of Altdorfer, he turned toward international Mannerism in the 1540's. From then onward his art has certain features in common with the School of Fontainebleau and Mannerism in Rome and Florence. Mielich visited Rome in 1541. The Mocking of Christ and the Entombment of 1543 in the church of Solna near Stockholm are the most striking testimonials of this change of style.
The attribution of this drawing to Mielich is a suggestion of the present author. The architectural setting clearly shows elements of the Bavarian Renaissance. The closely grouped round arches occur in works by Refinger and by Mielich himself (for instance, in the lower portion of the Eck epitaph in the Bayerisches Nationalmuseum, Munich). The drawing technique reveals an artist deriving from the Danube School, and influenced by Altdorfer and Huber. The type of composition is that of early German Mannerism. The elongated proportions of the figures can be found in the Solna paintings. The nude near the left margin of the drawing is reminiscent of the "Ignudi" in Michelangelo's Sistine ceiling.

WENZEL JAMNITZER I
Born Vienna 1508, died Nuremberg 1585.

96 The Apotheosis of the Emperor Maximilian II.
Pen and Indian ink, greenish gray wash over preparatory drawing in chalk; explanatory inscriptions — the Latin ones added in the course of the execution of the drawing with the same Indian ink, the German ones inserted later in black ink.
Watermark: Briquet 925.
679 : 486 mm.
Inv. no. 14528.

From the Waitzenbeck Album.
Albertina Cat. IV, 502.

Preparatory drawing for the etching by Jost Amman dated 1571 (A. Andresen, Der Deutsche Peintre-Graveur, I, 1864, p. 126, no. 30).
The present drawing is Jamnitzer's design for an allegorical etching by Jost Amman dated 1571 (Andresen 30). The inventive genius of the great goldsmith reveals itself in the luxuriant scrollwork and in the decorative abundance of the figures. In spite of its surfeit of emblems and allegories, the whole work is indisputably a splendid achievement displaying numerous parallels with Jamnitzer's goldsmith's works. The

flying genii, for instance, are actually conceived as figures of the goldsmith's art.

The Emperor kneels upon the dome of the Temple of Peace, which is shaped like a tabernacle. Justice and Faith hold the edges of his cloak; the Emperor receives a sword and the Bible from the hands of genii. Other Virtues line the parapet of the semi-circular exedra. Figures of kings and judges from the Old Testament fill the niches. Wisdom, flanked by War and Peace, is seated at the foot of the tabernacle. In the foreground Theology and a man symbolizing the nations ruled by the Emperor are seen kneeling. In the clouds Christ is enthroned on the symbols of the Evangelists. Below him two genii lower the crown on the Emperor's head. With its wealth of allusive content and its crowded forms, this monumental drawing is a masterpiece of courtly Mannerist art. Amman's etching altered the model considerably in some parts.

HERMANN TOM RING
Born Münster 1521, died there 1596.

97 Christ as the Savior of Mankind.
Pen and brush in dark gray-brown; the artist's monogram on the cross.
261 : 184 mm.
Inv. no. 3020 (L. 174).

Albertina Cat. IV, 616; K. Hölker, "Die Malerfamilie Tom Ring", Beiträge zur westfälischen Kunstgeschichte, Heft 8, Münster, 1927, p. 35 and p. 68, no. 17, fig. 15.

Preparatory drawing for the painting, Hölker no. 18.

In 1555 the artist painted a double-sided panel representing the Last Judgment on one side, and Christ as the Savior of Mankind on the other (now in the Westfälisches Landesmuseum at Münster). The designs for both representations are in the Albertina. The present drawing shows an allegorical compilation of everything Christ has done for suffering mankind, the outstanding events of His life being grouped around the figure of the Savior and the towering cross. In the foreground Lazarus rises from his tomb. Before it Martha kneels and behind it the Magdalen anoints the Savior's feet. Seated on the edge of the tomb is the Dropsical Man. On the Savior's left there kneels one of the Emmaus disciples beside whom the Woman from Samaria stands. At the right are the kneeling Leper and the Good Captain. The cross is flanked on the left by the Good Thief, on the right by Matthew seated in the fig tree. Spread out in the background is a rich landscape in which the lame, the blind, the epileptic, and the infirm await the Savior's help. Overhead the sky opens up into several tiers of figures, prophets of the Old Testament, the Apostles, and the saints of the Church. In the top row angels adore Jehovah's name.

Hermann tom Ring derived his style as a draughtsman from Dutch Renaissance artists like Scorel, Jan Swart, and Teunissen; a clear, continuous linear design of ornamental effect is filled by soft modeling washes. But the character of the German artist reveals itself in his emphasis on the expressive, self-willed elements and in a certain exaggeration of the figures with their ghost-like, long, tapering fingers. As in Venetian Late Renaissance paintings, the figures loom oppressively large in the foreground and dwindle abruptly in the distance, creating a dramatic spatial effect. The "petrification" of the celestial universe overhead, even more evident in the Last Judgment, is one of the boldest formulations of expressive German Mannerism.

TOBIAS STIMMER
Born Schaffhausen 1539, died Strasbourg 1584.

98 Ahasuerus and Esther (Esther, chapter 5, 1—2).
Pen and brush, and Indian ink and white bodycolor on gray prepared paper. Signed and dated: Thobias Stymmer fecit (15)66.
436 : 323 mm.
Inv. no. 14529 (L. 174).

Albertina Cat. IV, 372; Schönbrunner-Meder 936; F. Thöne, Tobias Stimmer Handzeichnungen, Freiburg im Breisgau, 1936, Cat. no. 94, plate 49.

The rich architectural setting and ornamentation of the present drawing clearly show the origin of Stimmer's style in Holbein's decorative frescoes and designs for stained glass.

But while Holbein strove to free himself from the angular Late Gothic forms and achieve Renaissance harmony, Stimmer tends to unintelligible and startling effects of spatial setting as befits a Mannerist artist. He is the main Swiss representative of Mannerism, especially in his graphic work. Undoubtedly, the remains of the numerals underneath the signature are part of the date. They demonstrate that Stimmer had early become acquainted with the graphic art of the Dutch Renaissance, either by direct experience or at second hand. The group with King Ahasuerus clearly shows this.

In the old inventory and the catalogues of the Albertina and also in other publications the subject-matter of the present drawing has been regarded as Ahasuerus and Esther. Ivan Fenyö, following an assumption of A. Pigler, recently suggested with very good reason that another theme is represented here, namely "King Abimelech Restoring Sarah to Abraham with a Thousand Pieces of Silver" (Genesis 20, 9—18). See I. Fenyö, Acta Historiae Artium, Budapest, 1965, XI, Fasc. 2—3, p. 351; A. Pigler, Barockthemen, vol. I, Budapest, 1956, p. 46.

CASPAR FRAISINGER
Coming from Ochsenhausen, active in Ingolstadt, documented there from 1581 onward, died 1599.

99 Christ Sinking Beneath the Cross.
Pen and Indian ink, washed, heightened with brush and white bodycolor on green paper. Monogram: C F Ingolstadiensis, also inscribed with the number of the Station of the Cross: 9 and arrow.
456 : 366 mm.
Inv. no. 25379 (acquired 1928).

Albertina Cat. IV, 419; F. Thöne, Zeitschrift des Deutschen Vereins für Kunstwissenschaft 7 (1940), p. 61, no. 68.

Very little is known about the life and development of this artist. We know only that he was the city painter of Ingolstadt. The significance of his art becomes evident mainly in his drawings, of which a considerable number have survived; they are, however, widely scattered. They show Fraisinger to be first and foremost an eminent master of chiaroscuro modeling in space, who achieved his effects with loose strokes of the pen as well as a spotting with the brush. In this he follows Mielich's drawings (compare no. 95), so that he can be assumed to have studied in his native Bavaria. But he certainly visited Italy: the influence of Florentine and Venetian Late Renaissance is an essential element in the formation of his style. The jailers and the men accompanying the procession to Golgotha definitely reveal the influence of Schiavone and Bassano. But in the figure of Christ the artist has retained all the dramatic greatness characteristic of the scenes of the Passion in the classical era of German painting. In spite of the internationalism of the Mannerist idiom, an indigenous force lives on in this ugly and moving Man of Sorrows, which forms a bridge from the age of Dürer and Altdorfer to the popular art of Bavarian Late Baroque and Rococo.

HANS VON AACHEN
Born Cologne 1552, died Prague 1615.

100 Pietà with St. Mary Magdalene and Two Angels Carrying Torches.
Pen and bistre, washed, heightened with white.
309 : 184 mm (arched top).
Inv. no. 3310 (L. 174).

Albertina Cat. IV, 441; A. Peltzer, Jahrbuch der Kunsthistorischen Sammlungen des Allerhöchsten Kaiserhauses, XXX, Vienna, 1911/12, pp. 92—95 (reproduction of the painting) and 170, no. 22.

This drawing is a variation of the composition of the painting in the Residenz in Munich which the artist painted for the chapel of the Wilhelmsfeste, completed in 1597; it is thus not a preparatory drawing, but a further clarification and intensification of the idea. It is only in the drawing that the angels appear as a necessary complement to the central figure, whose essential lines are stressed by the angle of their torches.

The artist's career was typical of a leading representative of courtly Late Mannerism, combining northern and southern elements in an international idiom of style. Pupil of a Netherlandish artist in Cologne, he spent the years from 1574 to 1589 in Italy, particularly in Florence, Rome, and Venice. He was called thence to various artistically important courts, first to Munich, where Sustris and Candid worked along with him, and then to Prague where, together with Spranger (no. 141) and Heintz (no. 101), he formed the group of artists who set the style at the court of Rudolph II. From all these theatres of activity, he acquired elements for the formation of his style. His closeness to Sustris (no. XII) is obvious in the present drawing.

The prototype of this Pietà is Michelangelo's marble group in St. Peter's. Yet it has undergone a modification in the sense of the Gothic representation of the Virgin with the dead body of Christ: His head falls forward towards the spectator. Once again the Gothic tradition comes to the fore in the art of Late Mannerism north of the Alps, creating a work of deep solemnity of expression.

JOSEPH HEINTZ THE ELDER
Born Basle 1564, died Prague 1609.

101 Allegory on the Birth of a Prince.
Black and white chalk, charcoal stumped, on light blue paper.
373 : 261 mm.
Inv. no. 3317 (L. 174).

Albertina Cat. IV, 454; Schönbrunner-Meder 1285; Th. Muchall-Viebrook, Deutsche Barockzeichnungen, Munich, 1925, plate 2 (erroneously reproduced in reverse).

The composition appears in a simpler and earlier version in the Print Room in Budapest (Schönbrunner-Meder 1278). Its subject-matter is derived from the circle of courtly poetic allegory, but thanks to the draughtsman's genius it is expressed in a most direct and charming manner, as the play of adults with a small child, whose symbol of sovereignty — a crystal orb — they hold up to him as an ardently coveted toy. On the left we recognize Nike with the orb and Diana with her bow, behind them the Three Graces, and on the right Venus, Pan, and Demeter. In the lower half on the left recline the Four Seasons, on the right Amor approaches.

The fluidity and liveliness of the line show that Heintz' ability as a draughtsman equaled his gift as a painter; he was the only artist of Rudolph II's court of whom this can be said. Numerous pentimenti enable us to trace the development of the composition. Shadow accents with the stump supplement the modeling of the lines.

Heintz spent some time in Rome, but as a draughtsman he is superior to all his Roman contemporaries. He was also familiar with the drawing style of the North Italian masters (Correggio, Tibaldi), whose inspiration is noticeable in this **drawing**.

ADAM ELSHEIMER
Born Frankfort-on-Main 1578, died Rome 1610.

102 Bathsheba at the Bath.
Brush and Indian ink and white bodycolor on gray paper.
91 : 84 mm.
Inv. no. 3345 (L. 174).

Albertina Cat. IV, 513; see E. Bock, Zeichnungen deutscher Meister im Kupferstichkabinett, Berlin, 1921, I, p. 158, Inv. 4272, fig. 87; H. Weizsäcker, Adam Elsheimer, Berlin, 1936, Part I, Text, p. 144; W. Drost, Adam Elsheimer, Potsdam (1932), p. 141.

There is another version of this composition in the Print Room in Berlin (Inv. no. 4272), which was considered by E. Bock to be the later one, but was rightly regarded by Weizsäcker as the earlier one. In the Albertina drawing the composition is more mature, although it shows more of the character of the mannerist tradition of Rottenhammer's small-scale paintings. The Albertina drawing achieves its effect mainly through the sparkling white lights in bodycolor on a dark gray ground, which lend the scene a nocturnal aspect.

There is a variation of the Vienna drawing, in reverse, in the sketchbook in Frankfort (Weizsäcker, Die Zeichnungen im Skizzenband des Städelschen Kunstinstituts, plate 21). It is the latest and the most mature version, anticipating in highest degree Rembrandt's technique of drawing. The importance of this greatest of seventeenth-century German painters and draughtsmen is largely based on his role as a highly gifted precursor of Rembrandt.

103 A Crowd Moving towards the Left.
Pen and bistre. Upper left, inscribed in black chalk: Adam E f.
60 : 130 mm.
Inv. no. 3350 (L. 174).

Provenance: Charles, Prince de Ligne (Cat. p. 148, no. 1)

Albertina Cat. IV, 517; H. Weizsäcker, Adam Elsheimer, Berlin, 1936, Part I, Text, p. 278 (as by Goudt).

This drawing is attributed to Hendrik Goudt in the old inventory. The attribution to Elsheimer was advocated by A. Bredius. There are a series of similar sketches of crowds of people in the Frankfort sketchbook, which includes works by both Elsheimer and Goudt. The confusion of Elsheimer's drawn oeuvre with that of his imitator Goudt has not yet been conclusively resolved. In view of this fact the attribution in the old inventory of the Albertina is worth noting. Apparently Goudt was already known to the collectors of earlier centuries as Elsheimer's closest follower.

JOHANN ROTTENHAMMER
Born Munich 1564, died Augsburg 1625.

104 Jesus, the Friend of the Children.
Red and black chalks, washed in bistre, the figure of Christ heightened with white bodycolor. Squared and numbered.
246 : 297 mm.
Inv. no. 3328 (L. 174).

Albertina Cat. IV, 397; A. Peltzer, Jahrbuch der Kunsthistorischen Sammlungen des Allerhöchsten Kaiserhauses, XXXIII, Vienna, 1916, p. 324, Verzeichnis no. 82, plate XXXVIII.

Rottenhammer, whose career was more international than that of all the other late mannerists, worked in Venice from 1596 to 1606. There Tintoretto and Veronese in particular exerted their influence upon him; he was a friend of Palma Giovane's, and Elsheimer worked in his studio for a short time. The present drawing, probably made during the first years after his return to Augsburg, strikingly demonstrates the effect which Tintoretto and Palma Giovane had upon him. The diagonal development of the composition in space from the left foreground to the right background is an acquisition from Tintoretto. Rottenhammer also follows the Venetians in their technique of sketching a design for a picture. It is true that he does not achieve their clarity and plasticity, in whose place there is a confusion of agitated figures. But by this very profusion he with conscious artistic intent creates the effect of a tumultuous crowd. With consummate mastery the draughtsman makes the figure of Christ stand out as the strongest accent by modeling it in darker bistre and white bodycolor against the crowd fading into the distance. He thus lends it a radiating force of its own and marks it as the spiritual center of the scene.

JAN LISS (Lys)
Born Oldenburg about 1590, died Venice 1629.

105 Camillus and Brennus Weighing the Ransom (Plutarch LI).
Pen and bistre, washed. Pen trials, with the signature: Lys.
353 : 536 mm.
Inv. no. 25427 (acquired 1928).
Verso: The Elephant of Pyrrhus in the Battle against the Romans.
Technique as above.

Albertina Cat. IV, 625; E. Schilling, Festschrift für Karl Lohmeyer, Saarbrücken, 1954, p. 34, fig. 4.

The present drawing is a late work of the artist from his Venetian period. The curls and flourishes of the pen line show his descent from Late Mannerism, but the full-bodied

Baroque forms clearly reveal acquaintance with the art of Rubens' circle, in particular with Jordaens. Liss knew how to lighten the ponderous forms of the Flemish artists in terms of the airiness and luminosity of the Venetians. As a result his works, next to those of Elsheimer, are among the earliest documents of Baroque art in the history of German painting. The artificiality and interlace of Mannerism is transformed into a new feeling for life, which has a certain naturalness despite its lofty high-flown character. There is a sheet identical in size and style in the Gustav Schwarting Collection, Delmenhorst, which is covered on the recto and verso with studies for a "Fall of Phaëton" (see the essay by E. Schilling) and bears similar pen trials.

JOHANN HEINRICH SCHÖNFELD
Born Biberach 1609, died Augsburg 1682/83.

106 The Fall of Phaëton.
Red chalk, and brush and red chalk wash.
480 : 390 mm.
Inv. no. 27356 (acquired 1935).
Provenance: Artaria (as Gabriel Weyer).
H. Voss, Johann Heinrich Schönfeld, Biberach, 1964, p. 36; a painting, representing the same subject is reproduced by Voss, and mentioned on p. 34.
A comparatively modern conjecture assigned this drawing to Gabriel Weyer while it was in the Artaria Collection, but in point of fact it has nothing in common with him. It is the work of a contemporary of the great classic masters of the Baroque, not of a late mannerist like Gabriel Weyer. The attribution to Schönfeld was made by the present author. Not only the slender proportions of the figures but also the drawing of the foliage find close parallels in Schönfeld's work. The ample space and the transparency of the composition, which is full of expressive movement, are characteristic of his style. Neapolitan masters of the Baroque like Stanzioni and Cavallino, and even Poussin, inspired him. Yet his art never loses its strangely enchanted and dreamlike character, its suspended and remote quality that give it the lasting imprint of its German origin.

MICHAEL WILLMANN
Born Königsberg 1630, died Monastery of Leubus 1706.

107 Apotheosis of Joachim von Sandrart.
Design for a dedicatory page ("Titul-blädtgen"), 1682.
Pen and brush, and bistre and Indian ink, washed, heightened with white bodycolor on yellowish paper.
315 : 203 mm.
Inv. no. 3567 (L. 174).
Albertina Cat. IV, 1952; Th. Muchall-Viebrook, Deutsche Barockzeichnungen, Munich, 1925, p. 38, plate 28; E. Kloss, Michael Willmann, Breslau (1934), pp. 11, 100, 143, 149, Cat. no. 73, fig. 139.
Exhibition: Michael-Willmann-Jubiläumsausstellung, Breslau, 1930, Cat. p. 21, no. 106.
The draft of Willmann's letter to Joachim von Sandrart is printed in full in the Albertina Catalogue and in Kloss, op. cit., p. 149. This letter accompanying the drawing explains the meaning of the allegorical representation. In view of Sandrart's great age, the day will come when Chronos will take the brush from his hand. Then he will be crowned by the Olympic gods and will take his place as a new star in the circle of the heavens. Such was Willmann's expression of gratitude for the ample appreciation Sandrart had given him in his "Academie der Bau-, Bild- und Mahlerey-Künste". Instead of the inevitable journey to Italy, made by so many of his German contemporaries, Willmann undertook a journey to the Netherlands. He worked with J. A. Backer in Amsterdam and was in personal touch with Rembrandt. The spirited Baroque exuberance of Flemish art, to which Backer introduced him and with which he became well acquainted in the Huis ten Bosch at The Hague, admittedly dominates his paintings for Catholic churches and monasteries (Leubus), but the fantastic and mysterious magic of light which he displays in them and which also characterizes the present drawing, is derived from Rembrandt.

KAREL SKRETA (Screta von Ssotnowsky and Zaworzitz)
Born Prague about 1604, died there 1674.

108 Allegorical Representation of the Safe Voyage of the Arts and Sciences under the Auspices of Count Johann H. Nostitz in accordance with F. C. Scheydlern's Program.
Pen and bistre, washed, over preparatory drawing in leadpoint. Signed at lower left: Carl Screta f.; the letters and numerals accompanying the allegorical figures refer to the explanatory text of the engraving.
293 : 385 mm.
Inv. no. 3480 (L. 174).
Albertina Cat. IV, 1951.
Preparatory drawing for an engraving. It belongs to a series of allegorical representations for the glorification of the Nostitz regime, two of which, the present drawing and that of the preceding event (Cat. 1950, The Preparation for the Voyage) are in the Albertina. A third drawing, The Arrival, is known only from an engraving by B. Kilian (G. Pazaurek, Carl Screta, Prague, 1889, p. 100, no. 13).
A long stay in Italy thoroughly familiarized Skreta with Italian Baroque art. In addition to being an excellent painter, he also had a gift for illustration, which manifested itself in allegorical scenes like those of the present cycle. Literary concettism and a baroque wealth of allusion are imbued with the breath of life as if they were actual happenings. Power of invention and effective representation distinguish Skreta's sketches.

WILHELM STETTLER
Born Berne 1643, died there 1708.

109 Panorama of Berne.
Pen and bistre, watercolor and bodycolor; the paper joined at the center; signed and dated: W. Stettler fecit ad vivum 1683.
226 : 682 mm.
Inv. no. 3738 (L. 174).
Albertina Cat. IV, 694.
Stettler was one of the most powerful and important seventeenth-century illustrators. (For this aspect of his activity, compare K. T. Parker, Old Master Drawings, March, 1938, p. 58 ff.; Otto Benesch, Artistic and Intellectual Trends from Rubens to Daumier as Shown in Book Illustration, Cambridge, Massachusetts, 1943, p. 44.) The present watercolor reveals him also as an important landscape painter. Although he followed Merian's style of topographical painting, he renders the character of the landscape, its impression of light and atmosphere, in a unique manner. It is an early autumn day in Berne, with cool air coming from the mountains. The sky sparkles in a cold blue which is reflected in the steel-blue Aare. The green of the meadows and woods is grayish in the shadows on the left, and olive-green in the sunshine on the right. Between is the delicate pink of the tiled roofs. Stettler's whole power of representation is revealed in the laborers and their team of oxen tilling the field. Steel-grays and slate-grays are complemented by the terracotta of the oxen. A festive accent is established in the center of the drawing by the golden ochre and the flaming pink of Fame who blows a trumpet adorned with the municipal arms.

MELCHIOR MICHAEL STEIDL
Born Innsbruck, became master at Munich in 1687, died there 1727.

110 The Assumption of the Virgin.
Pen and bistre, washed, with some watercolor over preparatory drawing in leadpoint, creased in horizontal zones.
673 : 529 mm.
Inv. no. 14338 (L. 174).
Wickhoff Sc. V. 123.
Design for the fresco of a cupola. The lunette with the representation of the Battle of the Angel with the Demons, and the Creation of Adam, was cut out and pasted on about 5 mm higher up. In the pendentives: the Birth of

the Virgin, a Female Christian Martyr with a Palm, St. Peter, and St. Andrew.

In the old inventory of the Albertina this drawing is listed as a work by Tintoretto. Yet the first glance shows that it is not an Italian, but a German work, inspired by the Venetians. The watercolor scheme, crimson, lemon yellow, and purple, combined with the brown of the bistre in its manifold shades and variations, is typical of the Bavarian Baroque which developed from Late Mannerism. The Bavarian Mannerist tradition is quite evident here in the radial arrangement of the figures.

The present author suggests that this design is an early work of Melchior Michael Steidl. Bruno Bushart has greatly clarified the artist's oeuvre as a draughtsman by his investigation of the designs for the frescoes of the Schönenbergkirche at Ellwangen (1710—1712), (Festschrift für Eberhard Hanf-staengl, p. 95 ff.). In Steidl's drawing style the cubic, crystalline element is prominent. Heads are frequently shown steeply from below or wedge-shaped from above. These characteristics are also apparent in the present drawing, although, under the direct influence of the Venetians, they are not yet as strongly stressed as in the Ellwangen designs where the artist's personal manner is clearly revealed.

JOHANN GEORG PLATZER
Born Eppan 1702, died St. Michael in the Tyrol 1760.

XI   Drawing from the Model in the Studio.
Black chalk, pencil, watercolor and bodycolor; at lower right, collector's number in pencil: 20, and price: 9. fl.
424 : 539 mm.
Inv. no. 14551 (L. 174).
Albertina Cat. IV, 2015.

A favorite subject of Late Mannerism — Alexander having Campaspe's portrait painted by Apelles — is transferred here to the setting of the bourgeois Late Baroque. The mythological subject, for which the artist uses his own model, is the "Caritas Romana". In accordance with Baroque concettism, a genre painting is given an erotic meaning. The idea of the patron's counter-figure playing the lute during the sitting probably goes back to a precept in Leonardo's Treatise on Painting.

The watercolor is of the greatest pictorial charm, especially in the unfinished still-life on the right. Platzer represented an old-fashioned trend of the Late Baroque, now more bourgeois than courtly, in harking back to Late Mannerism. He painted his miniature-like pictures mostly on small copper plates, creating sparkling microcosms in which a profusion of capricious inventions is crowded into pictorial scenes of the richest fantasy. It is an artificial, highly stylized world in which pictorial observation becomes a decorative end in itself.

COSMAS DAMIAN ASAM
Born Benediktbeuern 1686, died Weltenburg 1729.

111   The Coronation of the Virgin.
Compositional design for an altarpiece.
Leadpoint, pen and brush and bistre, washed, heightened with white, and squared for transfer. Signed: Cos: D: Asam Inven.
408 : 257 mm.
Inv. no. 3825.
Albertina Cat. IV, 957; K. Garzarolli-Thurnlackh, Die Barocke Handzeichnung in Österreich, Vienna, 1928, p. 40, fig. 41; Great Drawings of All Time, New York, 1962, II, no. 449 (O. Benesch).

Design for an altarpiece. The curved shape of the frame is recognizable at the top. This sheet, perhaps the artist's finest extant drawing, reveals his experience in the mastery of forms at once decorative and expressive, an experience gained in the creation of the architectural, sculptural, and pictorial ensemble. In its late bourgeois phase the courtly mode of life of the Baroque was extended to the realm of religious representation in Bavaria and Austria. It is in the manner of a cavalier that Christ by order of the Almighty hands the ladylike Virgin her crown, a scene of glorification as well as of capricious grace.

JOHANN WOLFGANG BAUMGARTNER
Born Kufstein 1712, died Augsburg 1761.

112   The Coronation of the Virgin.
Pen and Indian ink, washed, with some white bodycolor, squared for transfer.
493 : 380 mm.
Inv. no. 32737 (acquired 1957).
Provenance: Dr. Ludwig Münz.
Exhibition: Neuerwerbungen alter Meister 1950—1958, Vienna, Albertina, 1958, Cat. no. 45.

The art of the South German Late Baroque and Rococo of the eighteenth century was significantly and increasingly reinforced by artists native to the North Tyrol. The resultant artistic coalescence of Bavaria and Swabia with Austria in this period was as close as at the time of the Danube School. On both sides of the frontier the painters busied themselves with the fresco decoration of the churches.

The present drawing is presumably a sketch for a choir fresco. All the groups and figures are composed in such a manner that they converge in the radiant symbol of the Holy Trinity as if concentrated by a lens. Here, too, the celestial scene is given the aspect of a court ceremonial (compare no. 111) and is thus brought closer to the understanding of the people. A visible object for pious admiration is required by the devout church-goer. The careful modeling shows a draughtsman skilled in designing for engraving.

MATTHÄUS GÜNTHER
Born Unterpeissenberg near Wessobrunn (Bavaria) 1705, died Auf der Haid near Wessobrunn 1788.

113   The Reception of St. Elizabeth into Heaven.
Pen and brush and Indian ink, heightened with white over preparatory drawing in leadpoint. Squared for transfer in leadpoint; inscription in the artist's hand: Elysawetinen / in München; later inscription: Dominik Günther in München / bei den Elisabet / dinern.
520 : 636 mm.
Inv. no. 30572 (acquired 1948).
Design for the fresco in the cupola of the hospital church of St. Elizabeth in Munich, 1765 (H. Gundersheimer, Matthäus Günther, Augsburg, 1930, p. 58).
Exhibition: Von der Gotik bis zur Gegenwart, Neuerwerbungen aus den Jahren 1947—49, Albertina, Vienna, 1949—50, Cat. no. 25.

The artist, a peasant's son who was brought up in the monastery school of Wessobrunn, may already from his early youth have been in touch with the Wessobrunn school of stucco-workers. Later he became a journeyman with Asam and assisted him in the execution of his commissions in Bavaria and the Tyrol. The art of this most sensitive and popular ecclesiastical painter of the Bavarian Rococo thus developed with delight in form and decoration, and a fervent style of narration. Günther made Augsburg his residence, but the open seasons of the year always found him travelling about decorating churches in Bavaria, Swabia and Austria with frescoes.

Günther prepared his frescoes with careful designs. Over a period of years the present author was successful in rediscovering a number of the most important drawings and also acquired some examples for the Albertina. (Art Bulletin, XXIX, New York, 1947, p. 49 ff.). In 1765, Günther decorated the church of St. Elizabeth in Munich with frescoes. The present drawing is the design for the cupola. The patron saint appears in Heaven as intercessor for the nuns of her order and their works of charity. The acute triangular rhythm of the Bavarian Rococo — a revival of the formal elements of Late Mannerism — is the determining factor in the invention of the figures and groups.

DANIEL GRAN
Born Vienna 1694, died St. Pölten 1757.

114   Allegory of the Wealth and Power of Moravia.
Inscribed in the clouds within the central diamond-shaped area of the composition: "Überfluss" (Abundance).

Below: studies for the zodiac sign of the Centaur.
Pen and bistre over preparatory drawing in leadpoint.
280 : 196 mm.
Inv. no. 26979 (acquired 1935).
Provenance: Artaria.
Sketch for the ceiling fresco in the great hall of the old "Landhaus" in Brno (Brünn).
Sketches in oil for the same ceiling fresco in Vienna, Barockmuseum, Painting Gallery of the Academy of Fine Arts, and in Brno (Brünn), Moravské Museum (Mährisches Landesmuseum).
E. Knab, Wiener Jahrbuch für Kunstgeschichte, XV (XIX), p. 148/49.
Exhibition: Daniel Gran, Gedächtnisausstellung, Albertina, Vienna, 1957, Cat. no. 29.

The master decorated with frescoes some of the major works of Austrian Baroque architecture, especially those of Fischer von Erlach and Prandtauer. He studied with Sebastiano Ricci in Venice and with Francesco Solimena in Naples. The ceiling fresco of the "Landhaus" in Brno (Brünn) was painted in 1737/39. In designs like the present one Gran sets the surface to vibrating through the optical effect produced by powerful pen lines over preliminary indications in leadpoint, as is typical of the technique of Solimena and his pupils (Fischetti, Conca, del Mondo).

PAUL TROGER
Born Zell in the Val Pusteria 1698, died Vienna 1762.

115 The Archangel Michael Fighting the Demons.
Pen and bistre, over preparatory drawing in leadpoint.
Above, in the aureole, the symbol of the Holy Trinity with the artist's own inscription: quis ut Deus.
294 : 202 mm; watermark: anchor within a circle.
Inv. no. 26996 (acquired 1935).
Provenance: Lanna; Artaria.
R. Jacobs, Paul Troger, Vienna, 1930, p. 153, no. 13; W. Aschenbrenner, P. Troger, Salzburg, 1965, p. 147.
Exhibitions: Franz Anton Maulbertsch und die Kunst des österreichischen Barock, Albertina, Vienna, 1956, Cat. no. 168; Paul Troger, Stift Altenburg, May to October, 1963, Cat. no. 141.

Design for an etching (?). This spirited sketch, hastily jotted down, demonstrates Troger's brilliant and expressive power of invention at its best. The pen lines, shooting over the surface like arrows, convey an impression of the liveliest movement. The fact that St. Michael carries his spear in his left hand leads one to suppose that the composition was intended for graphic reproduction.
The resoluteness, the intense thrust and wedge-like movement in the dynamics of Paul Troger's pictures developed from his contact with Venetian painting, in particular with Piazzetta, who was mentioned in Troger's obituary as an important source of inspiration for his art. The expressive chiaroscuro of his paintings also derives from Piazzetta.

MARTIN JOHANN SCHMIDT (called Kremser Schmidt)
Born Grafenwörth 1718, died Stein 1801.

116 Bust of a Woman with a Bonnet.
Chalk.
295 : 194 mm.
Inv. no. 24686 (acquired 1925).
Albertina Cat. IV, 2121.
Exhibitions: Österreichische Kunst 1700—1928, Preussische Akademie der Künste, Berlin, 1928, Cat. p. 25, no. 53; M. J. Schmidt, Krems-Stein, 1951, Cat. no. 134.
This drawing of unique quality justifies the artist's reputation as Austria's best eighteenth-century painter and draughtsman next to Maulbertsch. Its delicate pictorial softness and its enigmatic beauty revive something of Grünewald's portrait drawings. Although the artist's immediate teachers were the Venetians, the poetry of old German art again becomes apparent here. Like Tiepolo, Schmidt sold entire albums of his drawings to amateurs as far afield as Poland and Russia, and it was in one of these albums that the present sheet found its way back to Austria from the East.

FRANZ ANTON MAULBERTSCH
Born Langenargen on Lake Constance 1724, died Vienna 1796.

117 The Assumption of the Virgin.
Pen and Indian ink, washed, some accents in pen and bistre.
453 : 316 mm.
Inv. no. 25731 (acquired 1931).
Albertina Cat. IV, 2196; K. Garas, Franz Anton Maulbertsch, Budapest, 1960, p. 206, no. 107, fig. 82.
Exhibitions: Schönbrunn, Maria-Theresia-Ausstellung, Vienna, 1930, Cat. no. 17; Franz Anton Maulbertsch und die Kunst des österreichischen Barock, Albertina, Vienna, 1956, Cat. no. 15.
The subject of the Assumption of the Virgin occupied Maulbertsch as a religious painter all his life. Strongly influenced by Piazzetta and Bazzani (see Otto Benesch, Städel-Jahrbuch, 3, Frankfort-on-Main, 1924), he chose as his model, particularly for the altarpieces of the 1750's (Zirc, 1754; Mainz, St. Quintin, 1758), Piazzetta's altarpiece in the monastery of Königsaal near Prague, which must have been known to him, if not in the original, at least in an engraving. While in these early works pictorial structure is reduced to a ragged texture of flecks and flakes and vaporous chiaroscuro effects, a stronger crystallization sets in with the 1760's. Typical of this change are the Assumption scenes of Bohuslavice, 1763; Schwechat, 1764 (destroyed in World War II); Tišnov (Tischnowitz), 1766; and Székesfehérvár (Stuhlweissenburg), 1767.
The present drawing, like the altarpiece of Rastenfeld, Lower Austria, represents the intermediary stage between these two groups. Without giving up the expressive dissolution in light of the first group, it displays the most powerful dramatic action. It reveals this greatest genius of eighteenth-century German painting and draughtsmanship at the height of his mastery.

118 The Birth of the Virgin.
Pen and bistre, washed with Indian ink and olive-green over preparatory drawing in leadpoint.
339 : 424 mm.
Inv. no. 25132 (acquired 1927).
Albertina Cat. IV, 2202; K. Garas, Franz Anton Maulbertsch, Budapest, 1960, p. 216, no. 218, fig. 178.
Exhibitions: Österreichische Kunst 1700—1928, Preussische Akademie der Künste, Berlin, 1928, Cat. p. 24, no. 41; Künstlerhaus, Vienna, 1928, no. 40; Vienna, Albertina, 1933, no. 200; Kunsthaus, Zürich, 1955, no. 212; Franz Anton Maulbertsch, Vienna, Albertina, 1956, no. 24
Design for the ceiling fresco of 1767 in the nave of the former Carmelite (Seminary) Church at Székesfehérvár (Stuhlweissenburg).
This drawing, identified by the present author as a sketch by Maulbertsch for Székesfehérvár (Stuhlweissenburg), is one of those works by the great master of the Late Baroque in which the international idiom of the period is combined in a charming manner with elements of popular art. As in Gothic panel paintings, household furniture like St. Anne's yarnwinder and a carved peasant cradle are introduced as domestic notes in the magnificent Baroque setting.

KASPAR FRANZ SAMBACH
Born Breslau 1715, died Vienna 1795.

119 Grand Duke Leopold of Tuscany (later Emperor Leopold II) Conferring the Order of the Golden Fleece upon his Sons Franz (later Emperor Franz I of Austria) and Ferdinand (later Grand Duke Ferdinand III of Tuscany).
Pen and Indian ink, washed; above the various heads are the numerals 1 to 14 for an explanatory inscription.
373 : 502 mm.
Inv. no. 32972 (acquired from R. Miller-Aichholz, 1960).
This drawing was made in preparation for an engraving of which no copy can be traced. The ceremony took place in the Palazzo Pitti at Florence in 1772, when the children were four and three years old respectively. On the right of the main group are seated Leopold's wife, Maria Ludovica of

Bourbon, and Maria Theresa, their eldest daughter. The main figures are the Regent and his family (including the attendants on either side of the throne); they are accordingly marked with the numerals 1—7. The person next in importance is the lady standing on the right, indicated by an 8, who is recognizable as none other than the Regent's mother, the Empress Maria Theresa. That the Empress visited Florence in the course of the year 1772 is proven by other documents. In the same year Leopold called A. R. Mengs to Florence and had him paint single and double portraits of himself, his wife, and his children. In preparation for the court portraits, he made masterly studies from life, one of Maria Ludovica and another one of the Empress Maria Theresa (both in the possession of the Duke of Alba, Madrid). Maria Theresa's portrait was not further elaborated. The study is so lifelike that it can have been made only from the model. Mengs, however, was never called to the Vienna court for a portrait commission so the study can have been made only during the Empress' short visit to Florence.

As next in rank the Empress' sons, Joseph, the Co-Regent, and Ferdinand, Regent of Lombardy, appear behind her.

A few years later Sambach drew a group portrait of Leopold and his family that is also in the Albertina. The artist received his artistic training from the sculptor Georg Raphael Donner and the painter Paul Troger. This is why the clear, plastic forms and accentuation prevail in his drawings.

FRIEDRICH HEINRICH FÜGER
Born Heilbronn 1751, died Vienna 1818.

120 The Artist's Son with Palette and Brush.
Pen and bistre.
358 : 232 mm.
Inv. no. 5272.

Etching after the present drawing by Adam Bartsch, F. de Bartsch, Catalogue des Estampes de J. Adam de Bartsch, Vienna, 1818, p. 49, no. 112.

Mentioned by A. Stix (H. F. Füger, Vienna—Leipzig, 1925) in connection with the portrait of the artist's son (no. 62).

Füger's son Heinrich was born in 1792. His father portrayed him in the same pose with his painting tools, in a blue suit, about 1796 (Österreichische Galerie, Vienna). The present drawing, of which Füger himself made a replica (also in the Albertina), was made about 1798.

Füger, the principal artist of Vienna classicism, originated in the Baroque tradition of his teachers Guibal and Oeser. It was not until he went to Rome and studied antiquity, the masters of the Renaissance, and the neo-classicists that he became, under the influence of Mengs and David, an "historical painter." Nevertheless his essential artistic achievement is in the field of portraiture, particularly in miniature painting.

ANTON RAPHAEL MENGS
Born Aussig 1728, died Rome 1779.

121 Self-Portrait of the Artist at the Age of Twenty-Two.
Silverpoint and graphite on white prepared paper.
174 : 130 mm.
Inv. no. 4617 (L. 174).
Albertina Cat. IV, 1899.

Preparatory study for the youthful self-portrait in oil, painted in 1750 and engraved by C. G. Rasp in Dresden in 1784. A related drawing in chalk and of somewhat larger size (563 : 443 mm) is in the Kupferstichkabinett, Dresden (Inv. C 185); it is reproduced in Deutsche Zeichnungen, Der Bürger und seine Welt 1720—1820, Exhibition 1958—1959 of the Lucas-Cranach Kommission, Weimar, Cat. no. 197.

Notwithstanding his role as a rediscoverer of classical art, a role praised by Winckelmann, Mengs' main importance lies in his portraits. Through them he influenced even Goya. For all the simplicity and the straight lines of the graphic structure, the pictorial tradition of the Baroque is still fully alive in the present drawing. As with Füger, the technique of drawing recalls that of the miniature painters. The delicate soft modeling of the face by contrast with the open crosshatchings of its surroundings actually achieves an effect of color.

ANTON GRAFF
Born Winterthur 1736, died Dresden 1813.

122 Self-Portrait at the Age of Seventy-Six.
Charcoal and white chalk on brownish paper; monogram, dated twice: 1812.
377 : 273 mm.
Inv. no. 5383 (L. 174).
Albertina Cat. IV, 1894.

Graff was linked to the tradition of the Baroque through his years of apprenticeship with the engraver Haid in Augsburg. He was exclusively a portrait painter. He developed from the Baroque bourgeois convention of his youth into an eminent painter of men, a portraitist of psychological insight who has transmitted to us a faithful picture of many figures of German intellectual life from the era of classical poetry. The objectivity of his portrayal led to an ever increasing realism that culminated in the true inner greatness of this late self-portrait painted one year before his death. The only other artists to paint such moving portraits in their old age were David and Goya.

NETHERLANDISH MASTERS

A NETHERLANDISH MASTER
About 1450—1460.

123 Christ Carrying the Cross.
Pen and bistre.
204 : 277 mm.
Inv. no. 3025 (L. 174).
Albertina Cat. II, 22; Schönbrunner-Meder 1021; G. J. Kern, Die verschollene „Kreuztragung" des Hubert oder Jan van Eyck, Separatum, Berlin, 1927, p. 9, fig. 3; F. Winkler, Nederlands Kunsthistorisch Jaarboek 9, (1958), pp. 83 ff.; E. Panofsky, Kritische Berichte zur kunstgeschichtlichen Literatur 1927/28, p. 74; O. Benesch, Jahrbuch der Preussischen Kunstsammlungen 46 (1925), p. 181; L. Baldass, Jan van Eyck, London, 1952, p. 96, footnote 2 and p. 290, no. 80; E. Panofsky, Early Netherlandish Painting, Cambridge, Mass., 1953, pp. 233, 237, 242, 350, fig. 304.

This drawing has been so widely discussed by scholars ever since the present writer first brought it to the attention of art historians in 1925, that it is impossible to deal with it in extenso here. Among the main conclusions reached are these: the drawing is a copy of an important early painting that was in its turn connected with a lost painting by Hubert or Jan van Eyck, preserved in a painted copy in Budapest. While in Van Eyck's composition the procession went from right to left, here it moves from left to right. At the same time the basic elements of the composition have been changed in accordance with mid-fifteenth century art and have become more "progressive". The drawing is undoubtedly a copy in which the group of the Three Marys with Veronica was not quite completed. The copyist was an important artist, who here created a work of high quality. Another work by his hand is The Fall of the Damned in the Louvre, likewise a copy of an older work. The lost original goes back to Hubert or Jan van Eyck just as does the original of the Carrying of the Cross, a conclusion supported by a comparison with the wing of the "Last Judgment" in New York. Some figures in the Paris drawing also recur in a Fall of the Damned by Dirck Bouts in the Louvre.

All these factors led the present writer to conclude that the prototypes of the two drawings are to be sought in Dutch painting about the middle of the fifteenth century or shortly thereafter, and he has tentatively put forward the name of Ouwater. The dating of the drawings is still an open question. Probably they should be placed about 1500. J. Q. Van Regteren Altena referred (orally) to Juan de Flandes, a name which the present writer, perhaps on the basis of a comparison with the "Ecce Homo" painting in Prague, finds quite meaningful.

The most recent hypothesis, that of F. Winkler, attributes the original of Christ Carrying the Cross to Jean Fouquet, the original of the Fall of the Damned to one of the brothers Van Eyck; in the drawings he sees the hand of Pieter Bruegel the Elder. This takes the high quality of the two drawings

into account, and, with reference to the date of the original of the "Carrying of the Cross", coincides with the present writer's suggestion.
A painting in the Suermondt Museum in Aachen is a weaker copy of the present composition, omitting the drawing's unfinished Veronica group.

PETRUS CHRISTUS I (CRISTUS)
Native of Baerle, master at Bruges in 1444, died there 1473.

124 Portrait of a Man.
Silverpoint on white prepared paper.
266 : 186 mm.
Inv. no. 4845 (L. 174).

Albertina Cat. II, 15; Schönbrunner-Meder 307; J. Meder, Albertina-Facsimile, Handzeichnungen vlämischer und holländischer Meister, Vienna, 1923, plate 1; Great Drawings of All Time, New York, 1962, II, no. 463 (E. Haverkamp-Begemann).

Exhibition: London, 1948, no. 44.

The attribution to this artist was suggested by the present writer on the basis of a comparison with paintings by Petrus Christus. The strong accentuation of the head in comparison with the summary treatment of the body is in accordance with the style of this artist's portraits. The powerful angularity of the modeling has also given rise to the conjecture that this is a German drawing made after a Netherlandish painting. This hypothesis was strengthened by the fact that there is a second version, also in silverpoint, in the Kupferstichkabinett in Hamburg. As far as its bad state of preservation will permit us to judge, it is inferior in quality to the drawing in the Albertina. The drawing of the hands in the latter is freer than is usual in copies.

HIERONYMUS BOSCH
Hertogenbosch about 1450—1516.

125 The Tree Man.
Pen and bistre. Inscribed by a later hand, lower left: BRVEGEL.
277 : 211 mm.
Inv. no. 7876 (L. 174).

Albertina Cat. II, 26; O. Benesch, Jahrbuch der Preussischen Kunstsammlungen, 58, Berlin, 1937, pp. 258—266; Ch. de Tolnay, Hieronymus Bosch, Basel, 1937, p. 111, no. 7 and Baden-Baden, 1965, no. 7; M. J. Friedländer, Die Altniederländische Malerei, V, pp. 124 and 125, no. 7; L. Baldass, Hieronymus Bosch, Vienna, 1959 (2nd edition), p. 247, no. 152 (reproduced); O. Benesch, Jahrbuch der Kunsthistorischen Sammlungen in Wien, 53 (1957), p. 14, fig. 6; O. Benesch, Konsthistorisk Tidskrift XXXVI (1957), pp. 126 and 127, fig. 39; Great Drawings of All Time, New York, 1962, II, no. 476 (E. Haverkamp-Begemann).

Exhibitions: Exposition Jerôme Bosch, Rotterdam, Museum Boymans, 1936, no. 14; London, 1948, no. 37.

This important drawing, a work of Bosch's later years, transplants to a broad river landscape a motif which first occurs in the wing representing Hell in The Garden of Earthly Delights, in the Prado. The drawing, formerly attributed to Bruegel on the basis of the apocryphal signature, was identified by the present writer as a work by Bosch. He has further demonstrated that the motif of the "Tree Man" is a kind of "disguised" self-portrait of the artist, who identified himself with tree and wood (Bosch) in order to escape persecution by his tormentors. The explanation is furnished by the drawing of "The Seeing Field and the Listening Wood" in the Berlin Kupferstichkabinett, which was provided with a Latin inscription by the artist. The human features of the hybrid creature approximate his own. Another charade-like self-personification of the artist is found in the owl pursued by mocking magpies, a motif which we encounter twice in this drawing, in the rigging of the Tree Man and on a spit of land at the right. The spacious scenery goes back to models from the beginning of the fifteenth century (compare the landscapes in the Turin Prayerbook).

JAN DE BEER
Became disciple of Gillis van Everen in 1490, master at Antwerp in 1504, died there before 1536.

126 The Tree of Jesse. In two parts: (a) lower part, Jesse and the Tree; (b) upper part: King David and King Solomon, the Virgin and Child Enthroned.
Black chalk, brush and Indian ink and white bodycolor on gray prepared paper mounted on canvas.
Lower part: 215 : 56 cm.
Upper part: 215 : 56 cm.
Inv. no. 32919, 32920 (acquired 1959).
Provenance: A. v. Lanna; Rudolf v. Gutmann.

M. J. Friedländer, Die Altniederländische Malerei, 11, Berlin, 1933, p. 24, no. 7; O. Benesch, Jahrbuch der Kunsthistorischen Sammlungen in Wien, 53 (1957), p. 16, figs. 8a—b.

Monumental painting in the Netherlands was concerned with stained glass and tapestry. As the only preserved example of a cartoon for a church window from the beginning of the Renaissance in the Netherlands, the present drawing has particular importance. The cartoon seems to take in only the middle zone of the window. The boughs branching off to the right and left and the gestures of the figures permit the conclusion that the window was wider.
Jan de Beer was the leading artist of the so-called first Mannerist movement in Antwerp, which combined late Gothic elements of Dutch origin (H. Bosch, Jan de Cock) with decorative features of the early Renaissance.

JAN GOSSAERT (Jan Mabuse)
Born Duurstede near Utrecht about 1478, died Middelburg between 1533 and 1536.

127 The Fall of Man.
Pen and bistre. On the left very faded inscription in black chalk: . . . . . Get(ekent) den 6. / 1525; below in the same chalk faded monogram MB (similar to Wurzbach, II, p. 86).
257 : 210 mm.
Inv. no. 13341 (L. 174).

Albertina Cat. II, 36; Schönbrunner-Meder 1189; J. Meder, Albertina-Facsimile, Handzeichnungen vlämischer und holländischer Meister, Vienna, 1923, plate 3; E. Weisz, Jan Gossaert, gen. Mabuse, Parchim i. M., 1913, p. 35, plate VII, fig. 17; M. J. Friedländer, Die Altniederländische Malerei, 8, Berlin, 1930, p. 64, no. 3.

Exhibitions: London, 1948, no. 51; Le Siècle de Bruegel, Musées Royaux des Beaux-Arts de Belgique, Brussels, 1963, cat. no. 285, ill. 273; Jan Gossaert genaamd Mabuse, Rotterdam, Museum Boymans-Van Beuningen, May-June 1965, cat. no. 61 and ill.

The earliest works of this artist show that his style derived from that of the Antwerp Mannerists, the so-called "Bles Group" (see no. 126). A visit to Rome acquainted him with classical antiquity and the Italian Renaissance, but it was chiefly Albrecht Dürer's influence that made him the first representative of true Renaissance art in the Netherlands. This fact is attested by the freedom of movement and the round forms of the modeling of the nudes in the present drawing which follows Dürer's example. (The drawing was identified as a work of Gossaert by J. Meder.) Nevertheless the twisting bodies still clearly reveal the late Gothic mannerist tradition. Adam's right leg seems to have been drawn twice. The artist turned the first, discarded version into the root of a tree.

DIRICK JACOBSSONE VELLERT
Became master in Antwerp in 1511, Dean in 1518 and in 1526, documented until 1544.

128 Hannah Brings the Little Samuel to Eli in the House of the Lord at Shiloh (Samuel I, chapter 1, verse 24).
Pen and bistre, washed with Indian ink. Dated in pen and bistre on the step near the lower margin: 1523, monogram with star, Aug(usti) 28.
Diameter: 284 mm.
Inv. 7803 (L. 174).

Albertina Cat. II, 40; Schönbrunner-Meder 997; G. Glück, Jahrbuch der kunsthistorischen Sammlungen des Allerhöchsten Kaiserhauses, XXII, Vienna, 1901, p. 23, no. 14; O. Benesch, Jahrbuch der Kunsthistorischen Sammlungen in Wien 53 (1957), p. 16, fig. 12.

Design for stained glass.

As in Switzerland, the art of designing stained glass windows also developed in the Netherlands, especially during the Renaissance. The majority of Vellert's extant drawings are designs for stained glass. They combine the formal vocabulary of the Renaissance, introduced by Gossaert, with the decorative tradition of the Antwerp Mannerists. This gave rise to works notable for their clever adaptation of the composition to the circular shape. They are as rich in ornamental charm as the master's engravings. A uniform formal rhythm pervades the whole drawing. (Decorative objects like the candlestick repeat the peculiar rhythm of the movement of the figures.)

LUCAS VAN LEYDEN
Born Leiden 1494, died there 1533.

129 Young Girl Reading.
Black chalk, with monogram L.; moisture stain and retouching on the gown; along the upper margin a strip of paper (13 mm wide) was added at a later date and the head dress completed in leadpoint.
316 (including added strip): 192 mm.
Inv. 17550 (L. 174).

Albertina Cat. II, 60; Schönbrunner-Meder 356; J. G. van Gelder, Dutch Drawings and Prints, London, 1959, Cat. no. and fig. 10; Great Drawings of All Time, New York, 1962, II, no. 485 (J. G. van Gelder); M. J. Friedländer, Lucas van Leyden, Berlin, 1963, p. 76, no. 24.

Exhibition: Exposition Jerôme Bosch, Rotterdam, Museum Boymans, 1936, p. 72, no. 56, fig. 36.

The date "about 1520" suggested by the present writer in the Albertina catalogue was confirmed by Friedländer's "um 1522 entstanden" (compare, however, the far too early date proposed by J. G. van Gelder: "Lucas, not even eighteen years of age, when he made this drawing"). A good possibility for comparison is offered by the engraving of St. Catherine of 1520 (Bartsch 125).
Still impressive in spite of much damage, this drawing shows Lucas' style of draughtsmanship in a phase shortly before his adherence to Dürer in his portrait drawings. The two artists met and Dürer drew a portrait of Lucas in 1521. The precocious artist played a role in North Netherlandish art, similar to that of Gossaert in South Netherlandish art, namely as a propagator of Dürer's style and, in his last phase, of Italian Renaissance art.

PIETER CORNELISZ KUNST
Born Leiden about 1490, documented until 1542.

130 The Good Samaritan.
Pen and bistre.
249 : 184 mm.
Inv. 24755 (acquired 1926).

Provenance: private property of Archduke Frederick.

Albertina Cat. II, 62; L. Baldass, Die Graphischen Künste, Mitteilungen der Gesellschaft für vervielfältigende Kunst, XXXVIII, Vienna, 1915, p. 25 ff.

The artist was the eldest son of Lucas van Leyden's teacher Cornelis Engelbrechtsen. According to Van Mander's testimony he was a friend of Lucas and practised drawing together with him so that he eventually became an outstanding glass painter. Pieter Cornelisz is known above all as a draughtsman. Many of his drawings are designs for stained glass. Stylistically, he stems from Jan de Cock, a Dutchman who settled in Antwerp and was important for the development of the first phase of Antwerp Mannerism.
In the art of Pieter Cornelisz, landscape plays an increasingly prominent role, and, as in the works of the Danube School, human, animal, and vegetable forms merge with one another.

BARENT VAN ORLEY
Born Brussels 1491/92, died there 1542.

131 The Triumph of Heroic Woman.
Pen and bistre, washed. Inscribed by a later hand on upper margin: F 89 (according to Meder the mark of a series). A missing narrow strip of paper on the upper right margin has been restored.
365 : 536 mm.
Inv. 15468 (L. 174).

Albertina Cat. II, 43; J. Meder, Die Handzeichnung, Vienna, 1919, p. 337 and note 9; O. Benesch, Jahrbuch der Kunsthistorischen Sammlungen in Wien, 53 (1957),)p. 16, fig. 11.

The subject of this drawing was taken from Petrarch's "Trionfi", namely from the "Triumphus Famae". Jael and Sisera, Lucretia Romana, and Judith are lined up in front. There are three further drawings in the same series: Dresden, Kupferstichkabinett (Friedländer, Jahrbuch der Preussischen Kunstsammlungen 30 [1909], p. 159, fig. 44, 370 : 561 mm); Berlin, Kupferstichkabinett (Inv. 12301); Collection Rodrigues (sale catalogue Mensing, 1921, no. 186).
Design for a tapestry. M. J. Friedländer has described Orley's activity for the tapestry manufactory in Brussels in his authoritative essay on the artist (Jahrbuch der Preussischen Kunstsammlungen 29 [1908] and 30 [1909]). Tapestry, like stained glass, played the same monumental part in the Netherlands as frescoes did in Italy. It was an event of decisive importance for the development of Netherlandish art when the Vatican commissioned Pieter van Aelst's workshop in Brussels to weave the tapestries from Raphael's cartoons. They led to a complete revolution of composition and pictorial organization in the works of the Northern artists as can clearly be traced in Orley's oeuvre. The connection with the older decorative style of an artist like Vellert shows itself only in the technique of the pen drawing, in the trembling, vibrating "wire-like outline" which the Flemish Romanists also retained and passed on to the Dutch (see nos. 132 and 133).

PIETER COECKE VAN AELST (Alost)
Born Alost 1502, died Brussels 1550.

132 The Money-Changer.
Pen and bistre, washed. Lower left corner, later inscription in pen and ink: Peter Van Alst.
171 : 180 mm.
Inv. 7852 (L. 174).

Albertina Cat. II, 50; M. J. Friedländer, Jahrbuch der Preussischen Kunstsammlungen, 38 (1917), p. 86.

This drawing demonstrates the importance of genre, interiors, and still-life for Netherlandish painting from Van Eyck and Petrus Christus onward. The present representation is mainly influenced by Quentin Massys and Dürer. The bull's-eye pattern, reflected by the sunlight on the embrasure of the window on the right, was inspired by Dürer's "St. Jerome in his Study".
Pieter Coecke was a pupil of Orley, from whose technique of drawing he took over the trembling "wire outline". His most important works were designs for tapestries, which demonstrate the strong influence exerted by Raphael on Netherlandish Romanism.

JAN SWART VAN GRONINGEN
Born Groningen about 1500, died Antwerp (?) after 1553.

133 Boaz Beholds Ruth in the Fields.
Pen and bistre, washed; lower right inscription in pencil: Swartz Joh.
274 : 203 mm.
Inv. 7841 (L. 174).

Albertina Cat. II, 93; L. Baldass, Die Graphischen Künste, Mitteilungen der Gesellschaft für vervielfältigende Kunst, XLI, Vienna, 1918, p. 14, fig. 6, no. 69 (the nos. 22 and 70 belong to the same series).

This drawing is a design for stained glass. Together with another drawing in the Albertina and one in the Städelsches

Kunstinstitut, it is part of a series illustrating the story of Boaz and Ruth. Many drawings by this prolific artist are designs for stained glass. His style is derived from the art of Jan van Scorel, and as in his works landscape plays a prominent part whenever the subject demands it. The technical peculiarity of the trembling pen lines is a feature shared by the early Dutch with the Flemish Romanists. It is the result of a slow and deliberate manipulation of the pen. With the Dutch, however, it is combined with the equally important work of the brush in light tones that not only models shadows but frequently also draws oblique hatchings, thereby achieving an unusually airy effect, as in this attractive landscape.

DIRCK PIETERSZ CRABETH
Born Gouda, documented 1545—1552, 1555—1571, died Gouda 1577.

134 Judith and Holofernes.
Pen and brush and bistre, washed, over preparatory drawing in black chalk, flesh tinted red with the brush. Inscription by the artist's hand on the key-stone: Anno Dñi 15 . . .
502 : 332 mm.
Inv. no. 7847 (L. 174).
Albertina Cat. II, 105; Wurzbach I, p. 354.
Preparatory drawing for the stained glass window dated 1571 in the Cathedral at Gouda.

The brothers Dirck and Wouter Pietersz Crabeth were the most important Dutch glass painters during the period of highly developed Romanism. They were responsible for numerous windows in Dutch churches, including those of the Oude Kerck in Amsterdam. Their principal work was the window decoration in the cathedral of their home town Gouda, the project for which the present drawing was intended. The besieged city of Bethulia and the camp in front of it are rendered in detail. In the background on the left, Judith returns to town after having killed Holofernes, while on the right Holofernes' head hanging from a tower causes the besieging army to turn and flee.
Old Testament scenes as subjects for church windows are typical of Protestant Holland. In the period of the great religious wars a subject like the present one was particularly pertinent. The style of the figures has been influenced by that of the Raphaelesque Mannerists, presumably transmitted to the artist through Heemskerck.

MAERTEN VAN HEEMSKERCK
Born Heemskerck 1498, died Haarlem 1574.

135 Job Tormented by a Demon.
Pen and bistre. Lower left signature on a small card: Martinus Heemskerck; dated on the corbel of the pillar buttress: 1548.
259 : 384 mm.
Inv. no. 7826 (L. 174).
Albertina Cat. II, 99.
Engraved in reverse direction with the inscription: Martinus Heemskerck Inventor. L. Preibisz, Martin van Heemskerck, Leipzig 1911, p. 100, no. 185 (attributed by Preibisz to the engraver Cuerenhert [D. Coornhert]).

Heemskerck, who was a pupil of Scorel, represents the climax of Dutch Romanism. He spent four years in Rome (1532—36), studying especially the ancient ruins and forming his style on the works of Raphael, Michelangelo, and the Mannerists. All these elements can be clearly recognized in the present drawing. An area of Roman ruins is the scene of action. The nudes follow the models of Michelangelo and Giulio Romano. By reason of Heemskerck's settling in Haarlem this town became the center of the Italianate movement in Dutch art for half a century.
Like most of Heemskerck's extant drawings, the present sheet is a design for an engraving. The role of reproductive graphic art in the dissemination of artistic achievements and as a general means of education developed strongly in the Netherlands about the middle of the century. The leading artists, Bruegel among them, were active as draughtsmen for engravings.

ADRIAEN THOMASZ KEY
Born Antwerp about 1544, died there after 1589.

136 Portrait of a Lady with Ruff.
Black and white chalk; watermark: Briquet 8066.
382 : 224 mm.
Inv. no. 14269 (from an album).
Albertina Cat. II, 129; J. Meder, Handzeichnungen alter Meister aus der Albertina und aus Privatbesitz, Neue Folge, Vienna, 1922, no. 37.

The present drawing was considered a portrait of Queen Anne of Spain from the hand of Antonis Moro by J. Meder. This attribution was doubted by Friedländer. The fact that the soft, fused modeling of the drawing resembles the portraits of A. Th. Key, a follower of Moro, prompted the present writer to suggest this artist as its author. A. Th. Key was a portrait painter much in demand. In addition to the abstract trend of Romanist Mannerism in the Netherlands about the middle of the century, there was a powerful revival of naturalism, which found a special outlet in portraiture and was often practised by the same artists who created the Mannerist compositions.

PIETER BRUEGEL THE ELDER
Born Breughel between 1525 and 1530, became master in Antwerp 1551, died Brussels 1569.

137 The Big Fish Eat the Little Ones.
Pen and Indian ink; dated and signed lower right: 1556 brueghel; the cross hatching in pen and bistre under the tree added later; the two lower corners restored.
215 : 307 mm.
Inv. no. 7875 (L. 174).
Engraved by Pieter van der Heyden (R. v. Bastelaer, Les Estampes de Peter Bruegel, Brussels, 1908, no. 139) with the inscription:

Hieronymus Bos.   Cock. excu. 1557 etc.
inventor.

Copy in reverse direction after the engraving with some alterations: C. Visscher excud. P. Breugel inven:

Illustration of the proverb: De groote visschen eten de cleyne, which the man in the boat is explaining to his small son. (R. v. Bastelaer and G. Hulin de Loo, Peter Bruegel, Brussels, 1907, pp. 68, 69 and p. 194, no. 90.)

Albertina Cat. II, 76; A. L. Romdahl, Jahrbuch der Kunsthistorischen Sammlungen des Allerhöchsten Kaiserhauses 25 (1904), p. 123; L. Burchard, Amtliche Berichte 34, columns 224—226; M. J. Friedländer, Pieter Bruegel, Berlin, 1921, pp. 62 to 64; Ch. de Tolnay, Die Zeichnungen Pieter Bruegels, Zurich, 1952, no. 44, plate XXIV; Ch. de Tolnay, Pierre Bruegel l'Ancien, Brussels, 1935, pp. 18, 19, fig. 170; O. Benesch, The Art of the Renaissance in Northern Europe, Cambridge, Massachusetts, 1947, p. 93, fig. 54, and revised edition, London, 1965, p. 107, fig. 55; O. Benesch, Jahrbuch der Kunsthistorischen Sammlungen in Wien 53 (1957), p. 21, fig. 14; L. Münz, Bruegel, The Drawings, London, 1961, p. 225.
Exhibition: London, 1948, no. 39.

The inscription on the engraving mentioning Hieronymus Bosch as its inventor is, according to Friedländer, the publisher's attempt to make Bruegel's oeuvre sail under the flag of the famous and popular Bosch for commercial reasons. According to other scholars the drawing may actually be based on an invention of Bosch. Certainly the moralizing and didactic meaning of the representation is much closer to Bruegel's manner than to that of his great predecessor. The soldier who is slitting the fish's belly wears a soldier's helmet; his knife bears as hallmark the symbol of the world turned upside down. The scene is a satire on war, which kills even the biggest predatory fish. The drying of flounders on the tree in the background is clearly an allusion to the gallows. The gesture of the peasant in the doorway signifies lamentation rather than command. The small predatory fish in front of him suddenly assumes human shape and wanders off with its prey.

Like most of Bruegel's free inventions, this drawing was intended as a model for an engraving: hence the careful shading and modeling technique, which anticipates the work of the burin while preserving all the colorful vibrance and closeness to life characteristic of the paintings of this greatest of sixteenth century Netherlanders. The engraving was published by Hieronymus Cock, himself known as an etcher of Roman ruins and Romanist landscapes.

138 Painter and Art-Lover.
Pen and bistre; apocryphal signature in bright bistre: BRVEGEL; the pupils of the painter's eyes slightly strengthened in the same bistre.
250 : 216 mm.
Inv. no. 7500 (L. 174).

Albertina Cat. II, 84; Schönbrunner-Meder 358; A. Romdahl, Jahrbuch der Kunsthistorischen Sammlungen des Allerhöchsten Kaiserhauses 25 (1904,) p. 147 (opposite p. 148), plate XXIV; J. Meder, Albertina-Facsimile, Handzeichnungen vlämischer und holländischer Meister, Vienna, 1923, plate 4; Ch. de Tolnay, Die Zeichnungen Pieter Bruegels, Zürich, 1952, no. 118, fig. LXXIII; L. Münz, Bruegel, The Drawings, London, 1961, p. 224; C. G. Stridbeck, Bruegelstudien, Stockholm, 1956, pp. 15—42; O. Benesch, The Art of the Renaissance in Northern Europe, Cambridge, Massachusetts, 1947, p. 94, fig. 53, and revised edition London, 1965, p. 108, fig. 56; O. Benesch, Bulletin, Koninklijke Musea voor Schone Kunsten 1—2, Brussels, Mars-Juin, 1959, pp. 35—42; Great Drawings of All Time, New York, 1962, II, no. 138 (E. Haverkamp-Begemann).

Exhibition: London, 1948, no. 41.

This drawing is a monumental work of Bruegel's late years. Although it bears neither signature nor date, it was already famous in the sixteenth century, as is attested by a number of copies, among them those by Jacques Savery and Hoefnagel. It was not intended as a preparatory drawing for an engraving, but as an independent work of art of self-revealing character, which perhaps remained in the artist's possession all his life. It was intended to illustrate the artist's relation with the world: a moral and philosophical reflection in pictorial form. The artist is poor, badly dressed, ill-groomed; the connoisseur is rich, as his money-bag indicates, and dressed with bourgeois elegance. The artist's expression is bitter, disillusioned with the world, but his eyes burn with the sacred fire of creation. The connoisseur's face expresses surprise and astonishment to the point of silliness, but this does not upset his materialistic calculations, as is demonstrated by his right hand which almost automatically reaches into the money-bag. Artistic ethos is immediately reduced to hard cash, certainly to his own and not the artist's advantage.
This is the general idea of the drawing. On the grounds of its revealing character, Tolnay has assumed it to be a disguised self-portrait. The present writer supposes it to be an apotheosized portrait of Bosch, whom Bruegel revered. (That Bosch did not have a beard became known only through the engraved portrait of Lampsonius, published after Bruegel's death and based on a drawing in the Codex Arras.) Both concepts may have inspired the general idea of the drawing, which is definitely much more real than Stridbeck assumes when he sees in it an allegory of painting, its essence and its relationship to the public.

CRISPIN VAN DEN BROECK
Born Malines 1524, died Antwerp 1591.

139 Open Air Meeting of Netherlandish Protestants at the Time of the Religious Wars.
Pen and brush and bistre, blue watercolor on light brown paper.
378 : 534 mm.
Inv. no. 15472 (L. 174).
Old Inventory: Inconnu.
Attribution by the present writer.
The artist, a pupil of the Romanist Frans Floris, has so far been known only as the creator of Mannerist compositions of a religious, allegorical or classical content. The present

drawing, however, is an impressive depiction of everyday life in the Netherlands as it was familiar to all during the difficult eighty years of the religious wars. From the human point of view it must have been more important to the artist than the creation of compositions in the classical manner. The broad field, fortified by a barricade of wagons, is filled with four simultaneous Protestant meetings. The entrance to the camp and the surrounding rampart of hills are watched by soldiers with loaded rifles. In the foreground the kind of life normally associated with such events goes on: leaflets are distributed, a woman rents out chairs, Protestant books are sold at an improvised book-stall; families come and go. The whole drawing is a masterly genre piece with a serious undertone, worthy of the age of Pieter Bruegel and his intellectual friends, an age in which spiritual and religious freedom were obliged to express themselves in cryptic pictures and were threatened by dangers from all sides.

FRIEDRICH SUSTRIS
Born Italy (?) about 1540, died Munich 1599.

XII St. Michael.
Pen and Indian ink, and watercolor; grid for the sculptural execution of the work.
353 : 227 mm.
Inv. no. 3275 (L. 174).

Albertina Cat. II, 150; K. Steinbart, Die Graphischen Künste, Neue Folge III, 1938, p. 118 ff.

Attribution by K. Feuchtmayr, who first identified the drawing as the design for a silver statuette in the Reiche Kapelle of the Residenz in Munich.
The son of a Romanist painter from the Netherlands, this artist was given an international education and was a pupil of Vasari in Florence (see no. 42). He worked for the Fugger family in Augsburg and for Duke William V of Bavaria in Munich and Landshut, and was the leading Mannerist artist in South Germany during the second half of the sixteenth century. His style, like that of the artists at the court of Rudolf II in Prague, was a synthesis of Netherlandish, Italian and German elements. The present drawing exhibits the precious and subtle play of forms, adequately matched by the cool, bright iridescent colors, in a most attractive arrangement. The slender proportions of the figure correspond to the formal ideal of Late Mannerism. The colors suggest that the silver statuette was intended to be enamelled. The idea of the figure influenced even the bronze statue of St. Michael by Hans Reichle on the Armory in Augsburg, and on this account the drawing was attributed to that artist in the old inventory of the Albertina.

JOOS VAN WINGHE
Born Brussels 1542, died Frankfort-on-Main 1603.

140 The Last Supper.
Pen and brush and bistre, heightened with white bodycolor on greenish-brown paper; signed lower left: Jodocus van Winghe.
467 : 428 mm.
Inv. no. 15116.

Provenance: Charles, Prince de Ligne (Cat. p. 242).

Albertina Cat. II, 194; Wurzbach II, p. 888.

According to a note in the old inventory of the Albertina this drawing is the design for a painting in the Church of St. Gery in Brussels, where the artist was still living in February, 1585, as court painter to Governor Alessandro Farnese.
Joos van Winghe was one of the most highly gifted and inventive draughtsmen of Late Flemish Mannerism, his drawings being far superior to his paintings. He spent a number of years in Italy and in Paris, blending elements of Italian and French Mannerism with those of the Netherlandish. The expressive composition with its flickering light is strongly influenced by Tintoretto. Towards the end of the century traveling Northern artists were influenced more strongly by Venice than by Florence and Rome. Van Winghe spent the last years of his life in Frankfort; he probably emigrated to this city for religious reasons.

BARTHOLOMAEUS SPRANGER
Born Antwerp 1546, died Prague 1611.

141 Apollo.
Pen and bistre, washed, flesh-color slightly tinted in red, the ground lightly shaded with chalk; signed: B. Spranger F.
203 : 140 mm.
Inv. no. 7996 (L. 174).

Albertina Cat. II, 283; Schönbrunner-Meder 1064; O. Benesch, The Art of the Renaissance in Northern Europe, Cambridge, Massachusetts, 1947, p. 133, fig. 76, and revised edition, London, 1965, p. 152, fig. 79; O. Benesch, Jahrbuch der Kunsthistorischen Sammlungen in Wien 53 (1957), p. 23, fig. 17.

Exhibition: Le Siècle de Bruegel, Musées Royaux des Beaux-Arts de Belgique, Brussels, 1963, Cat. no. 299, ill. 285.

Spranger was the principal artist in the group of painters summoned by Rudolf II to his court at Prague (see nos. 100 and 101). He was first and foremost a gifted draughtsman whose impromptu pen sketches contain the quintessence of the labile interplay of forms characteristic of Late Mannerism. His brittle linear configurations seem to generate a sort of centrifugal force. The Late Mannerism of Rome and Florence (Zuccari, Zucchi) exerted a decisive influence on him during the ten years of his stay in Italy. But like his contemporaries he succeeded later on in the North in imparting a fantastic, expressive note to what he had learned in Italy; as a result his art appears as the legitimate heir of the Late Gothic style. What he had learned in his younger days from the Bosch follower Mandijn, and Bruegel's contemporary Cornelis van Dalem, asserted itself again in his mature years.

HENDRIK GOLTZIUS
Born Mühlbrecht near Venlo 1558, died Haarlem 1617.

142 Self-Portrait.
Black and colored chalk, brush and Indian ink, red chalk, flesh-color reddish, background yellowish-green, stone frame tinted brownish. Monogram by the artist's hand.
430 : 323 mm.
Inv. no. 17638 (L. 174).
Provenance: D. Muilman; C. Ploos van Amstel.

Albertina Cat. II, 375; E. K. J. Reznicek, Die Zeichnungen von Hendrik Goltzius, Utrecht, 1961, no. 256.

Exhibition: Hendrik Goltzius, Rotterdam, Museum Boymans 1958, no. 42, plate 46.

This artist was German by birth. At Duisburg his first teacher was his father, a glass painter. At Xanten and Cleve he was a pupil of the engraver Coornhert, a friend of Bruegel, whom he followed in 1577 to Haarlem where he settled and became the most distinguished engraver of the Netherlands. Prolific as an engraver and draughtsman, he was also active later on as a painter. Only when he was a mature artist did he travel to Italy where he was in contact with the famous artists of his day, the Zuccari, Barocci, Giovanni da Bologna, and others.
In Haarlem, together with Carel van Mander and Cornelis Cornelissen, he founded the group of the so-called "Haarlem Academicians", a circle of artists who cultivated the study of the model in the Italian manner and publicized Spranger's art (see no. 141). Goltzius engraved numerous compositions by his colleagues and by Spranger. Thus he developed his style, which combined the artificiality of the figure composition of Late Mannerism with a refreshing naturalness in portraiture. His portraits, whether drawn in colored chalks or engraved with technical brilliance, are among the most vivid representations of personalities of the time.

JACQUES DE GHEYN
Born Antwerp 1565, died The Hague 1629.

143 Rocky Landscape with the Flight into Egypt.
Pen and bistre. Lower left signed and dated 1599.
209 : 318 mm.
Inv. no. 8155 (L. 174).
Albertina Cat. II, 391.

Jacques de Gheyn, an excellent engraver and draughtsman, was Goltzius' (see no. 142) most important pupil and, together with Matham, Saenredam and Muller, belonged to his circle. In his drawing style he harks back remarkably to Dürer, Lucas van Leyden, and the northern masters of their time. He thus developed an uncommonly expressive and individual style, which in some aspects anticipates Callot. A sombre seriousness dominated by the idea of death and the hereafter is the fundamental mood of his art, which sometimes, especially in his scenes of witches, rises to a splendid fantasy akin in spirit to Shakespeare.

DAVID VINCKBOONS I (Vinckeboons)
Born Malines 1576, died Amsterdam 1629.

144 Paradise with the Fall of Man.
Pen and bistre, washed, and tinted gray-blue.
436 : 680 mm.
Inv. no. 15091 (L. 174).
The artist, who was born in Flanders, settled in Amsterdam in 1591 at the same time as Hans Bol and Jacques Savery. He was a member of the group of artists who emigrated for religious reasons and became important for the blending of the Flemish tradition of landscape painting, as formulated by Bruegel, with the Dutch and German. The brothers Jacques and Roelant Savery (see no. 145) and Gillis van Coninxloo exerted a particular influence on him in Amsterdam. The conception of Paradise as a zoological garden, with an almost textbook-like profusion of species, is also to be found with Roelant Savery. The artist's vibrant manner of drawing fits especially well with the depiction of the Garden of Eden as a complete world, ahum with a thousand voices.

ROELANT SAVERY
Born Courtrai 1576, died Utrecht 1639.

145 Rocks and Pines on the Banks of a Mountain Torrent.
Black chalk and watercolor in green, blue, and reddish terracotta.
309 : 203 mm.
Inv. no. 17547 (L. 174).

K. Erasmus, Roelant Savery, Thesis, University of Halle-Wittenberg, Halle a. S., 1908, no. 81.

Exhibition: Roelant Savery, Museum voor Schone Kunsten, Gent, 1954, Cat. no. 123.

This artist, who like many others emigrated for religious reasons (see no. 144), worked as court painter for Rudolf II in Prague from 1604 to 1612. The Emperor sent him to the Tyrol to make studies from nature, which afterwards were used in the free compositions of his small cabinet paintings so treasured by Rudolf's court. Numerous magnificent drawings from nature originated in this way, continuing the landscape painting tradition of the Danube School and Bruegel. The present drawing is one of them. After Rudolf's death, Savery entered the service of the Emperor Matthias in Vienna in 1614. In the following years he made studies from nature in Salzburg and again in the Tyrol. Although Savery's paintings manifest the fantastic and unreal landscape concept of Late Mannerism, his drawings show its relaxation and gradual supersedure by a new and direct visual relationship with nature. Seventeenth-century landscape painting is foreshadowed here.

JAN BRUEGHEL THE ELDER
Born Brussels 1568, died Antwerp 1625.

146 Landscape with the Temple of Vesta (by Ercole Sassano) at Tivoli, and a Draughtsman.
Pen and bistre over preparatory drawing in black chalk, washed with bistre and blue watercolor. Lower left, signed and dated: i breugel 15 . . . Upper right, in pencil by a later hand: Jean Breugel.
253 : 202 mm.
Inv. no. 8424 (L. 174).
Jan Brueghel, also called "Fluweelen" (Velvet) Brueghel, was the second son of the great "Peasant Bruegel". Famous during his lifetime and appreciated by Rudolf II and Albert

of the Netherlands, he enjoyed the friendship of Rubens, with whom he frequently collaborated. He also readily participated in common projects with other artists such as Rottenhammer (see no. 104), Francken (see no. 147), Balen and Momper. Landscapes, still-lives, and animal paintings were his forte. From 1593 to 1594 he sojourned in Rome, studying the landscape and the ancient buildings. The present drawing, a study from nature surprising in its freshness and unconventionality and far ahead of its time, dates from this period. It was only Elsheimer and his followers who were to recapture such a direct feeling for nature.

FRANS FRANCKEN II
Born Antwerp 1581, died there 1642.

147 Witches' Sabbath.
Pen and bistre, some watercolor in purple, crimson, yellow, brown, gray, blue and gold. Several magic formulas in pen and bistre by the artist's own hand. Signed upper right on the frame of the small cupboard: di. FFrancken iv.
190 : 269 mm.
Inv. no. 7971 (L. 174).

Wurzbach I, p. 552; W. Bernt, Die Niederländischen Zeichner des 17. Jahrhunderts, Munich, 1957, I, no. and fig. 237.

Scenes with witches were, ever since Bruegel's "Dulle Griet", a frequent subject of Netherlandish painting and graphic art, particularly about the turn of the century. The reawakened interest in German art of Dürer's time probably was influential in this. While with de Gheyn such scenes assume a demoniac and ominous character, a delightful sense of humor is evident in Francken's drawing. The diableries, as lavish as a still-life in their profusion, are suitably rendered by the flourishes and gay improvisations of the pen.

Like Jan Brueghel, Francken is one of the artists of Rubens' era who stands in the twilight between Mannerism and Baroque art. While the intricacy of his figure-rich compositions heralds the demise of the former, the fluent mastery of light and shade is already a symptom of the latter.

PETER PAUL RUBENS
Born Siegen 1577, died Antwerp 1640.

148 A Miraculous Image of the Virgin and Child, Carried Skyward by Putti and Venerated by Angels.
Pen and brush and bistre, washed, some white bodycolor in the clouds; lines on left and right margins and center line in leadpoint, further traces of leadpoint.
267 : 152 mm. (a strip of paper, about 5 mm. wide, added along the right and left margins by the artist's own hand.)
Inv. no. 8231 (L. 174).

Provenance: P. J. Mariette (L. 2097); L. Lempereur.

G. Glück and F. M. Haberditzl, Die Handzeichnungen von Peter Paul Rubens, Berlin, 1928, no. 54; F. M. Haberditzl, Jahrbuch der Kunsthistorischen Sammlungen des Allerhöchsten Kaiserhauses XXX, 1912, p. 271 and fig. XXVII (fig. 10 altarpiece); J. S. Held, Rubens, Selected Drawings, London, 1959, no. 17, plate 19; M. Jaffé, P. P. Rubens and the Oratorian Fathers, Proporzioni IV, Florence; see also O. Benesch, Neue Beiträge zum Werk des Rubens, W. Friedländer zum 90. Geburtstag, Berlin, 1965, p. 43.

Design for the central panel of the altar of 1608 by Rubens in S. Maria in Vallicella, Rome.

When Rubens was given leave by the Duke of Mantua and stayed in Rome in 1606, he signed a contract with the Congregation of the Oratorian Fathers on September 25th, to paint a picture for the high altar of the church of S. Maria in Vallicella (Chiesa Nuova) on the occasion of the transference of the miraculous image to this altar. The artist agreed to conditions that were very favorable to the Order, as it meant a great increase in prestige for him to be able to install a monumental altar painting in a prominent place in Rome. The first version was that now in the museum at Grenoble, with the saints Gregorius, Marius and Papianus, Domitilla, Nereus and Achilleus below the miraculous image held by angels. Although Rubens declared the painting to

be his best work, both he and the Congregation found the light so unsatisfactory after its installation that he devised another version of the iconographic subject in three panels and submitted designs for it (probably at the beginning of the year 1608).

The present drawing is the design for the central panel, which represents the miraculous image adored by angels. A detailed sketch of the image with the flying angels, in the Pushkin Museum in Moscow, is far superior to the identical version in the Louvre. The oil sketch for the painting is in the Academy of Fine Arts in Vienna.

The present drawing shows the ingenious facility and inventive power of the master's sketches, which are jotted down in loose, apparently unsystematic strokes of the pen and accents of the brush, but which nevertheless convey a perfect idea of a well-balanced whole floating in light and atmosphere. Baroque art is fully and completely present here—earlier than in the works of the Italians. It is significant that the drawing is ahead of its time in its asymmetrical composition, which, however, in the oil sketches gives way to a greater symmetry more in accordance with the principles of the Late Renaissance.

149 PORTRAIT OF RUBENS' SON NICOLAS.
Black and white chalk, red chalk, brush and bistre in the eyes. Lower right in pen and bistre by a later hand: P P Rubbens, lower left in another later hand, obliterated inscription in leadpoint, of which only the date of 1621 is legible.
252 : 203 mm.
Inv. no. 17650 (L. 174).

Glück-Haberditzl, loc. cit. 116; Schönbrunner-Meder 435; M. Rooses, L'Oeuvre de P. P. Rubens, Anvers, 1892, no. 1520; J. S. Held, Rubens, Selected Drawings, London, 1959, no. 98, plate 100.

Exhibition: London, 1948, no. 69.

Used for the head of the Infant Christ in the painting of the Madonna and Child with Seven Holy Penitents, Gemäldegalerie, Kassel.

Nicolas, Rubens' second son by Isabella Brant, was born on March 3, 1618. Both the drawing and the altar painting for which the present study served as a model for the Infant Christ were presumed to date from about 1619. For the little St. John the Baptist in the same painting Rubens used a study of his elder son Albert, also in the Albertina (Glück-Haberditzl 117). It is true that in the present drawing, Nicolas already seems past the first years of childhood, and that eleven seems to be not too advanced an age for the boy portrayed in the other drawing, so that the old inscription (1621) may perhaps be correct.

The drawing is one of the finest portrait studies by Rubens, perhaps even the loveliest drawing of a child whatsoever, unsurpassed in the delicate peach-like softness of the cheeks and the golden fluff of the curls.

XIII Portrait of Susanna Fourment, the Artist's Sister-in-Law.
Black and white chalk, red chalk; eyes, eyebrows, and eyelashes strengthened with pen and brush in black-brown bistre. Along the upper margin, inscription in red chalk by the artist's own hand: suster van Hela Rubbens. Lower left in pencil by a later hand: no. 8, lower right seventeenth-century inscription in bistre by a hand also found on a number of other drawings from the artist's estate: P. P. Rubbens.
344 : 260 mm.
Inv. no. 17651 (L. 174).

Glück-Haberditzl, loc. cit. 162; Rooses, loc. cit. 1506; G. Glück, Rubens, Van Dyck und ihr Kreis, Vienna, 1933, p. 136 ff.

Exhibition: London, 1948, no. 71.

G. Glück assembled the portraits of Hélène Fourment's sister and discussed them in detail. Susanna Fourment was born in 1599. She married Raimondo Delmonte in 1617; her second husband, whom she married in 1622, was Rubens' friend Arnold Lundens. After Rubens' death, his son Albert married Clara Delmonte, her daughter by her first marriage. As many as seven portraits of Susanna painted by the artist were found in his estate. The artist's name was inscribed on this drawing and on no. 149 by a hand which sorted the drawings of the estate. The spirited young woman was evidently very close to Rubens, as her portraits date from the time when his first wife, Isabella Brant, was still alive and Hélène was still a child. There is a portrait drawing of Susanna of the same high quality as the present one in the Museum Boymans-Van Beuningen in Rotterdam (Glück-Haberditzl 161). Both drawings were made about 1625.

150 Costume Study for the Portrait of Hélène Fourment.
Black chalk, heightened with white bodycolor, the hand in red chalk.
400 : 288 mm.
Verso: Portrait of Hélène Fourment, three-quarter length figure (Glück-Haberditzl 232).
Inv. no. 8255.
Glück-Haberditzl, loc. cit. 233; Rooses, loc. cit. verso of 1540; G. Glück, Rubens, Van Dyck und ihr Kreis, Vienna, 1933, p. 133 ff.

Exhibition: London, 1948, no. 74.

Study for the painting representing Hélène Fourment, in the Collection of Baron Alphonse de Rothschild, Paris, R. Oldenbourg, P. P. Rubens, Klassiker der Kunst V, 425.
Glück dated the painting and the drawing in the master's last period: 1639. The vitality, simplicity and inner greatness, the mastery in the handling of color and light in this drawing justify the late date, as Rubens' art was a continuous climax right to the end. In the painting Hélène is represented leaving her house, followed by her little son Frans, and about to step into an approaching carriage. The expression of the movement is also fully captured by the drawing. Hélène is holding a handkerchief or a glove in her left hand, while the painting shows her gathering her wrap.
The drawing on the reverse is a sketch for a half-length portrait of Susanna Fourment (Leningrad, Hermitage), although the soft features, quite different from the sharp ones of the painting, make it seem more probable that Hélène was the model.

151 **SIR ANTHONY VAN DYCK**
Born Antwerp 1599, died London 1641.

The Arrest of Christ.
Pen and brush and bistre, touches of white bodycolor, the two lower corners damaged.
218 : 230 mm.
Inv. no. 17537 (L. 174).
Schönbrunner-Meder 696; J. Meder, Albertina-Facsimile, Handzeichnungen vlämischer und holländischer Meister des XV. bis XVII. Jahrhunderts, Vienna, 1923, plate 12; H. Rosenbaum, der junge Van Dyck, Thesis, Munich, 1928, p. 71; M. Delacre, loc. cit., p. 76, fig. 42; O. Benesch, Die Graphischen Künste, Vienna, 1938, N. F. 3, p. 19 ff.; O. Benesch, Jahrbuch der Kunsthistorischen Sammlungen in Wien 53 (1957), p. 32, fig. 25; H. Vey, Die Zeichnungen Van Dycks, Brussels, 1962, no. 83.

Exhibition: Antoon Van Dyck, Rubens Huis, Antwerp, 1960, Cat. no. 42.

Sketch for the painting formerly with Lord Methuen, Corsham Court, England (G. Glück, Van Dyck, Klassiker der Kunst, XIII, 1931, p. 70), a variation of the version in the Prado, Madrid.
In 1622 Van Dyck left the Netherlands for a sojourn of several years in Italy. Shortly before his departure the "Arrest of Christ" now in the Prado was made, a picture of which there exist two further versions by the artist's hand. It is a work full of passionate emotion, a dramatically agitated chiaroscuro composition which demonstrates the astounding mastery of the young artist at the height of his powers. There are a series of preparatory drawings for this painting which allow one to follow step by step the development from a horizontal to a vertical composition. The movement went first from right to left, with Judas standing on the right of Christ. In the present drawing the movement and the position of the group of Judas and Christ are reversed, a motif which became the essential feature of the painting. The final version appears

in a drawing in the Hamburg Kunsthalle. While the latter drawing stresses graphic accuracy and is provided with a grid of lines for transfer, it is in the present drawing that the impetuous flickering chiaroscuro comes to the fore. It models the hard, angular figures, which are so characteristic of Van Dyck's style of drawing, in a magnificent rhapsodic manner. The trees on the left were omitted by Van Dyck in the final version.

XIV Pentecost.
Pen and brush and bistre, washed, watercolor and white bodycolor. Signed lower left (illegible except for the word: Fecit).
340 : 260 mm.
Inv. no. 7574 (L. 174).
Provenance: P. H. Lankrink (L. 2090).
J. Meder, Albertina-Facsimile, Handzeichnungen vlämischer und holländischer Meister des XV. bis XVII. Jahrhunderts, Vienna, 1923, plate 13; J. Meder, Die Handzeichnung, Vienna, 1923, p. 636, fig. 315; J. Guiffrey, Antoine van Dyck, Paris, 1882, p. 34; G. Glück, Van Dyck, Klassiker der Kunst XIII, 1931, p. 525; H. Rosenbaum, Der junge Van Dyck, Thesis, Munich, 1928, p. 70; M. Delacre, Le dessin dans l'Oeuvre de Van Dyck, Académie Royale de Belgique, 2e reeks III, 1, Brussels, 1934, p. 118, fig. 64; A. J. J. Delen, Flämische Meisterzeichnungen des 17. Jahrhunderts, Basel, 1949, no. 29; M. Rooses, Onze Kunst II, Antwerp-Amsterdam, 1903, p. 136; H. Vey, Die Zeichnungen Van Dycks, Brussels, 1962, no. 66.

Exhibition: Antoon Van Dyck, Rubens Huis, Antwerp, 1960, Cat. no. 33.

Design for the painting in Potsdam, Schloss Sanssouci (G. Glück, Van Dyck, Klassiker der Kunst XIII, 1931, p. 56).
When Van Dyck had finished his apprenticeship with Van Balen, he worked independently for a short time (about 1615), but soon entered Rubens' workshop as an assistant. There Lord Arundel saw him as late as 1620. It was during these years that the painting of "Pentecost" originated. The artist created a number of designs in brush and pen for it. There are also two studies of details in black chalk for the apostles (Museum Plantin-Moretus, Antwerp, Delen, plate LXXII and Berlin, Bock-Rosenberg, plate 94). The present drawing is the most mature of all the known preparatory versions. Yet the painting shows a number of further alterations made by the artist in the course of his work. The ecstatic and expressive note, peculiar to the early Van Dyck, is emphasized more strongly in the drawing than in the painting.

152 Portrait of the Antwerp Painter Artus Wolfart.
Black chalk, brush and Indian ink.
281 : 175 mm.
Inv. no. 8659 (L. 174).
H. Vey, Die Zeichnungen Van Dycks, Brussels, 1962, no. 304.
Exhibition: Paris, 1950, no. 99.

Engraved by Cornelis Galle the Elder for the Iconography, the first edition of which was published by Martinus van den Enden in 1636, the second by Gillis Hendricx in 1645. F. Wibiral, L'Iconographie d'Antoine van Dyck d'après les recherches de H. Weber, Leipzig, 1877, no. 27; Wurzbach I, p. 466.

On his return from Italy in 1626 Van Dyck conceived the plan for an iconography of portraits of his famous contemporaries. The first edition contained 80 plates of engraved portraits. Eighteen portraits for the work were etched by the master himself; the others were made by contemporary engravers from the models he had drawn or painted in grisaille. The work is a testimonial of the growing historical and anthropological interest of the period. Along with portraits of statesmen, generals and princes of the Church, there are a considerable number of artists' portraits which are of particular interest to us. They convey a lively picture of the appearance of the leading exponents of this flowering of Flemish Baroque painting.
Artus Wolfart (1581—1641), a pupil of F. Francken, was a painter of religious history. His right hand, outlined in a telling gesture in the drawing, was omitted in the engraving.

PETER LELY (Pieter van der Faes)
Born Soest near Utrecht 1618, died London 1680.

153 Two British Heralds.
Black and white chalk on blue paper; inscribed in leadpoint: herauten (heralds); in pen and bistre, the numeral: 486.
513 : 274 mm. (a strip of paper 25 mm. wide originally added below).
Inv. no. 17594 (L. 174).

Provenance: Moriz v. Fries (L. 2903).

Schönbrunner-Meder 8 (as Van Dyck); J. Meder, Albertina-Facsimile, Handzeichnungen vlämischer und holländischer Meister des XV.—XVII. Jahrhunderts, Vienna, 1923, plate 16; F. Lugt, Jahrbuch der Preussischen Kunstsammlungen, 52, Berlin, 1931, p. 47; De Verzameling van Mr. Chr. P. van Eeghen, s' Rijksprentenkabinet, Amsterdam, 1958, p. 31; E. Croft-Murray and P. Hulton, Catalogue of British Drawings, London, British Museum, 1960, I, p. 409 ff.

Exhibition: London, 1948, no. 50.

On the coats are the three leopards and the fleur-de-lis of Britain, the harp of Ireland and the fleur-de-lis tressure of Scotland. This drawing belongs to a series of about thirty known studies representing figures at the ceremony of the Order of the Garter on St. George's Day (April 23rd). Sixteen of these drawings are in the British Museum, the remainder in other European and American collections.
The artist was Dutch by birth and a pupil of Frans Pietersz de Grebber in Haarlem. He was called to England in 1641 and settled there as a court portraitist. His style is so close to Van Dyck's that his fine drawings in black chalk on blue paper, like the present one, formerly often went under Van Dyck's name.

ARTUS QUELLINUS I
Born Antwerp 1609, died there 1668.

154 St. Peter with a Pair of Keys and a Cock, Embracing the Cross.
Oily chalk, heightened with white bodycolor on blue paper.
522 : 260 mm.
Inv. no. 8227 (L. 174).

Design for the statue of St. Peter in St. Andrew's Church at Antwerp, 1658 (J. Gabriels, Artus Quellien, Antwerp, 1930, plate XXXVI).

R. Oldenbourg, Peter Paul Rubens (Veröffentlichungen und Abhandlungen), Munich-Berlin, 1922, p. 198 and fig. 121; M. Rooses, L'Oeuvre de P. P. Rubens, no. 1455, pl. 411 (as Rubens).

As a work of the leading Flemish sculptor among Rubens' followers, this drawing gains special interest. Its technical medium was frequently used in the early drawings of Van Dyck. The drawing shows the figure still bound to the block in the manner of a high relief; in the finished work the sculptor completely freed it on all sides. The drawing further depicts St. Peter nude under his cloak, while in the sculpture he wears a long tunic.

THEODOR VAN THULDEN
Born Hertogenbosch 1606, died there 1669.

155 Cavaliers Departing.
Brush and bistre and watercolor, red and black chalk; the corners trimmed diagonally and restored.
287 : 397 mm.
Inv. no. 8912 (L. 174).

The scene corresponds to the iconographic scheme of the "Departure of the Prodigal Son", who is being given the farewell drink, although the genre element certainly dominates the biblical illustration. The garden portal before which the scene takes place is a replica of the central arch of the garden portal of Rubens' house at Antwerp.
As a pupil of Rubens the artist was not only employed on large decorative commissions like the Medici cycle and the triumphal arches for the entry of the Cardinal-Infant, he also developed, particularly in his sketches and genre pic-

tures like the present one, a highly individual note of his own. This spirited drawing is based on Rubens' genre pictures like the "Garden of Love" or the "Landscape with the Castle of Steen", which are modified by Mannerist elements derived from the art of Callot.

JACOB JORDAENS I
Born Antwerp 1593, died there 1678.

XV Mother with Baby and a Maidservant Holding a Candlestick.
Watercolor, brush and bistre and bodycolor over preparatory drawing in black and red chalk; the composition enlarged with pieces of paper added on upper, lower and right margins by the artist.
357 : 479 mm.
Inv. no. 15126 (L. 174).

Schönbrunner-Meder 725; R.-A. d'Hulst, De Tekeningen van Jacob Jordaens, Brussels, 1956, p. 331, no. 32; M. Rooses, Onze Kunst II (1903), p. 156; W. Bernt, Die Niederländischen Zeichner des 17. Jahrhunderts, Munich, 1957, I, no. and fig. 326.

In Jordaens' realistic art biblical story and genre painting blend without any noticeable boundaries. An early sketchy drawing by the master in pen and brush in the Siegfried Philippsohn Collection, New York (d'Hulst no. 21) depicts Mary with the Child, and Joseph and Anne by the light of a candle held by a young servant girl. Later, in the present watercolor, an independent picture in itself, he represented the Virgin with only the Child and the servant. Scenes by candle- or torch-light are part of the basic repertory of Caravaggesque painting in the Netherlands. A drawing in the Louvre closely related in subject and style was identified by F. Lugt in his catalogue (no. 722) as a study for the early painting in Warsaw and dated 1618—24. Yet like the present drawing it may also have been made later than the painting as a variation of it.

ADRIAEN BROUWER
Born Oudenaerde 1605 or 1606, died Antwerp 1638.

156 Scene in a Tavern.
Pen and bistre, washed with bistre and Indian ink.
140 : 183 mm.
Inv. no 9033 (L. 174).

J. Meder, Albertina-Facsimile, Handzeichnungen vlämischer und holländischer Meister des XV.—XVII. Jahrhunderts, plate 17; Wurzbach I, p. 198.

Design for the painting in the collection of Sir Hickman Bacon, W. v. Bode, A. Brouwer, Berlin, 1924, p. 156; G. Knuttel, A. Brouwer, The Hague, 1962, p. 113.

Brouwer grew out of the Bruegel tradition in Antwerp, but his removal to Holland and a stay in Haarlem (1626—31) brought him in touch with the art of Frans Hals, which led to a strong relationship with Dutch painting. On the other hand his genius as a painter and a draughtsman influenced the Dutch genre painters, for example, Ostade (see no. 187). After his return to Antwerp he became the leading influence in Flemish genre painting (Teniers, Craesbeeck). Brouwer was by far the most important Netherlandish peasant painter of the seventeenth century. Even Rembrandt owned some of his works. He combines the exuberant vitality and monumentality of the Flemish with the sketchy terseness and psychological acuteness of Frans Hals.

JACOB PYNAS
Born Haarlem, 1597 in Amsterdam, mentioned there until 1643, signed works until 1648.

157 Wooded Mountain Road with a View of a Castle on the Water and a Lake in the Distance.
Pen and bistre, some watercolor.
218 : 311 mm.
Inv. no. 8332 (L. 174).

Old inventory: Roelant Savery.
C. Müller and J. Q. Van Regteren Altena, Jahrbuch der Preussischen Kunstsammlungen 52 (1931), p. 197, fig. 44 and p. 199.

Exhibition: Die holländische Landschaft im Zeitalter Rembrandts, Vienna, Albertina, 1936, no. 1.

Elsheimer found a group of followers among the Dutch who as the generation of Rembrandt's teachers gained special importance. The brothers Jan and Jacob Pynas belonged to this group; the latter, along with Lastman, is mentioned as Rembrandt's teacher.

The present drawing is a typical example of the composed, Italianate landscape derived from Elsheimer. The peculiarly pointillist rhythm of the pen technique was anticipated in the landscape sketches of the Haarlem academicians. It reached its climax in the landscape drawings and etchings of Seghers, Buytewech, and the early Van de Veldes, and even determined the graphic aspect of many woodland representations by Vroom (see no. 167).

HENDRIK AVERCAMP
Born Amsterdam 1585, died Kampen after 1663.

158 Canal with Sail Boats in the Vicinity of Amsterdam.
Pen and bistre, and watercolor.
179 : 257 mm.
Inv. no. 8591 (L. 174).

Exhibition: Die holländische Landschaft im Zeitalter Rembrandts, Vienna, Albertina, 1936, no. 3.

The 1580's and 1590's saw the birth of the generation of artists who brought about the definitive change from the composed, Italianate landscape to the true rendering of Dutch landscape and life. Arent Arentz, Cl. J. Visscher, and Hendrik Avercamp were the eldest among them. Their development, in which drawing and etching played a special part, took place mainly in Amsterdam. Avercamp, called "de Stomme van Kampen", because he was deaf-and-dumb and had settled at Kampen, was a pupil of the Late Mannerist Pieter Isaacsz in Amsterdam in 1607. He may also have been influenced by the emigrant Flemish landscape painters who had settled in Amsterdam. Yet his works and those of his contemporaries mark the beginning of a new trend in art which strove to mirror the real world and so gained outstanding national and sociological importance. It is the hour of the birth of the unique Dutch art of the seventeenth century.

Avercamp's watercolors with their gay tints, which, however, are still set within a tonal unity, give a homely picture of life on land and water in old Holland.

ESAIAS VAN DE VELDE I
Born Amsterdam about 1591, died The Hague 1630.

159 Landscape with a Ruined Tower and Pilgrims.
Black chalk. Signed and dated: E. V. Velde. 1624.
192 : 303 mm.
Inv. no. 8682.

Exhibition: Die holländische Landschaft im Zeitalter Rembrandts, Vienna, Albertina, 1936, no. 5.

The strongest impulse in the new art of landscape painting emanated from Haarlem, once the seat of the Late Mannerist academicians, even though artists like Esaias and his cousin Jan van de Velde (see no. 164) spent only part of their lives in this city. In the circle of the great portraitist Frans Hals there developed not only a new kind of genre picture, but also a new landscape painting. In both categories W. Buytewech (see no. 161) gained special importance; he had a decisive influence on both Esaias and Jan van de Velde, who painted and etched not only landscapes, but genre subjects as well.

The numerous landscape drawings of the Van de Veldes render a plain and unadorned picture of the Dutch countryside. Yet motifs and pictorial elements are chosen and combined in a manner as deliberate as it is inconspicuous so that they embody the principles of Early Baroque composition.

BARTHOLOMEUS BREENBERGH
Born Deventer about 1599-1600, died Amsterdam 1659.

160 Group of Houses Erected on the Ruins of a Wall in the Vicinity of Rome.

Pen and brush and bistre, washed. Signed and dated at lower left: Bartholomeus Breenberch. ANo 1627.
243 : 329 mm.
Inv. no. 9366 (L. 174).

G. Naumann, Die Landschaftszeichnungen des B. Breenbergh (Thesis, Heidelberg 1933).

Another drawing of the same subject in a German private collection was published by W. Bernt, Die Niederländischen Zeichner des 17. Jahrhunderts I, no. 124; E. Knab, Jahrbuch der Kunsthistorischen Sammlungen 56, Vienna, 1960, pp. 99, 100.

Breenbergh sojourned in Rome from 1619 to 1629. The Netherlandish landscape painters working in Italy at this time not only created fantastic compositions, but also tried in their drawings to render a true picture of the southern scenery surrounding them. A drawing like the present one could only have originated face to face with nature. The draughtsman has sought out a quiet corner on the outskirts of Rome where picturesque little houses had established themselves on the ruins of an ancient wall. The concept of the "picturesque" appears here for the first time as a selected motif. In an effective contrast the artist makes the houses stand out in dazzling sunshine behind the shadow zone of the foreground. Although observed in nature, this strong contrast of light and shade is typical of Baroque art and also occurs in religious figure painting.

Breenbergh was a friend of Paul Bril. His Italian landscape studies are closely related to those of Cornelis van Poelenburgh.

WILLEM BUYTEWECH
Born Rotterdam 1591-92, died there 1624.

161 Portrait Sketch of a Seated Lady, Full Length.
Pen and brush and Indian ink, washed, over preparatory drawing in black chalk; lower left, later inscription: F. Hals.
186 : 123 mm.
Inv. no. 8402 (L. 174).

Old inventory: Frans Hals.

In the Albertina catalogued as Buytewech since F. Lugt's correct attribution in 1924. In the earlier inventory listed as Frans Hals.

Wurzbach I, p. 640 (Frans Hals); E. Haverkamp-Begemann, Wilhelm Buytewech, Amsterdam, 1959, no. 65. .

The present drawing is a masterly example of the work of this most ingenious artist who started out under the influence of Frans Hals. Buytewech excelled first and foremost as an etcher and draughtsman who was equally conversant with historical illustration and allegory, genre and landscape painting. All his works reveal a direct relationship to nature, as in this portrait where he placed his model in bright sunlight, so that it is modeled by the shadows of the body and of the room — an anticipation of Rembrandt's technique in handling light. Problems of light, atmosphere, and color, which make every object part of a comprehensive whole, begin to play an increasing part in Dutch drawing. The strokes of the pen and the accents of the brush are spirited and light as in Hals' paintings, apparently unrelated but actually connected by light and atmosphere. On the basis of the costume this sheet is to be dated in the 1620's.

WILLEM CORNELISZ DUYSTER
Born Amsterdam 1598-99, died there 1635.

162 Theorbo Player.
Red chalk.
159 : 144 mm.
Inv. no. 13074 (L. 174).

Old inventory: Velazquez. Attribution by the present author. W. C. Duyster was probably a pupil of Pieter Codde and as such a typical painter of Amsterdam "company pieces" at the time when this branch of painting flourished in Haarlem. No drawings of his have so far come to light. The attribution of this drawing is made by the present author on the basis of a comparison with his paintings. A characteristic feature of the artist is the keen and steep incidence of light (it is sometimes artificial) and the low point of vision, which give his figures a lean, elongated appearance: their expression is one of melancholy, even ecstatic earnestness, a somewhat unexpected quality in a painter of mundane society, and one which lends his works a highly personal note. His paintings, which are not very numerous, are always of high quality. All these features are encountered in the present drawing, which creates the impression of a direct transposition of a Duyster painting into drawing. Very probably Duyster was one of the first teachers of Terborch (see no. 200), whose early works are still imbued with the mood of his paintings.

GERRIT CLAES BLECKER (Bleker)
Mentioned in Haarlem from 1628 to 1656.

163 Carriage with Two Ladies Followed by a Horseman with Greyhounds.
Pen and bistre, washed with Indian ink over preparatory drawing in leadpoint; lower center signed in pen and bistre: blecker; lower left the name repeated in pencil at a later date; upper left the numeral 66.
190 : 288 mm.
Inv. no. 10182 (L. 174).

Wurzbach I, p. 104; W. Bernt, Die niederländischen Zeichner des 17. Jahrhunderts I, no. 68.

As a painter Blecker represented in Haarlem the Caravaggesque realism of Elsheimer's stamp. But this most ingenious study of a group observed amid the activity of a main road is more in the vein of Callot and Buytewech. It is a delightful Dutch counterpart of Van Thulden's "Cavaliers' Excursion on Horseback" (no. 155), but more matter-of-fact and closer to reality, a delight for the historian of culture.

JAN VAN DE VELDE II
Born Rotterdam 1593, died Enkhuizen 1641.

164 Landscape with Herds and Two Wayfarers Resting, in the Background the Ruins of a Castle.
Pen and bistre.
101 : 314 mm.
Inv. no. 8084.

J. G. van Gelder, Jan van de Velde, s'Gravenhage 1933, no. 69, fig. 26.

Exhibition: Die holländische Landschaft im Zeitalter Rembrandts, Albertina, Vienna, 1936, no. 6.

Compare the title-page of the series of landscapes, Original Etchings of 1616, published by C. J. Visscher (D. Franken—J. P. van der Kellen, L'Oeuvre de Jan van de Velde, Amsterdam—Paris, 1883, no. 295).

In this drawing and in another closely related one in the Albertina, probably intended as a companion piece (Inv. no. 8083), the artist has tried to capture the boundless breadth of the Dutch landscape by choosing a new and unusual format, one he also used for his etchings. The way in which the gentle progression of the lines of the terrain creates a slight, but irresistible movement from the right foreground to the left background is remarkable. In the same manner the strokes of the pen diminish in strength so that the delicate outlines of the castle ruins appear like a mirage on the horizon. This mastery of spatial illusion prepares the way for Rembrandt's landscape etchings. The close resemblance of both Albertina drawings to Buytewech's work has occasionally led to their attribution to this artist. The calligraphic precision of line clearly reveals that Jan van de Velde grew up in the tradition of Late Mannerist engraving at Haarlem. He was a pupil of Jacob Matham.

JAN JOSEPHSZ VAN GOYEN
Born Leiden 1596, died The Hague 1656.

165 The Beach of Egmond aan Zee.
Black chalk, washed with Indian ink.
163 : 288 mm.
Inv. no. 17538 (L. 174).

Van Goyen's most important period of apprenticeship was with Esaias van de Velde, whose works obviously influenced his early paintings. Similarly, Esaias' technique of drawing in chalk (see no. 159) is continued in Van Goyen's drawings. But Van Goyen added a new note: a closer connection with the optical picture of reality and a stronger rejection of "landscape recipes". The tonal unity of atmosphere which is so characteristic of his paintings also prevails in his drawings, where wash is frequently added to chalk. Van Goyen initiated the reduction of the human figure in landscape to an effective cipher, a process which eventually led to Canaletto's and Guardi's "vedute" and could be called "impressionism", though the basic structure of the lively little figures is completely Baroque.
The scene is the beach of Egmond aan Zee, which Van Goyen also represented repeatedly in his paintings.

SIMON JAKOBSZ DE VLIEGER
Born Rotterdam about 1600, died Weesp 1653.

166 Northern Fjord Landscape.
Black chalk, washed with light Indian ink; lower left signed: S DE VLIEGER.
186 : 297 mm.
Inv. no. 9167 (L. 174).

Although this artist frequently changed his place of residence, there is no evidence that he ever visited Scandinavia. Everdingen (see no. 191) undertook a journey to Sweden and Norway shortly after 1640 and introduced the popular northern motifs into Dutch landscape art. The present drawing may possibly have originated under their influence. De Vlieger was first and foremost a marine painter who was influenced by Porcellis (see no. 168). That an arm of the sea with sea-going ships should be dammed off by a wooden barrier against an inland body of water with a lower level is contrary to all hydrographic probability. This therefore seems to be a free composition rather than a study from nature.

CORNELIS HENDRICKSZ VROOM
Born Haarlem about 1591, died there 1661.

167 View from an Enclosure into the Interior of a Forest.
Pen and bistre. Signed on the horizontal board of the fence: VROOM.
286 : 302 mm.
Inv. no. 8168 (L. 174).

Schönbrunner-Meder 843; Wurzbach II, p. 833; J. Rosenberg, Jahrbuch der Preussischen Kunstsammlungen 49 (1928), p. 110, no. 9.

Exhibition: Die holländische Landschaft im Zeitalter Rembrandts, Albertina, Vienna, 1936, no. 11.

The artist was probably a pupil of his father, the marine painter Hendrik Cornelisz Vroom. Together with the Van de Veldes and Buytewech, he was one of the most important representatives of early landscape painting in Haarlem. Among his finest works are the drawings of woodland scenery, of which the Albertina owns three; there is a fourth in the Hamburg Print Room. For the pointillist technique of the pen drawings, see the note to no. 157.
When Vroom created these forest pieces, Jacob van Ruisdael was probably his pupil and received vital inspiration from his teacher's works of this kind.

PIETER JANSZ SAENREDAM
Born Assendelft 1597, died Haarlem 1665.

XVI Interior of the Groote Kerk at Alkmaar with a View towards the Organ.
Pen and bistre, washed with Indian ink and watercolored; on the back of the choir-stalls inscription in the artist's own hand: Anno 1661, in de Maent Maij, heb ick Pr, Saenredam dese teeckening tot Alkmaer in de kerck gemaeckt.
453 : 605 mm.
Inv. no. 15129 (L. 174).

Schönbrunner-Meder 1009; Wurzbach II, p. 547; J. Six, Bulletin van den Nederlandschen Oudheidkundigen Bond 2. Serie, III, 1910, pp. 18—25; M. D. Henkel, Le dessin hollandais, Paris, 1931, p. 63.

Exhibition: Pieter Jansz Saenredam, Utrecht, Centraal Museum, no. 3, fig. 2.

The present watercolor and the view of the interior of St. Mary's Church at Utrecht in the local Gemeente Archief there, are probably the two most impressive drawings of this great architectural painter which have been preserved. He was the son of Jan Pietersz Saenredam, an important Late Mannerist engraver of the Goltzius school. Following the Netherlandish painters' inclination towards thematic specialization, he became the most important architectural painter Holland had in the first half of the seventeenth century. Like the landscape painters, he sought to give an accurate picture of optical reality. In so doing he followed mathematically precise perspective calculations and also had recourse to geometrical construction. This, however, was not an end in itself. He strove to achieve the representation of an enclosed space flooded with light, whose bounding surfaces are of a shimmering transparency. He was one of the most amazing plein-air painters of interiors. This watercolor is the basis for a painting now in the Stedelijk Museum at Alkmaar. During the same visit to Alkmaar he created on May 27 and 28, 1661, a watercolor drawing of the big organ with its wings thrown open (Albertina Inv. no. 8566). The instrument was the work of the organ-building brothers van Hagerbeer and the architect Jacob van Campen. Saenredam, who visited Alkmaar several times during the 1630's, drew an elevation of the front of the organ for the architect.

JAN PORCELLIS I
Born Ghent about 1584, died Soeterwonde near Leiden 1632.

168 Beach with a Signal Post and Fishing Boats, at Low Tide.
Black chalk, pen and bistre, washed with Indian ink.
86 : 143 mm.
Inv. no. 8583 (L. 174).
Wurzbach II, p. 346.

The artist, a native of Flanders, received his most significant inspiration in Haarlem and Amsterdam. He was the most important marine painter of the early period. Rembrandt thought highly of him and owned some of his works. Like Van Goyen (see no. 165) he progressed from the bright color scheme of the older naturalists to a tonal unity of space. It is remarkable how he succeeds in rendering the mood of a quiet gray day by the sea through the monochrome medium of drawing. A signal post and the masts of the sail boats are used as measurements of distance. The thickening and thinning of the line of the horizon and the slightest elevations of the ground are sufficient to create an impression of unlimited depth. A scarcely noticeable spatial movement runs diagonally to the right towards the point of vision.

PHILIPS KONINCK (Koning)
Born Amsterdam 1619, died there 1688.

169 Landscape with Dunes, a Farm House and a Windmill, on the left a Manor House by a Pond.
Pen and bistre, washed, on brownish paper; upper left collector's number in pencil: 29.
98 : 183 mm.
Inv. no. 9358 (L. 174).
H. Gerson, Philips Koninck, Berlin, 1936, p. 147, Z. 82; Wurzbach I, p. 325; Kunstmuseets Aarskrift XVI—XVIII (1931), p. 140.
Sale S. Feitama, Amsterdam, October 16, 1758, Kunstb. I, no. 83.

Exhibition: Die holländische Landschaft im Zeitalter Rembrandts, Albertina, Vienna, 1936, no. 52.

Philips Koninck was the most important landscape painter among the inner circle of the pupils of Rembrandt, in whose studio he worked during the second half of the 1630's. He became famous through those of his paintings which give a wide panoramic view of the Dutch plain. He imbued them with a powerful, one might almost say "global", spatial effect by piling the various zones of distance on top of each other like slightly curved friezes, thereby producing the impression of the curved surface of the earth. Even a modest motif like the windmill in the present drawing becomes the center of a circular spatial development, ebbing away towards the horizon in ever flatter curves. Rembrandt's etchings were the models for spatial effects of this kind.

REMBRANDT HARMENSZ VAN RIJN
Born Leiden 1606, died Amsterdam 1669.

170 An Elephant.
Black chalk; signed and dated: Rembrandt ft. 1637.
233 : 355 mm.
Inv. no. 17558 (L. 174).
O. Benesch, The Drawings of Rembrandt, vol. I—VI, London, 1954—57, no. 457; C. Hofstede de Groot, Die Handzeichnungen Rembrandts, Haarlem, 1906, no. 1469; Schönbrunner-Meder 263; C. Neumann, Rembrandts Handzeichnungen, Munich, 1919, no. 19; O. Benesch, Rembrandt, Werk und Forschung, Vienna, 1935, p. 28; J. Rosenberg, Rembrandt, Cambridge, Mass., 1948, p. 154 and London, 1964, p. 261, fig. 226; O. Benesch, Rembrandt as a Draughtsman, London, 1960, p. 20, fig. 27; Great Drawings of All Time, New York, 1962, II, no. 578 (J. G. v. Gelder).
Exhibitions: Rembrandt Tentoonstelling, Rijksmuseum, Amsterdam, 1935, no. 42; London, 1948, no. 54; Paris, 1950, no. 105; Rembrandt, Nationalmuseum, Stockholm, 1956, no. 89; Rembrandt Tentoonstelling, Museum Boymans, Rotterdam-Rijksmuseum, Amsterdam, 1956, no. 67; Rembrandt, Albertina, Vienna, 1956, no. 28.

Rembrandt excelled not only in his own main spheres — religious narrative and portraiture — but in all the others in which Dutch painters used to specialize; he surpassed all the specialists including the animal painters, even though in this area there were great masters like Potter.
In 1637 he made several drawings of elephants, for which a traveling menagerie probably furnished the models. The present example is the best of them. It is admirable how Rembrandt with loosely executed chalk strokes characterizes not only the external appearance of the animal, its thick, wrinkled silver-gray hide, but also its inner nature, the slow, deliberate movements and the cunning look in its small eyes. The elephant was included in a religious work: it appears in the background of the etching "Adam and Eve" of 1638, Bartsch 28.

171 Portrait of Baldassare Castiglione.
Pen and bistre, some white bodycolor.

Inscribed and dated 1639 by the artist's own hand, above left and right: de Conte batasar de Kastijlyone von raefael / verkooft voor 3500 gulden; below: het geheel caergesoen tot Luke van Nuffeelen / hefd gegolden f 59456 :—: Ano 1639 (Count Balthasar Castiglione by Raphael sold for 3500 florins / the whole shipload of Lucas van Nuffeelen brought 59456 florins. In the year 1639).

163 : 207 mm.
Inv. no. 8859 (L. 174).

A drawing after Raphael's painting (about 1519) in the Louvre, Paris, which was brought to Amsterdam by Lucas van Uffelen. It was sold there on April 9, 1639, at an auction at which Rembrandt apparently was present. He used the pose for his etched self-portrait, also dated 1639, A. Bartsch, Catalogue raisonné de toutes les estampes ... de Rembrandt, Vienna, 1797, no. 21; A. M. Hind, A Catalogue of Rembrandt's Etchings, London, 1923, no. 168.

Benesch loc. cit. 451; Hofstede de Groot loc. cit. 1430; W. R. Valentiner, Rembrandt, Des Meisters Handzeichnungen, Klassiker der Kunst 31, 32, no. 626 B; Schönbrunner-Meder 324; Benesch, Werk und Forschung, pp. 27, 28; J. Rosenberg, Rembrandt, Cambridge, Mass., 1948, I, p. 27 and London, 1964, p. 42; O, Benesch, Rembrandt as a Draughtsman, London, 1960, p. 19, fig. 33.

Exhibitions: Rembrandt Tentoonstelling, Rijksmuseum, Amsterdam, 1935, no. 46; Paris, 1950, no. 107; Rembrandt, Nationalmuseum, Stockholm, 1956, no. 94; Rembrandt Tentoonstelling, Museum Boymans, Rotterdam-Rijksmuseum, Amsterdam, 1956, no. 91; Rembrandt, Albertina, Vienna, 1956, no. 43.

Rembrandt, the most universal artist of his era, had a closer relationship with the art of other centuries and nations than any of his contemporaries. He was particularly attracted by the great classic masters of the Renaissance, but ancient and medieval art also greatly fascinated him. This instantaneous sketch after Raphael's "Castiglione" — perhaps made from memory, as it varies considerably from the original — demonstrates how Rembrandt at once creatively transformed his models, even if they were works of art. He has in this instance approximated his own likeness, and the drawing in its turn influenced the etched self-portrait of the same year. Rembrandt's keen interest in ancient art was the reason for his enthusiastic activity as a collector. It was indulgence beyond his means that contributed to his financial débâcle in 1657. His judgement as a connoisseur was widely sought, and he was a constant visitor at art auctions in Amsterdam.

172　Self-Portrait.
Pen and bistre, the paper slightly tinted with Indian ink, only the cap left free.
84 : 71 mm.
Inv. no. 25449 (acquired 1927).

Benesch loc. cit. 1177; Valentiner loc. cit. 667; Benesch, Werk und Forschung, p. 65; Benesch, Mitteilungen der Gesellschaft für vervielfältigende Kunst 55 (1932), p. 30.

Exhibitions: Rembrandt Tentoonstelling, Rijkmuseum, Amsterdam, 1935, no. 92; Paris, 1950, no. 127; Rembrandt, Nationalmuseum, Stockholm, 1956, no. 187; Rembrandt Tentoonstelling, Museum Boymans, Rotterdam-Rijksmuseum, Amsterdam, 1956, no. 244; Rembrandt, Albertina, Vienna, 1956, no. 140.

In 1660 Rembrandt painted the "Self-Portrait with the Easel" in the Louvre. Preparatory for this painting is this little sketch which the author discovered as an unidentified work on the art market many years ago. The edge of the easel appears as a dark line at the right edge of the small sheet. The painting most movingly manifests the inner greatness of the artist who suffered grievously from the adversities of fate, yet remained unbroken in his artistic power. Although the drawing is small in size, the spiritual force emanating from it is enormous. Its lines are drawn, as in the late landscapes, in incoherent pen strokes, yet they create an almost uncanny effect of totality and reality. The eyes are like black coals; their absorbing depth casts a magic spell over the spectator. The light effects of the painting are already indicated; the strongest light falls on the white linen cap. It may therefore be assumed that the gray tint of Indian ink was applied by Rembrandt himself. In the course of this process the paper became soft and rough in spots (e. g., between the head and the easel). An impression of darkness surging around the figure was thereby created, and received its final pictorial form in the painting.

The greatness of an artist can be judged by the force with which he compels the onlooker to enter into a dialogue, into an exchange of questions and answers from man to man. This compulsion is with no artist of modern times as strong as it is with Rembrandt. A small sheet of paper like the present one often reveals this quality even more strongly than a large painting.

173　Beggar Family with a Dog.
Black chalk.
105 : 100 mm.
Inv. no. 8839 (L. 174).

Benesch, loc. cit. 751; Hofstede de Groot loc. cit. 1456; Benesch, Werk und Forschung, p. 41.

Exhibitions: Rembrandt Tentoonstelling, Rijksmuseum, Amsterdam, 1935, no. 61; Rembrandt, Albertina, Vienna, 1956, no. 77.

While Rembrandt's drawings from the 1630's (nos. 170, 171, XVII) derive their effect from strong Baroque contrasts, his work undergoes a complete change about 1648. Its outward aspect becomes quieter, more subdued, more balanced; its human experience and inner significance gain in depth.

The present drawing is a telling example of this change. A beggar family with its little dog is wandering along the road. The movement of the group pushes almost perpendicularly into the depth of the space so that all Baroque diagonals are avoided. The group has the shape of a block, which appears to the onlooker as the plane of a relief. The chalk traces only basic lines and avoids hatchings as much as possible. Space is rendered solely by the white surface of the paper. But how very clear is the expression of movement, of the exhausting, eternal travel along an unending road! How close is the bond with the atmosphere, which causes the figures to appear veiled in a slight haze, as if they were plunged in mist. The mature Rembrandt conceals and hints rather than raises his voice pathetically as in his earlier works. The figures turn their backs on us, but by doing so they tell us all the more plainly of the burden of poverty and of the sad fate of the homeless, condemned to eternal wandering without rest or repose.

The drawing was probably made about the same time as the etching entitled "The Beggar at the Door", Bartsch 176, dated 1648, to which it is closely related in style.

XVII　Young Woman at her Toilet.
Pen and bistre, washed with bistre and Indian ink.
233 : 180 mm.
Inv. no. 8825 (L. 174).

Benesch loc. cit. 395; Hofstede de Groot loc. cit. 1453; Valentiner loc. cit. 682; Schönbrunner-Meder 215; J. Meder, Albertina-Facsimile, Handzeichnungen flämischer und holländischer Meister des XV.—XVII. Jahrhunderts, Vienna, 1923, plate 21; O. Benesch, Werk und Forschung pp. 16, 22; J. Rosenberg, Rembrandt, Cambridge, Mass., 1948, p. 212; London, 1964, p. 340, fig. 280; O. Benesch, Rembrandt as a Draughtsman, London, 1960, no. 6.

Exhibitions: Rembrandt Tentoonstelling, Rijksmuseum, Amsterdam, 1935, no. 36; De Jérôme Bosch à Rembrandt (F. Schmidt Degener), Palais des Beaux-Arts, Brussels, 1937 to 1938, no. 68; London, 1948, no. 59; Paris, 1950, no. 103; Rembrandt, Nationalmuseum, Stockholm, 1956, no. 75; Rembrandt Tentoonstelling, Museum Boymans, Rotterdam-Rijksmuseum, Amsterdam, 1956, no. 33; Rembrandt, Albertina, Vienna, 1956, no. 11.

Rembrandt, who in 1632 had settled in Amsterdam in the course of his work on the "Anatomy of Dr. Tulp", diligently applied himself not only to his portrait commissions and religious representations, but also to drawing from the model. Everyday life inside and outside the house furnished him with the models which pass before our eyes in a wealth of studies from the early 1630's. These in turn provided Rembrandt with the inspiration for his representations of religious and profane history. The present drawing is one of the finest of this kind. It is not impossible that it inspired the 1632 painting "Bathsheba at her Toilet" in the National Gallery of Ottawa. The model in this case was probably Rembrandt's sister Lisbeth, whose features can be recognized in the painting. It has also been supposed that Saskia was the model of the drawing; if so, this could only have been after the artist's marriage (July 10, 1634).

In the first stage, the drawing was sketched with the pen. Then with quick, sure strokes of the brush the master rounded out the group into a picture. He makes the group stand out in bright light; the contrasting effect is intensified by the shadows of the bodies and the cast shadows, enlivened by reflections on the left, and the shadows of the room on the right. Originally he painted the latter in gray Indian ink over which he later spread the richer and darker bistre.

174　"Het Molentje", Seen from the Amstel Dike.
Pen and bistre, washed.
96 : 213 mm; on the right a strip of paper, 26 mm wide, added by the artist.
Inv. no. 8870 (L. 174).

Benesch loc. cit. 1354; Hofstede de Groot loc. cit. 1494; Benesch, Werk und Forschung, p. 57.

Exhibitions: Rembrandt Tentoonstelling, Rijksmuseum, Amsterdam, 1935, no. 85; Die holländische Landschaft im Zeitalter Rembrandts, Albertina, Vienna, 1936, no. 42; Paris, 1950, no. 124; Rembrandt, Nationalmuseum, Stockholm, 1956, no.143; Rembrandt Tentoonstelling, Museum Boymans, Rotterdam-Rijksmuseum, Amsterdam, 1956, no. 195; Rembrandt, Albertina, Vienna, 1956, no. 110.

From the second half of the 1630's onward, Rembrandt consistently drew Dutch landscapes from nature. About 1650 his output of landscape studies increased to a new high that was maintained until the middle of the decade. It was on long walks to the outskirts of Amsterdam, the itinerary of which F. Lugt has successfully traced in his book "Wandelingen med Rembrandt", that the artist set down his impressions. Among his favorite motifs was the river Amstel with its popular excursion spots. One of these was a group of houses with an inn and a windmill called "Het Molentje", a popular place for outings with the inhabitants of Amsterdam. It appears in a number of Rembrandt's pen drawings.

This is one of his most mature drawings, made about 1654—55. All of Rembrandt's late landscape studies were drawn with the reed pen, which permitted him to develop a sort of shorthand, a telegraphic style of drawing in short, intermittent lines and dots, with scratches of the semi-dry pen which impart a strong atmospheric vibration to the surface of the paper. A few additional brush tones fully conjure up the mood of the time of day and of the weather. The unpretentious simplicity of the representation produces an effect of reality impossible to surpass. The breath of Nature itself seems to have been caught.

JAN LIEVENS
Born Leiden 1607, died Amsterdam 1674.

175 The Departure of Lot and his Family from Sodom.
Pen and brush and bistre over preparatory drawing in black chalk.
204 : 162 mm.
Inv. no. 9547 (L. 174).

Provenance: Charles, Prince de Ligne (Cat. p. 215, no. 1, as "Gerbrand van den Eeckhout").

Attribution by the author.

Lievens, like Rembrandt a pupil of Pieter Lastman, was in his early days in Leiden (up to 1631) a comrade of Rembrandt, who worked with him in a common workshop. Their relationship was one of mutual inspiration. Thus Lievens' early work from his Leiden period clearly shows features which we find in Rembrandt's early drawings, particularly the shallow relief of the body achieved by the fine and heavy strokes of the brittle pen, and the modeling by granular dots. The fluctuating chiaroscuro effect, produced by a combination of chalk and wash, is familiar to us from other early drawings of Lievens, e. g., from the "Presentation in the Temple" in the Louvre (included by F. Lugt in his Rembrandt catalogue under no. 1126, but with reservation of the decision between Lievens and Rembrandt).

FERDINAND BOL
Born Dordrecht 1616, died Amsterdam 1680.

176 Marcus Curius Dentatus Refusing the Samnites' Gifts.
Pen and bistre, washed, and brush and Indian ink over preparatory drawing in black chalk.
384 : 323 mm (L. 174).
Inv. no. 9554.

Schönbrunner-Meder 958 (as Gerbrand van den Eeckhout); Wurzbach I, p. 483; H. Schneider, Jahrbuch der Preussischen Kunstsammlungen 47 (1926), p. 79 and fig. 7.

Attribution by G. Falck.

Design for a painting in the Amsterdam Town Hall. The ceremonial chambers of the Amsterdam Town Hall, which was built by Jacob van Campen and dedicated in 1655, were by decision of the town council to be decorated with paintings representing examples of Roman civic virtue and scenes from national history. The realization that Rembrandt's school was especially proficient in historical painting led the town council to commission its representatives Bol and Flinck to paint scenes from Roman history for the mantle-pieces in the Mayor's room.

The present drawing is Bol's design for one of them. It depicts Marcus Curius Dentatus at his meal of turnips, rejecting the attempt of the Samnites to bribe him. The Roman milieu which the classicists of the Baroque strove to introduce into their paintings with faithful accuracy has been ruthlessly transformed in terms of Dutch realism: Marcus Curius sits by the fireplace like an old pater familias or biblical patriarch. Perhaps this was the reason why Bol's design was never executed. In its stead is a painting by Flinck.

JACOB ADRIAENSZ BACKER
Born Haerlingen, Friesland, 1608, died Amsterdam 1651.

177 Self-Portrait.
Black chalk; inscription in pen and bistre by the artist's own hand: Jacob A. Backer / fecit 1638. / In Vlissingen.
143 : 147 mm.
Inv. no. 9038 (L. 174).

Provenance: v. Neale; C. Ploos van Amstel; v. d. Schley. Wurzbach I, p. 40, no. 3; K. Bauch, Jacob Adriaensz Backer, Berlin, n. d., no. 59, and plate 1 (frontispiece).

Etched in the original size in the same direction by A. Bartsch with the inscription: Jacobus de Backer, but without Backer's own inscription on the drawing; F. de Bartsch, Catalogue des Estampes de J. Adam Bartsch, Vienna, 1818, p. 29, no. 65.

Backer was Rembrandt's oldest Amsterdam pupil and probably entered his studio immediately after the master settled there. Previously he had been studying with the painter Lambert Jacobsz at Leeuwarden. He was first and foremost an important portraitist, excelling in the lively human characterization of his models. It is in this capacity that the present drawing shows him. Technically he follows Rembrandt's early drawing style from his transitional Leiden-Amsterdam period. The relief of the fine and heavy strokes, the delight in rounded curves and flourishes still reveal the indirect connection with Callot.

GOVAERT FLINCK
Born Cleve 1615, died Amsterdam 1660.

178 Young Girl Sewing, Half-Length.
Black and white chalk on blue paper; signed upper right corner: G. Flinck, f.
291 : 252 mm.
Inv. no. 9327 (L. 174).

Schönbrunner-Meder 259; Wurzbach I, p. 538.

Like Backer (see no. 177), Flinck began his career as a pupil of Lambert Jacobsz at Leeuwarden before entering Rembrandt's Amsterdam studio. Perhaps Backer persuaded him to join him in his change of studio. He studied with Rembrandt from about 1632 to 1635, at the same time as Bol (see no. 176) and Jan Victors. They all belonged to the first generation of Rembrandt's Amsterdam disciples.

Among Rembrandt's disciples Flinck was the most vigorous and direct realist in the human sense. He was therefore given the lion's share in the decoration of the new Amsterdam Town Hall, a commission which was interrupted by his early death. He adhered most consistently to the style of the Italian Renaissance artists and the followers of Caravaggio. His masterly drawings, carried out, like the present one, in black and white chalk on colored paper, continue in some ways the tradition of the great Venetian masters. They combine a highly accurate, yet pictorially broadly-conceived depiction of reality with Dutch contemplation.

As a distinguished and wealthy Amsterdam citizen, Flinck was also an important collector who at the auction of Rembrandt's property was able to acquire a great many of his finest drawings.

GERBRAND VAN DEN EECKHOUT
Born Amsterdam 1621, died there 1674.

179 A Boy Standing behind a Chair.
Brush and bistre, some preparatory drawing in chalk.
182 : 147 mm.
Inv. no. 9559 (L. 174).

Schönbrunner-Meder 1019.

The old attribution of the present drawing to Eeckhout is correct. Like Philips Koninck (see no. 169), the artist belonged to Rembrandt's second generation of pupils in Amsterdam who worked with the master during the second half of the 1630's. Houbraken mentions him as Rembrandt's best friend along with the landscape painter Roghman (see no. 184). He produced numerous masterly pen drawings of youths in the studio and studies of nudes, rendering with a few large strokes what is visually essential in the appearance of a figure modeled by light. They demonstrate *ad oculos* the instructions given by Rembrandt to his pupils for drawing from the model and later theoretically set forth by Samuel van Hoogstraten, another pupil of Rembrandt's, in his "Inleyding tot de Hooge Schoole der Schilderkonst" of 1678. He recommends looking at the model with half-closed eyes, so as not to be distracted by details, and indicating the hollow shadows of the eyes, nose, and mouth by loose strokes and dots.

NICOLAES MAES
Born Dordrecht 1632, died Amsterdam 1693.

180 Old Woman at a Spinning-Wheel.
Black chalk, and brush and Indian ink.
206 : 167 mm.
Inv. no. 17557 (L. 174).

Schönbrunner-Meder 613; Wurzbach II, p. 90.

Etched by A. Bartsch 1782, F. de Bartsch, Catalogue des Estampes de J. Adam Bartsch, Vienna, 1818, p. 80, no. 185 (Rembrandt).

Provenance: Imperial Library, Vienna.

While Rembrandt's pupils who worked with him in the 1630's were mainly interested in the interplay of expressively charged lines, the constructive value of light and color began to assume increasing importance for the pupils of the 1640's, the generation to which Maes belonged. Some of Maes' finest early paintings are pictures of interiors with old women engaged in domestic pursuits, especially in spinning (Amsterdam, Rijksmuseum). A strong incidence of light sets them off against the dark of their surroundings. The present drawing is connected with these early paintings. The incidence of light which makes the old woman stand out against the dark background is so intense that one might well imagine some artificial source of light. The inner concentration with which the old woman runs the thread through the fingers of her left hand while her right hand turns the wheel is as masterfully rendered as the wheel itself, which, in spite of the brio of draughtsmanship, is shown clearly in all its details.

ABRAHAM FURNERIUS
Born Amsterdam (?) about 1621, died Rotterdam 1654.

181 Barn with Open Door on a Road near Utrecht, with Draughtsman Seated in the Road.
Pen and bistre, washed; lower left corner damaged.
130 : 260 mm.
Inv. no. 9030 (L. 174).

Schönbrunner-Meder 496 (as Rembrandt); C. Hofstede de Groot, Die Handzeichnungen Rembrandts, Haarlem, 1906, no. 1482 (as Rembrandt); F. Lugt, Mit Rembrandt in Amsterdam, Berlin, 1920, p. 149; O. Benesch, Gazette des Beaux-Arts XXXIII, New York, May 1948, p. 287, fig. 4.

Exhibitions: Die holländische Landschaft im Zeitalter Rembrandts, Albertina, Vienna, 1936, no. 54; London, 1948, no. 48.

The artist, who is known to us only as a draughtsman, was according to Hoogstraten's report a fellow-student of his in Rembrandt's studio. As this was in the first half of the 1640's, his date of birth was more likely 1621 than 1628. But

Rembrandt's landscape drawings impressed Furnerius beyond the period of his apprenticeship. The present drawing was undoubtedly made under the influence of Rembrandt's mature landscape art of about 1650. Its outstanding quality makes an attribution to the master himself quite understandable; indeed it was generally accepted as being by Rembrandt until the present author suggested an attribution to Furnerius on the basis of stylistic comparison; Doomer (see no. 182), too, was at one time proposed as its author.

The drawing, with its effects of space, light, and atmosphere, is a masterpiece. The barn and path with their dark shadows merging on the left with the brightly lighted group of buildings, which open up into the dark gaping doorway that reveals another area of light beyond it, are a splendid achievement of colorful luministic illustration. The group of trees was washed with the brush when still moist, so that it blends with the atmosphere without losing its shape. It is a humid day on which the sun struggles to break through the clouds, a picture full of the nostalgia and warmth of the Dutch love of Nature which the silent draughtsman is experiencing. We are approaching the period of classical Dutch landscape art during which the pictorial conquest of Nature was increasingly changed into a spiritual experience. Landscape becomes a receptacle for the expression of ethical values and moods. The artist is attempting its interpretation as a moral precept.

LAMBERT DOOMER
Born Amsterdam 1622—1623, died there 1700.

182 City Wall with a Small Gate and a Canal Passage.
Pen and bistre, washed; inscription in leadpoint below (partly cut off): Doomer f^t.
199 : 294 mm.
Inv. no. 8887 (L. 174).

Old inventory: Rembrandt.

Exhibition: Die holländische Landschaft im Zeitalter Rembrandts, Albertina, Vienna, 1936, no. 56.

Doomer was the son of Rembrandt's frame-maker, whose portrait and that of his wife Rembrandt painted in 1640. Shortly thereafter Doomer seems to have entered Rembrandt's studio where he was Furnerius' fellow-student. The two artists' style is frequently very close, as is shown by a comparison with no. 181. Both laid great stress on tonal effects and mood in their drawings.

Doomer, too, was first and foremost a draughtsman, although attractive paintings by his hand have also been preserved. There were forty portfolios of drawings in his estate, many of them dating from his extensive journeys. About 1645 he visited his brothers at Nantes and traveled the Loire to Paris. This trip was followed by a Rhine journey.

Doomer's landscapes are marked by a serious, sometimes almost melancholy mood. He liked to plunge his landscapes in shadow. By contrast the effect of light becomes all the more delightful, breaking, as it does here, through the dusky trees and suggesting the presence of a friendlier region filled with brightness.

JOHANNES LEUPENIUS
Born Amsterdam 1647—1648, died there 1693.

183 A Group of Trees by the Water Concealing a Manor House.
Pen and bistre, washed; signed and dated lower right: J Leupenius 1665, and: no 6.
193 : 313 mm.
Inv. no. 10105 (L. 174).

Wurzbach II, p. 30.

Exhibition: Die holländische Landschaft im Zeitalter Rembrandts, Albertina, Vienna, 1936, no. 59.

A drawing very closely related to the present one, and dated 1665, is in the Rijksprentenkabinet at Amsterdam (Cat. Henkel p. 99, no. 3). It was identified as a view of the Castle of Nijenrode on the Vecht. Leupenius repeatedly drew this castle. The present drawing does not show enough of the building to permit identification. The Amsterdam drawing, however, probably dates from the same period. These landscapes, broadly sketched with the reed pen, are typical of Leupenius in the diagonal strokes of the foliage.

In view of his late birth date, Leupenius must have been one of Rembrandt's last pupils. His style of drawing was so closely moulded by that of the master that a personal teacher-pupil relationship must be postulated. He was a surveyor and a map-maker by profession.

ROELAND ROGHMAN
Born about 1620, died Amsterdam 1686.

184 The Castle of Zwieten with a Draughtsman.
Pen and black-brown ink, washed with Indian ink over preparatory drawing in chalk; signed lower left: R. Rogham.
388 : 528 mm.

Provenance: Charles, Prince de Ligne (Cat. p. 199, no. 1).
Inv. no. 15130 (L. 174).
Schönbrunner-Meder 844; Wurzbach II, p. 464.

Exhibition: Die holländische Landschaft im Zeitalter Rembrandts, Albertina, Vienna, 1936, no. 57.

Roghman in the years 1646 and 1647 drew a series of 241 views of castles in Holland, Utrecht, and Gelderland. The present drawing was probably one of the series. Roghman, along with Eeckhout, was Rembrandt's best friend and, although his style did not derive from Rembrandt but rather from Seghers and the Flemish painters, his work, serious and meaningful, was greatly enriched by his friendly relations with the master.

JAN VAN DE CAPPELLE
Born Amsterdam 1624—25, died there 1679.

185 Seashore with Flagship and Sailing Boats.
Brush and bistre over preparatory drawing in chalk.
203 : 259 mm.
Inv. no. 10040 (L. 174).

Jan van de Cappelle, who, together with Porcellis, was Holland's most important marine painter, represents the classic high point in the depiction of these subjects which are so dear to the Dutch. The quiet balance of the composition in its verticals and horizontals permits the diagonals of the Baroque to assert themselves only in the spatial arrangement of the ships lying motionless in the harbor. It avoids the uproar of the elements driving the storm-whipped sailing vessels diagonally over the surface of the water as represented in the early and late seventeenth century. A lull lies over most of his paintings, which are filled with a solemn calm. In harmony with this mood is the silvery light, as typical of his paintings as of his drawings, so often lightly washed in gray with the brush. A painting related in composition to the present drawing was formerly in the Lippmann Collection.

Cappelle derived artistically from Simon de Vlieger (see no. 166), but seems to have developed further through self-instruction. He was befriended by Rembrandt, who painted his portrait. He owned a considerable art collection, including 500 drawings by Rembrandt.

AERT VAN DER NEER
Born Amsterdam 1603—04, died there 1677.

186 Moonlit Pond with Fishing Boats and a Village in the Background.
Brush and bistre and white bodycolor on blue paper; monogram by the artist's own hand (Wurzbach II, p. 223).
205 : 276 mm.
Inv. no. 9095.

Wurzbach II, p. 223.

Exhibition: Die holländische Landschaft im Zeitalter Rembrandts, Albertina, Vienna, 1936, no. 63.

The artist, who, by profession, was an innkeeper in Amsterdam, seems to have been a self-taught painter who formed his style under the influence of older masters like the Van de Veldes, Buytewech, and Pieter de Molijn. He was famous for the atmospheric and luminescent mood of his paintings which is more important to him than the composition. Sunrises and sunsets, landscapes by moonlight and the firelight of conflagrations, frosty winter mornings —

through which he also influenced Cappelle — were his favorite subjects. He was more successful in evoking the magic of silvery moonlight in his drawings through the employment of blue paper than in his smoky night paintings.

ADRIAEN VAN OSTADE
Born Haarlem 1610, died there 1684.

187 Interior of a Tavern with Twelve Peasants Drinking, Talking, and Playing Draughts.
Leadpoint, pen and bistre and Indian ink, washed with Indian ink.
173 : 220 mm.
Inv. no. 9134 (L. 174).

Wurzbach II, p. 280.

Genre painting of peasant life, the glory of Flemish sixteenth century art because of Bruegel, became an especially popular field of Dutch art in the seventeenth century, particularly at Haarlem. Its most prominent representatives were the brothers Adriaen and Isaack van Ostade. According to Houbraken's report Adriaen was a pupil of Frans Hals at the time when Brouwer (see no. 156) was working with the master. Rural genre painting was cultivated in the circle of Frans Hals' pupils, for instance, by his own sons and perhaps Molenaer. These as well as Brouwer's influence determined Ostade's style. But he was increasingly influenced by Rembrandt's art; it manifests itself not so much by an acceptance of external elements of style as by a certain emotional quality in the depiction of the life of simple people. His interiors particularly combine keen observation with sympathy for the subject matter and thus with a sense of humor. He was also an eminent etcher. Many of his drawings and watercolors were created as independent works of art. In the present drawing the cool note of the leadpoint drawing and Indian ink combine with the warm tonality of the bistre in an attractive colorfulness within the monochromy.

JAN STEEN
Born Leiden 1626, died there 1679.

188 Tavern Arbor with Revellers.
Pen and brush, and bistre and Indian ink, preparatory drawing in leadpoint on brownish paper, some white bodycolor; both corners on the right damaged.
211 : 249 mm.
Inv. no. 10140 (L. 174).

Schönbrunner-Meder 376; Wurzbach II, 658; J. Meder, Albertina-Facsimile, Handzeichnungen vlämischer und holländischer Meister des XV.—XVII. Jahrhunderts, Vienna, 1923, plate 30; J. Q. Van Regteren Altena, Oud Holland LX (1943), pp. 97, 98, figs. 1, 2; J. G. van Gelder, Dutch Drawings and Prints, London, 1959, no. and fig. 98.

Preparatory drawing for the painting formerly in the Lilienfeld Collection, Vienna. G. Glück, Die Sammlung L. Lilienfeld, Vienna, 1917, p. 25 with fig., p. 68, no. 66.

Together with the Ostades, Jan Steen was the most important painter of Dutch folk life, yet far superior in the pictorial quality of his pictures. The common people as well as the modest middle-classes were the subject of his pictures. He did not confine himself to a rendering of a simple, stationary situation like the Ostades, but imbued his scenes with a fictional emphasis, sometimes even theatrical character — the latter being especially true in his historical paintings. It was correctly assumed, therefore, that he had received his inspiration from the Dutch stage and from the "Rederijkers". He especially liked satirical scenes, and his mocking sense of humor makes him a worthy successor of Hieronymus Bosch. The present drawing, which depicts soldiers amusing themselves with women in an outdoor tavern by evening light — it might be the light of a torch as well as the setting sun — reveals the highly gifted draughtsman who, however, seldom practised his art.

Houbraken, the oldest source of information, calls Steen a pupil of Van Goyen at The Hague (see no. 165). He became his son-in-law. According to Weyerman he was also a pupil of Nicolaus Knüpfer at Utrecht and of Adriaen van

Ostade at Haarlem (see no. 187). He lived in Haarlem from 1661 to 1670. He had previously owned a brewery at Delft, but the local painters' school flourishing at that time became more important to him than his bourgeois trade. His wonderful sense of color prospered in this environment. His artistic development seems to have been fairly independent.

MICHAEL (Michiel) SWEERTS
Born Brussels 1624, died Goa, India, 1664.

189 Young Man in a Plumed Hat, Seated at a Table, Holding a Glass of Wine.
Red chalk over preparatory drawing in black chalk; dated: 1647.
337 : 237 mm.
Inv. no. 9252.

Old inventory: Gerard Dou. Attribution to Giovanni Battista Weenix by J. Q. van Regteren Altena (notation on the mount).

This fine study from nature reveals a power and a freedom peculiar to artists working in the South. In correct recognition of this fact, J. Q. van Regteren Altena assumed Giovanni Battista Weenix to be its author. But the drawing is simpler and less pretentious, less calligraphically decorative than Weenix' unquestioned drawings. The present author, therefore, would like to suggest one of the most important Netherlanders working in Italy during the seventeenth century: Sweerts, who is both unpretentious and monumental. The artist, who is of Flemish descent, came to Rome in his early years. Caravaggio's realism keynotes his thoughtful manner of observing the life of the Italian people around him as well as the everyday life of the Netherlandish colony of artists. In his uncompromising realism, there is an almost religious earnestness. It was also on grounds of faith that the Roman Catholic artist joined a missionary order as a lay brother. In this capacity he died in India at a relatively early age. The influence of his art on the Dutch artists working in Italy was considerable.

CORNELIS VISSCHER II
Birth and death dates assigned to Visscher vary between 1619—1629, and 1658—1662; Haarlem and Amsterdam are mentioned as the places where he was born and died.

190 Portrait of the Poet Joost van den Vondel.
Black chalk on vellum; irregularly arched at top; signed on the column at right, dated on pedestal: C de Visscher fecit./ Aº 1657.
328 : 267 mm.
Inv. no. 17601 (L. 174).

Schönbrunner-Meder 1330; Wurzbach II, p. 796.

The artist made a portrait engraving of the poet in the same year. J. Wussin, Cornel Visscher, Leipzig, 1865, no. 46; Wurzbach II, p. 797, no. 46.

Cornelis Visscher was Holland's most important portrait engraver and draughtsman after Goltzius. His drawings in black chalk on vellum are independent works of art, even though they were occasionally used as models for his engravings. They are extremely lively likenesses of his contemporaries. Holland's greatest poet is represented here in a manner which, though it probably does not do full justice to his intellectual importance, renders his bourgeois appearance with complete fidelity. Human warmth and directness in portraiture — a common Dutch heritage — greatly distinguish Visscher's work.

ALLART VAN EVERDINGEN
Born Alkmaar 1621, died Amsterdam 1675.

191 Norwegian Fjord Landscape with a Wooden Watch Tower.
Black chalk, brush and bistre and white bodycolor; monogram: A. V. E.
178 : 262 mm.
Inv. no. 9586 (L. 174).

Exhibition: Die holländische Landschaft im Zeitalter Rembrandts, Albertina, Vienna, 1936, no. 66.

Everdingen was a pupil of Roelant Savery in Utrecht (see no. 145) and of Pieter de Molijn in Haarlem. He was thereby heir to the romantic mountain scenery derived from Bruegel as well as to the discovery of the tonal beauty of Holland's flat landscape with its wide expanse of sky. Both components are effective in the drawings and paintings that were the fruits of a journey to Sweden and Norway in the early 1640's. In the power and freshness of its conception, the present drawing testifies that it was made on the spot under the direct impression of nature. After his return to his native country, Everdingen continued in Haarlem and Amsterdam to render northern mountain landscape motifs in his drawings, etchings, and paintings, and thereby exerted great influence on his contemporaries, particularly on Ruisdael.

JAN ASSELIJN
Born Dieppe 1610, died Amsterdam 1652.

192 Old City Wall with Round Tower Overgrown with Creepers, and Houses by a River.
Pen and brush and bistre, washed with Indian ink and bistre over preparatory drawing in black chalk.
281 : 441 mm.
Inv. no. 10107 (L. 174).

Old inventory: J. van Ruisdael.

Attribution by the present author.

An important group of Dutch landscape painters lived in Italy for a number of years, especially in Rome where they had their own social circle called "de Bent". Asselijn was one of the most gifted among them. With him were Pieter van Laer, Jan Both, Pijnaker, Swanevelt, Weenix, Dujardin, Berchem (see no. 198), and others. Poelenburgh and Breenbergh (see no. 160) were their precursors. The group was also in touch with the Flemish artist Jan Miel and with Claude Lorrain. They depicted the southern landscape and the life of the people with the same love and devotion to reality as their contemporaries in the North.

Asselijn, whom the Bent called "Krabbetje" because of his crippled left hand — his features were set down by Rembrandt in a portrait etching — knew how to lend great beauty of tone and light to his washed drawings and to his paintings. These constitute the merit of the present drawing, in which the artist causes the lightly veiled sunshine to strike the old tower in a marvelous manner. The brown of the bistre and the gray of the Indian ink and chalk combine to create a color scheme of symphonic richness.

Apart from Asselijn, an attribution to Herman Naiwinx might be considered; his drawings were often classified under the name of Ruisdael. Yet this little master scarcely ever attained the level of the present drawing.

ADRIAEN VAN DE VELDE
Born Amsterdam 1636, died there 1672.

193 Young Shepherd Boy.
Red chalk; signed A. v. d. Velde f. —
225 : 173 mm.
Inv. no. 10152 (L. 174).

Schönbrunner-Meder 295; Wurzbach II, p. 750.

Adriaen van de Velde, the son of Willem van de Velde the Elder and the younger brother of the marine painter Willem van de Velde the Younger (see no. 201), was in touch with the Haarlem school of painting through his teacher Jan Wijnants. But he seems also to have been in Italy in his youth, as can be deduced from the subjects of his early etchings and paintings. In any case he had much in common with the works of the other Dutch artists who traveled to Italy (see nos. 192 and 198). Equally proficient in the mastery of landscape and of figure and animal painting — in the latter he was influenced by Potter (see no. 194) — he left, in spite of his early death, a large oeuvre, not only of paintings, but also of etchings and particularly of drawings, including many fine studies from nature like the present one. This figure of a small "lazzarone", or shepherd lad, is connected with the work of Italianists such as Pieter van Laer, but is far superior in the freedom and mastery of the modeling in light. Because of his sure hand in figure drawing, he was asked by his teacher and by other landscape painters like Ruisdael, Van der Hagen, and Hackaert to supply the figures in their paintings.

PAULUS POTTER
Born Enkhuizen 1625, died Amsterdam 1654.

194 Stable Interior with a Cow Calving.
Black chalk and white bodycolor on brown paper; signed lower left: Paulus. Potter. f.
275 : 236 mm.
Inv. no. 9846 (L. 174).

Schönbrunner-Meder 303; Wurzbach II, p. 353; J. Meder, Albertina-Facsimile, Handzeichnungen vlämischer und holländischer Meister des XV.—XVII. Jahrhunderts, Vienna, 1923, no. 28.

Exhibition: Bestiaire hollandais, Institut Néerlandais, Paris, 1960, no. 150.

Paulus Potter was the son and presumably also the pupil of the still-life painter Pieter Symonsz Potter. His training took him to the schools of Delft and The Hague. His exclusive field of representation — he died young — was animal painting, to which he imparted true monumentality and nobility in spite of the triviality of the subject. Equally gifted as a painter and as a draughtsman, he studied the animal not as an isolated object, but in its connection with Dutch farm life and Dutch landscape. In the present drawing he has created one of the finest interiors, as rich in atmosphere and as complete in itself as the most intimate and unpretentious pictures of barns by Ostade, yet far superior to them in its monumentality and inner stability.

AELBERT CUYP
Born Dordrecht 1620, died there 1691.

195 A Group of Trees with a Distant View of Arnhem.
Black chalk, Indian ink and watercolor.
183 : 296 mm.
Inv. no. 8756.

W. Bernt, Die niederländischen Zeichner des 17. Jahrhunderts, Munich, 1957, I, no. 172. See H. P. R. Rosenberg, De Sint Walburgs Kerk te Arnhem, Nederlands Kunsthistorisch Jaarboek 12 (1961), p. 193 ff.

Exhibition: Die holländische Landschaft im Zeitalter Rembrandts, Albertina, Vienna, 1936, no. 74.

Cuyp was a member of a large family of painters, the son and pupil of Jacob Gerritsz Cuyp, who was chiefly active as a portraitist but also cultivated animal painting. Aelbert was primarily a great landscape painter, but he also mastered all the other pictorial themes of the "specialists". He knew above all how to blend animal painting and landscape into a truly monumental composition. As a landscape painter he continued the tonal unity of space of Van Goyen (see no. 165) and Pieter de Molijn, but he saturated it with light, a warmth and a golden glow that are unique even in Dutch painting. He cultivated pure landscape mostly in his chalk drawings, frequently tinted with watercolors; in them he was fond of producing the tonal unity of his paintings by applying a light golden olive-yellow. The present drawing shows a view of the city of Arnhem seen from the northeast with the Groote Kerck in the center and the two smaller towers of St. Walburg on the left.

JACOB ISAACKSZ VAN RUISDAEL
Born Haarlem 1628—29, died probably Amsterdam 1682 (buried at Haarlem).

196 Windmills on a Low Hill.
Black chalk, brush and Indian ink
144 : 190 mm.
Inv. no. 10109 (L. 174).

J. Rosenberg, Jacob van Ruisdael, Berlin, 1928, p. 115, no. 69, fig. 156.

Exhibition: Die holländische Landschaft im Zeitalter Rembrandts, Albertina, Vienna, 1936, no. 68.

Jacob van Ruisdael, the son and pupil of the landscape painter Isaack van Ruisdael, was, along with Hercules Seghers and Rembrandt, the greatest Dutch landscape painter of the seventeenth century. He created an image of the Dutch landscape in all its plainness and simplicity, its profound seriousness and inner greatness, which find expression in a pictorial structure of unique monumentality and in a dark, yet luminous color scheme. While his paintings and etchings are mostly free compositions and maintain an extensive freedom, even in the vedute, his drawings usually render an extant motif, although they are always compositionally complete. In the present drawing he raises the windmill on the low hill to monumental significance as if it were standing on a pedestal, and repeats the motif like an "echo" in the distance, comparable to a favorite artistic effect in seventeenth century organ music, embodying at the same time the Baroque compositional principle of the diagonal in space. An enormous tension and depth of space are thus achieved, and the lofty sky filled with dark autumn clouds actually seems to "vault". The importance of the vast sky applies particularly to Ruisdael's late and mature works, among which the present drawing is to be included.

JORIS VAN DER HAGEN
Born probably Dordrecht or Arnhem about 1615, died The Hague 1669.

197 View of the Bosch in The Hague.
Black chalk, and brush and bistre; inscription by the artist's own hand: Dit is int bosch buyte den Haegh Anno 1658 H f.; added by a later hand in the lower right corner: Hagen.
400 : 538 mm.
Inv. no. 15132 (L. 174).

Exhibition: Die holländische Landschaft im Zeitalter Rembrandts, Albertina, Vienna, 1936, no. 70.

Van der Hagen was a widely-traveled artist who took his motifs from the most diverse parts of Holland. Some of his best paintings and drawings are dedicated to the Bosch, the deer and forest park of The Hague, where he lived not far from Potter's domicile. The views of the Bosch by both artists show many points of affinity. The present drawing is one of Van der Hagen's finest works, depicting the Bosch in the morning light of an early autumn day, when the rising sun sheds its oblique rays over the meadows wet with dew. The leafy domes formed by the majestic old trees are masterfully rendered.

NICOLAES PIETERSZ BERCHEM
Born Haarlem 1620, died Amsterdam 1683.

198 Rocky Landscape with a Castle and Hunters at the Edge of a River.
Black chalk, pen and Indian ink; signed lower left: N Berchem. f.
298 : 510 mm.
Inv. no. 9808 (L. 174).

Ilse v. Sick, Nicolaes Berchem, Kunstwissenschaftliche Studien V, Berlin, 1930, p. 56, no. 86.

The artist stems from the Haarlem school of painters, but he also studied with Nicolaes Moeyaert in Amsterdam. Through this teacher he may have been directed to Italy. He lived in Rome from 1642 to 1645, at the same time as Asselijn, Dujardin and G. B. Weenix. He was one of the finest Dutch "Italianists", and his early landscapes display high pictorial quality.

Berchem was not only a very prolific painter, but also a most industrious draughtsman. In his late years the quality of his drawings is superior to that of his paintings. In drawings like the present one, which shows a fantastic landscape composition, there is already something of the lightness and grace of the Rococo.

GABRIEL METSU
Born Leiden 1629, died Amsterdam 1667.

199 Portrait Study of an Aristocratic Gentleman, Seen from the Front, Three-Quarter Length.
Black and white chalk on brown paper; lower left, later inscription in pen: G. Metsu.
363 : 239 mm.
Inv. no. 17585 (L. 174).

Schönbrunner-Meder 427; Wurzbach II, p. 151.

Houbraken calls Metsu a pupil of Gerard Dou, a statement which is corroborated by paintings like the "Fishmonger" in the Wallace Collection. While his early paintings show an affinity with the schools of Frans Hals and Rembrandt, he drew closer to the school of Delft (de Hooch, Vermeer) in the years of his maturity, as can also be noticed in the color scheme of his paintings. They are broadly painted and thus avoid the danger of the excessive smoothness to which other Dutch genre painters fell victim. The same fresh, loose execution which distinguishes his paintings is also to be found in his drawings. This briskly sketched portrait study is one of the finest of its kind and demonstrates the high level of its author. That he had Frans Hals in mind when he created this portrait study is obvious.

GERARD TERBORCH (Gerard ter Borch)
Born Zwolle 1617, died Deventer 1681.

200 Young Fortune Teller with her Cards.
Black chalk; signed and dated lower left in chalk: G T Borch naer leven geteekend anno 1669.
285 : 194 mm.
Inv. no. 17587 (L. 174).

Schönbrunner-Meder 383; Wurzbach II, p. 701; E. Plietzsch, Gerard Ter Borch, Vienna, 1944, p. 37, fig. 109; S. J. Gudlaugsson, Gerard Ter Borch, vols. I, II. The Hague, 1959, 1960.

In spite of a large number of drawings by all the members of the Terborch family in the sketchbooks and the family album which passed from the artist's family into the collection of L. F. Zebinden and from there for the most part into the Rijksprentenkabinet, research has made surprisingly little use of them in the identification of the drawings of this great painter. Incorrect attributions to Gerard Terborch the father, to his children Gerard, Moses and Gesina, and even to Metsu were still the order of the day in spite of all the differences in quality. And all this notwithstanding the basic essay by A. J. Moes-Veth "Mozes ter Borch als sujet van zijn broer Gerard" (Bulletin van het Rijkmuseum III, 1955, p. 37 ff.) beyond which research has never progressed. Thus, it could happen that this drawing of the great genre painter, clearly marked as Gerard's work and dated by his sister Gesina, was published by Plietzsch as the work of an "unknown artist". A critical catalogue of Gerard's drawings is urgently needed.

A closely related study in chalk representing a cavalier drinking, with an inscription and the date 1671 by Gesina's hand, is likewise in the Albertina. We also recognize Gesina's hand in the inscription on Gerard's copy of Bloemart's "Lamentation of Christ" of 1669 in the Albertina, and on studies of the head of the laughing Moses by Gerard's hand in the Albertina and in Amsterdam.

The solemn calm and meditative power of this inward-looking drawing should have led to the conclusion that none but a first-rate artist could have been its author, even without the contemporary confirmation of the inscription. Only Gerard Terborch's genre paintings reveal a similar concentration and calm in which the model's outward appearance and soul blend so wonderfully.

WILLEM VAN DE VELDE II
Born Leiden 1633, died London 1707.

201 The Destruction of the French Battleships in the Bay of La Hogue by Sir George Rooke.
Pen and bistre, washed with Indian ink. Monogram, lower left: W. V. V. J.; upper left: No. 2; also inscribed by the artist's hand: La Hogue 1692, 1. 2. 3. Juny.
295 : 464 mm.
Inv. no. 31521 (acquired 1954).

Three further representations of this subject are to be found in the Department of Prints and Drawings, British Museum, E. Croft-Murray & P. Hulton, Catalogue of British Drawings, Supplemented by ... Christopher White, London, 1960, I Text pp. 511, 512, nos. 49—51, plate 270.

This event took place on May 23 and 24, 1692. (The dates of June 1, 2 and 3 correspond, to the "New Style" chronology.) No. 51 of the London drawings is dated 1701, so that the series can only have originated at this time. The measurements of the present drawing are almost identical with those of no. 50 in London.
Willem van de Velde II was the elder brother of Adriaen (see no. 193) and a pupil of his father and of Simon de Vlieger (see no. 166). In 1673 he moved to England, where he lived until his death, mostly in London as a court painter. He was the most important Dutch marine painter after Cappelle. The finest among his paintings are those from his Dutch period with their clear color tones, for example, the famous "Cannon Shot" in Amsterdam. Later on the spirited drawings in which he anticipates the eighteenth century — Canaletto and Guardi may have known them — surpass the paintings in importance.

JAN DE BISSCHOP (Johannes Episcopus)
Born Amsterdam about 1628, died The Hague 1671.

202 View of The Hague from the Dunes, in the Distance the Towers of Delft.
Pen and brush, and bistre and Indian ink, watercolor.
245 : 401 mm.
Inv. no. 10112 (L. 174).

Old inventory: Jacob van Ruisdael. Attribution by F. Lugt. Wurzbach II, p. 521 (Ruisdael).

Bisschop was a lawyer by profession and a self-taught draughtsman and etcher. He went to Italy, where he drew not only landscapes, but also works of art. His studies based on the latter demonstrate his interest in the history of art. As an intellectual artist he occupied himself also with problems of art education and produced a model book for the teaching of drawing, the "Paradigmata". He was a friend of the Huygens family and his drawings show a great affinity to those of Constantin Huygens the Younger. His manifold intellectual interests did not impair his keen eye for nature, as is proved by this magnificent drawing showing The Hague on a cool day with a lofty cloudy sky and a vast perspective.

FRANS VAN MIERIS I
Born Leiden 1635, died there 1681.

203 Sick Woman in Bed (Probably the Artist's Wife).
Black chalk on vellum: signed and dated at lower right: F van Mieris. fecet / Anno 1663. (The numeral 3 is a correction of the numeral 4 which is still discernible.)
262 : 237 mm.
Inv. no. 17599 (L. 174).

Schönbrunner-Meder 304; Wurzbach II, p. 166.

Like Metsu, Terborch and the painters of Delft, Mieris rendered the life of the upper middle classes in his genre paintings. As a pupil of Gerard Dou he aimed at technical perfection and the little masters' polish in his paintings as well as in his drawings. He knew how to render the textural quality of surfaces in masterful fashion, and his works include one fine still-life after another.
This also applies to the present drawing which, moreover, strikes a winning human note in the weary expression of the sick woman, and reveals the artist as a subtle delineator of the soul.

JAN VAN HUYSUM
Born Amsterdam 1682, died there 1749.

XVIII Flower Piece.
Charcoal and watercolor.
333 : 245 mm.
Inv. no. 23130 (acquired 1923).

In Jan van Huysum's still-lives the decorative Baroque, which played only a secondary role in Dutch art, flares up once more before its extinction. He was the son and pupil of the flower-painter Justus van Huysum. While the glossy rendering of detail and the finely chiseled perfection of his paintings aroused the admiration of his contemporaries, the modern spectator will give preference to his watercolor drawings in which an outstanding gift of invention and observation manifests itself with an eruptive force.

ROMEYN DE HOOGHE
Born Amsterdam 1645, died Haarlem 1708.

204 The Conclusion of the Peace of Breda in August, 1667.
Brush and Indian ink and white bodycolor; traced with the stylus for transfer to the copperplate.
221 : 312 mm.
Inv. no. 10163 (L. 174).
Wurzbach I, p. 719.

Preparatory drawing for the etching with marginal scenes. F. W. H. Hollstein, Dutch and Flemish Etchings, Engravings and Woodcuts, Amsterdam IX, p. 119, no. 77.

Romeyn de Hooghe was the most brilliant Dutch illustrator of all time and also one of the most important etchers. He combined in his person the universality of the Baroque, being its last representative of European stature in Holland. He was an etcher, a painter, a sculptor, an engraver of medals, a cartographer, a mining engineer, an historian, an archaeologist and a jurist, a true representative of the age of Leibnitz. He towers like a giant above the increasing numbers of little masters of his time and environment. His inventions are of an incredible boldness and power of imagination. He cannot be connected with any teacher, but in his beginnings he etched after Berchem. He visited Paris in 1668; the great French etchers (Callot, Bosse and Silvestre) obviously influenced his work.

His vast etched work was devoted first and foremost to historical illustration. The Peace of Breda, represented here, ended the second naval war between England and The Netherlands after Admiral de Ruyter's victory in the Thames estuary. By its terms the colony of Nieuw Amsterdam was handed over to the English, who named it New York.

FRENCH MASTERS

FRANÇOIS CLOUET
Born Tours before 1520, died Paris 1572.

205 Portrait of a Young Man with a Ruff.
Black and red chalk (stumped).
324 : 222 mm.
Inv. no. 11185 (L. 174).

Anonymous collector's mark L. 1010.

Schönbrunner-Meder 340; J. Meder, Albertina-Facsimile, Handzeichnungen französischer Meister, Vienna, 1922, no. 1.

Exhibitions: Le Dessin français dans les Collections du XVIIIe siècle, Paris, Wildenstein, 1935, no. 198; London, 1948, no. 113; Meisterwerke aus Frankreichs Museen, Albertina, Vienna, 1950, no. 3.

The artist was the son and pupil of the court painter Jehan Clouet, who created the genre of the court portrait in colored chalks. It is assumed that Holbein's use of this technique for portrait drawing goes back to his impressions during a journey to France in 1524. It can be argued, on the other hand, that Holbein's attention had already been drawn to this technique by the portrait studies of his father and of the artists of Lombardy (see no. II), and that later he in his turn surely influenced the French artists.

The chalk court portrait was not only a preparatory study for a painting, but in many instances a work in its own right, its rapid execution offering a welcome substitute for the drudgery of portrait painting. François Clouet was a specialist in this field, succeeding his father as court painter in 1540. Catherine de' Medici admired and patronized him and avidly collected his chalk drawings. These drawings played an important part in French diplomacy, especially in the discussion of marriage proposals.

JEAN COUSIN THE YOUNGER
Born Sens about 1522, died Paris 1594.

206 Luna and Endymion.
Pen and bistre, washed with pinkish purple over preparatory drawing in black chalk; added by a later hand in pen and ink lower left: J. C.
288 : 396 mm.
Inv. no. 24468 (acquired 1925).
O. Benesch, Jean Cousin Fils, Dessinateur, Prométhée 20, Paris, 1939, pp. 271—280.

Exhibitions: Paris, 1950, no. 128; Meisterwerke aus Frankreichs Museen, Albertina, Vienna, 1950, no. 11.

While the "Livre de la Fortune" in the Bibliothèque de l'Institut has always been known as his work, most of the individual drawings of Jean Cousin the Younger sailed under false colors until the present author in the above mentioned essay tried to bring some order into the confusion. His starting point was the present drawing, which, with a few others by Cousin's hand in the Albertina, had been attributed to Blocklandt. This is one of Cousin's finest and most poetic works. His style derived from his father's art, which had been given its character mainly by the School of Fontainebleau (Rosso, Primaticcio, see no. 33), complemented by a strong Netherlandish influence, particularly of Jan van Scorel, in the representation of landscape.

MARTIN FRÉMINET (Fréminel)
Born Paris 1567, died there 1619.

207 Young Man Seated at a Table with a Lute.
Red chalk, pen and bistre; later inscription in ink: Martin freminet de. paris.
229 : 185 mm.
Inv. no. 11770 (L. 174).

Schönbrunner-Meder 1; P. Lavallée, Le Dessin français du XIIIe au XVIe siècle, Paris, 1930, p. 120, no. 92, pl. LXX; Silvie Béguin, L'École de Fontainebleau, Paris, 1960, p. 134.

Exhibitions: French Art, Royal Academy, London, 1932, no. 1008 and Commemorative Catalogue p. 1271, no. 563; Chefs d'oeuvre de l'art français, Paris, 1937, no. 458; Paris, 1950, no. 132; Meisterwerke aus Frankreichs Museen, Albertina, Vienna, 1950, no. 16.

In his youth, Fréminet lived in Italy for some time. He was in touch with Giuseppe Cesari in Rome and studied the works of the great Cinquecento masters. In 1604 he was appointed "peintre du roi" and subsequently summoned to take part in the decoration of Fontainebleau. Together with Dubreuil and Dubois, he founded the so-called "Younger (or Second) School of Fontainebleau" (see no. 33) which consisted mainly of native artists.

Like Bellange's drawings in red chalk (see no. 208), the present drawing is in its execution still connected with Rosso and the Late Gothic tradition of the older Mannerists. Yet in the interpretation of the subject there is already a touch of Caravaggio, with whom Fréminet may have been in contact through his friend Cesari. The ornamental flourish of the pen by which the cat is indicated, is altogether reminiscent of Bellange.

JACQUES BELLANGE
Documented Nancy 1602—1617.

208 The Three Marys at the Tomb of Christ.
Red chalk.
219 : 173 mm; later inscription in bistre: Pierre belange.
Inv. no. 11756 (L. 174).

Schönbrunner-Meder 16; P. Lavallée, Le Dessin français du XIIIe au XVIe siècle, Paris, 1930, p. 125, no. 101, pl. LXXVIII; O. Benesch, The Art of the Renaissance in Northern Europe, Cambridge, Massachusetts, 1947, p. 122, fig. 69 and London, 1965, p. 140, fig. 72; P. Lavallée, Le Dessin français, Paris, 1948, p. 291; J. Vallery-Radot, Le dessin français au XVIIe siècle, Lausanne, 1953, pl. 5 and p. 178; Great Drawings of All Time, New York, 1962, vol. III, no. 650 (A. Mongan).

Exhibitions: French Art, Royal Academy, London, 1932, no. 1010, Commemorative Catalogue no. 575; Paris, 1950, no. 134; Meisterwerke aus Frankreichs Museen, Albertina, Vienna, 1950, no. 17; French Drawings from Fouquet to Gauguin, Arts Council Gallery, London, 1952, no. 2.

The importance of this greatest of French Mannerists — apart from Duvet — has been fully recognized only in recent times when Expressionism has opened our eyes to the superior quality of his art. He was one of the greatest etchers and above all a draughtsman, who in various respects paved the way for Callot, his great fellow countryman from Lorraine (see no. 209). Examples of his once highly praised paintings — he was court painter at Nancy — have only lately become known; they are the subject of an essay which the present author is preparing.

This drawing — perhaps the finest by his hand that has been preserved — is identical in subject with a famous etching of his (Robert-Dumesnil 9), but without any closer relation to it. The elongated draped figures follow Rosso's pattern, but surpass by far the works of the Italian artist in the precious spiritualization that lends them something of the art of 1400. Gestures, costumes and the receptacles carried by the Marys are airy and unsubstantial; the figures themselves barely seem to touch the ground.

JACQUES CALLOT
Born Nancy 1592, died there 1635.

209 The Fair at Madonna della Impruneta near Florence.
Pen and bistre, washed, over preparatory drawing in leadpoint.
393 : 207 mm.
Provenance: Charles, Prince de Ligne (Cat. p. 333, no. 83).
Inv. no. 11218.

Schönbrunner-Meder 990; J. Meder, Albertina-Facsimile, Handzeichnungen französischer Meister des XVI.—XVIII. Jahrhunderts, Vienna, 1922, no. 35; L. Zahn, Die Handzeichnungen des J. Callot, Munich, 1923, p. 43 ff., fig. 18, p. 97 ff.; D. Ternois, Jacques Callot, Catalogue complet de son oeuvre, Paris, 1962, no. 173; L'art de Jacques Callot ib. 1962, pl. 226.

Preparatory drawing for the etching in the reverse direction, E. Meaume, Recherches sur la vie et les ouvrages de Jacques Callot, Paris, 1860, no. 624; J. Lieure, J. Callot, Paris, 1924, no. 361.

Exhibitions: French Art, Royal Academy, London, 1932, no. 1011, Commemorative Catalogue p. 130, no. 580; Artistes français en Italie, Paris, 1934, no. 378; Chefs d'oeuvre de l'art français, Paris 1937, no. 467; Paris, 1950, no. 133; Meisterwerke aus Frankreichs Museen, Albertina, Vienna, 1950, no. 25.

The large etching of 1620 is Callot's main work from his Florentine period (1611—1621), created before his return to Nancy, where he worked for the Court of Lorraine as Bellange had done previously (see no. 208). But while Bellange was also active as a painter, Callot was exclusively a draughtsman and etcher who left a prodigious graphic oeuvre, a true "orbis pictus" of his time.

In Italy he associated himself chiefly with the progressive Florentine artists, who strove to render a true picture of real life. But his links with Late Mannerism were also very strong, as is revealed by his drawings in particular; in many respects his art was a continuation of that of Bellange. On the other hand his oeuvre made him the teacher of many draughtsmen and etchers of the seventeenth century and won him European influence. The young Rembrandt and Lievens were among his followers.

For the etching of the Fair at Impruneta there are, apart from numerous studies of details, three more designs of the complete stage in the collection of drawings at the Uffizi (Ternois 172, 174 and 175). Ternois 172 is a sketch of the actual scene, which does not yet take into consideration the reversal of the printing process. Ternois 174 renders the main layout of the etching. The present drawing is already squared for transfer to the copperplate. Finally, Ternois 175 is a detailed and pricked working drawing, although the artist even at this stage altered some details on the plate.

NICOLAS POUSSIN
Born Villers 1594, died Rome 1665.

210 Walk in a Park.
Pen and brush and bistre, washed.
185 : 252 mm.
Provenance: P. J. Mariette (L. 2097); Charles, Prince de Ligne (Cat. p. 335, no. 8).
Inv. no. 11446 (L. 174).

W. Friedländer, Belvedere, 10. Jg., Vienna, 1931, p. 61.

Exhibitions: Paris, 1950, no. 136; Meisterwerke aus Frankreichs Museen, Albertina, Vienna, 1950, no. 42.

Side by side with his strictly organized figure compositions, there are some wonderful studies of the Roman landscape by Poussin; in these last the Titianesque element in his art reaches magistral development through experience with Nature. The Albertina is rich in such landscape studies. The present drawing is one of the finest, magnificent in its blending of the variegated foliage of an old park with its dense growth of trees through which the sunlight sparkles. The powerful, dusky screen of trees on the left was drawn with the brush and completed by accents of the pen, while in the more distant and lighter parts the primary drawing in pen was subsequently spatially organized by washing with the brush. The rendering of the crumbling garden wall overgrown with moss and creepers is incredibly colorful; its merging with the shrubbery — as a change of form and space — anticipates effects found in Cézanne's watercolors.

211 The Ponte Molle near Rome.
Pen and brush and bistre over preparatory drawing in leadpoint.
187 : 256 mm.
Provenance: P. J. Mariette (L. 2097).
Inv. no. 11443 (L. 174).

O. Grautoff, Nicolas Poussin, Munich, 1914, plate 23; W. Friedländer, Belvedere, 10. Jg., Vienna, 1931, p. 61.

Exhibitions: Paris, 1950, no. 137; Meisterwerke aus Frankreichs Museen, Albertina, Vienna, 1950, no. 43.

See comment on no. 210. In the present drawing the groups of trees in the foreground were also merely sketched with broad strokes of the brush, while the view into the distance was firmly outlined with the pen, therein revealing the draughtsman's experience with the different focuses needed for the close and the distant view. At the same time a firm architectural structure is created which, instead of doing away with the Baroque system of diagonals within the picture space, uses them to give the picture an inner tension. The brushwork continues the ductus of Callot's late landscape studies, which seem to have been known to Poussin.

CLAUDE LORRAIN (Claude Gellée)
Born Chamagne 1600, died Rome 1682.

212 A Group of Trees by a Brook against a Wooded Background.
Black chalk, brush and bistre; lower left inscription in leadpoint by a later hand: Claude Lorrain.
263 : 195 mm.
Inv. no. 11530 (L. 174).

M. Pattison, Claude Lorrain, Paris, 1884, p. 297, no. 288.
E. Knab's identification of the present drawing with one in the collection of Charles, Prince de Ligne (Cat. p. 337, no. 4) is doubtful, as the rocks mentioned by Bartsch in his description are not to be seen here (Alte und Neue Kunst, 2. Jg., Vienna, 1953, 4. Heft, p. 127, no. 23).

Whereas Poussin in his landscape studies drawn from nature, gives primary importance to firm tectonics, notwithstanding the colorfulness of their effect, Claude aims exclusively at tone and atmospheric mood. Atmosphere with him becomes an almost palpable fluid, a lighter or darker mist which permits objects to emerge and disappear again. While Poussin is linked with the constructed landscape of the classical masters of Italian Baroque (Carracci, Domenichino) and with French tradition, Claude has an obvious affinity with the Netherlandish and German artists working in Rome. Claude was, however, superior to every contemporary landscape artist in the mastery of atmosphere. There was only one equal to him in the seventeenth century, Rembrandt (see no. 174).

This mastery is even more admirable in the monochrome of his drawings than in his paintings. A cool gray and a warm brown display more shades and tints than the richest color scheme. In the present drawing, for instance, the preparatory work in black chalk represents a cool color value. The draughtsman first set down with the brush the more delicate silhouettes of the trees as a dark note on the paper. He then washed the whole background with a lighter tone, whereby washes of the clouded sky were unconcernedly spread over the tops of the trees, causing some of their outlines to run. In this way the foreground was atmospherically blended with the background, and in this way there was created the silvery tone of the air for which Claude's works are famous.

XIX Tiber Landscape with Rocky Slope.
Pen and brush and bistre, with traces of stumping in black chalk; collector's inscription in pen and bistre added later: M. Le Gros ma Envoye de Rom ce dessein en 1719. Claudio Lorin (referring to the sculptor Pierre Le Gros, 1666—1719, who arrived in Rome in 1690).
198 : 266 mm.
Provenance: P. J. Mariette (L. 2097, Vente Mariette 1774, no. 1255); Paillet; Le Gros; M. v. Fries (L. 2903).
Inv. no. 11513 (L. 174).
Pattison loc. cit. p. 296, no. 269; W. Friedländer, Claude Lorrain, Berlin, 1921, p. 190; J. Vallery-Radot, Le dessin français au XVIIe siècle, Lausanne, 1953, no. 75; E. Knab, Alte und Neue Kunst, Vienna, 1953, p. 128, no. 28; W. Hofmann, Revue des Arts, Paris, 1955, pp. 75 ff.
Exhibitions: Le dessin français dans les collections du XVIIIe siècle, Wildenstein, Paris, 1935, no. 202; Paris, 1950, no. 140; Meisterwerke aus Frankreichs Museen, Albertina, Vienna, 1950, no. 51.
The monumental structure of this landscape and the melancholy mood of an evening or a thunderstorm overlying it, make it a paradigm of the heroic-classical landscape. In contrast to no. 212, which is a direct study from nature, this is a free composition. W. Hofmann has demonstrated that it is a combination of two studies from nature, one rendering the view into the distance, the other showing the rocky screen of the foreground. Both drawings are in the collection of the British Museum (Hind 25 and 141). The indication of a hermit at prayer on the upper left underscores the meaning of the invention.

SIMON VOUET
Born Paris 1590, died there 1649.

213 Study of a Deacon Saint with Martyr's Palm.
Black and white chalk; squared for transfer; lower left inscribed in pen and ink: S. Voüet.
304 : 218 mm.
Inv. no. 11197 (L. 174).
Design for an altarpiece.
The artist, who lived in Italy from 1612 to 1627, mainly in Rome, combined in his work the Caravaggesque realism of studies from the model and the idealism of the classical Baroque masters of Bologna. He was thus a significant factor, not only in the development of French art, but also in the rise of the great decorative Baroque painting in Rome. His finest drawings are his powerful studies from the model; like the present study they were often transferred directly to the canvas. He followed therein the Carracci's manner of working.

CLAUDE GILLOT
Born Langres 1673, died Paris 1722.

214 The Birth of the Infant Pan.
Pen and Indian ink, brush and red chalk wash and white bodycolor on paper tinted with red chalk.
217 : 326 mm.
Inv. no. 11966 (L. 174).

Exhibitions: Watteau und sein Kreis, Albertina, Vienna, 1934, no. 3 (O. Benesch); Meisterwerke aus Frankreichs Museen, Albertina, Vienna, 1950, no. 63.

Gillot, a pupil of J. B. Corneille, was stage-manager of the Paris Opera. Many of his representations are chosen from the world of the theatre and are stage-like in their invention. He further transmitted this dream world of the stage, of bucolic and ornamental fantasy, to his main pupil Watteau, who is greatly indebted to him for inspiration, not only in subject-matter, but also in formal expression and conception. Another drawing in the Albertina (Inv. no. 11965) which is related to the present one represents a Wedding of Pan. Both sheets are completely traced with the stylus, pointing to their use as models for engravings.

ANTOINE WATTEAU
Born Valenciennes 1684, died Nogent-sur-Marne 1721.

XX A Young Girl Standing and a Woman Seated.
Red, white and black chalk on brownish paper; lower right inscription in bistre: Wateau.
269 : 214 mm.
Inv. no. 12009 (L. 174).
Schönbrunner-Meder 200; J. Meder, Albertina-Facsimile, Handzeichnungen französischer Meister des XVI. — XVIII. Jahrhunderts, Vienna, 1922, no. 4; K. T. Parker and J. Mathey, Antoine Watteau, Paris, 1957, II, 560; G. Lafenestre, Cinquante dessins de Watteau, Paris, 1907, no. 5.
Exhibitions: Antoine Watteau, Albertina, Vienna, 1934, no. 21 (O. Benesch); London, 1948, no. 120; Paris, 1950, no. 142; Meisterwerke aus Frankreichs Museen, Albertina, Vienna, 1950, no. 76.

Watteau was the greatest French draughtsman of all time and can be compared only to the very greatest artists of other nations, like Rubens or Rembrandt. Significant though his painted oeuvre is, his drawings are by far superior. Practically all of Watteau's drawings are studies from the model or studies after other works of art, made as an end in themselves for the sake of drawing and studying, and originating in the enjoyment of drawing itself. From them the artist later chose and combined the elements and details of his pictures. There are only a few composition sketches among his drawings. All the more important in his creative activity was the role of free copies after the works of other masters, mainly of the Flemish and the Venetians. As a guest of the collector Crozat he assiduously studied his host's collection of drawings.

It was above all Rubens who set the example for him; he adopted Rubens' system of drawing in red, black, and white chalk on chamois-colored paper and carried it to the utmost refinement. The battle between the "Poussinists" and the "Rubenists" in French painting took place in his time and was decided primarily by Watteau in favor of the latter. Watteau himself, who came from a Flemish family and a town which had only shortly before, as a consequence of the War of Succession, been handed over to France by the Netherlands, was considered a "peintre flamand" by his contemporaries.

His studies from nature, brilliant observations of reality, frequently cover the surface of the paper like loose, accidentally strewn patterns, but testify to an arrangement of the utmost decorative refinement.

JACQUES ANDRÉ PORTAIL
Born Brest 1695, died Versailles 1759.

215 Young Woman with a Negro Servant.
Black, red and brown chalk. Inscribed in leadpoint lower right: N. Portail fec.
402 : 317 mm.
Inv. no. 12100 (L. 174).
G. Swarzenski, Französische Meister des XVIII. Jahrhunderts, Munich, Marées Gesellschaft, no. 125; E. Gradmann, Französische Meisterzeichnungen des 18. Jahrhunderts, Basle, 1949, no. 20, fig. 54.

Exhibitions: Le Dessin français de Fouquet à Cézanne, Brussels, 1949, no. 69; Meisterwerke aus Frankreichs Museen, Albertina, Vienna, 1950, no. 87.

Little is known about this artist, his origin and his activity. He was appointed "Garde des plans et tableaux de la Couronne" at Versailles in 1740, and from 1741 on was entrusted with the arrangement of the annual exhibitions of the Salon in the Louvre. He became a member of the Academy as "peintre de fleurs" in 1746, and Natoire praised him as a landscape painter in a letter from Rome. These scanty dates in no way explain his outstanding figure studies and genre scenes from the intimate world of the eighteenth century, in which he appears as one of the most gifted artists among Watteau's followers. The delicacy of his drawings in red and black chalk is difficult to surpass. His drawings tend towards a conception of the human figure as still-life, a conception which had its greatest representative in Chardin. Some of his delightful drawings have not yet been identified and pass under the names of other artists.

JEAN-BAPTISTE OUDRY
Born Paris 1686, died Beauvais 1755.

216 The Terrace of the Park at Arcueil.
Black chalk, partly stumped, heightened with white bodycolor, on blue paper. Lower left inscription in leadpoint: Oudry.
314 : 538 mm.
Inv. no. 12020 (L. 174).
Exhibition: Meisterwerke aus Frankreichs Museen, Albertina, Vienna, 1950, no. 86.

Oudry, a pupil of his father and of Largillière, was famous as a painter of still-lives and animal pieces, in which he continued the tradition of the great Flemish artists. He was entrusted with the direction of the Beauvais tapestry manufactory and appointed "surinspecteur" of the Gobelins, for which he designed magnificent hunting scenes and established the international reputation of these workshops. He was also active as a book illustrator, and his views of the fine old parks of French castles rank among the most attractive landscape drawings of the eighteenth century.

CHARLES JOSEPH NATOIRE
Born Nîmes 1700, died Castel Gandolfo 1777.

XXI Italian Autumn Landscape with Pastoral Scene and Offering to Pan.
Black and red chalk, pen and bistre, washed with Indian ink and bistre, watercolor, white bodycolor on bluish paper; signed in Indian ink: C. NATOIRE and inscribed (probably by the artist himself): monte Porcio al 10 octobre 1763.
281 : 423 mm.
Inv. no. 12079 (L. 174).
Exhibition: Meisterwerke aus Frankreichs Museen, Albertina, Vienna, 1950, no. 88a.

Natoire belonged to those French artists who were mainly active on Italian soil. In his youth the Prix de Rome took him to Italy. In 1751 he was appointed director of the French Academy in Rome, and after leaving this position stayed on in the South. He was a pupil of Le Moyne and displayed great taste in the solution of decorative tasks, which made him the rival of Boucher. A series of attractive landscapes in watercolor in the Albertina from his later Italian period seem to have been made from nature, judging from the exact notation of place and time, but they were nevertheless transformed into decorative stage scenery with mythological figures.

FRANÇOIS BOUCHER
Born Paris 1703, died there 1770.

217 Corner of a Courtyard.
Black chalk, stumped.
238 : 349 mm.
Inv. no. 12190 (L. 174).
J. Meder, Die Handzeichnung, Vienna, 1919, p. 520, fig. 242.
Exhibition: Meisterwerke aus Frankreichs Museen, Albertina, Vienna, 1950, no. 95.

It is surprising to meet this great decorator (see no. 218) here as the author of a quiet and unpretentious study from nature, engrossed in this plain corner of reality with more inner sympathy and concentration than he had expended on his large scale routine projects. Yet it is just these works of Boucher, devoted to the bourgeois side of French life, where he is so near to Chardin's domain, that are among his most beautiful achievements.

218 Hermes Entrusting the New-Born Dionysus to the Care of the Nymphs of Nysa.
Brown chalk, stumped; lower right, faded inscription in bistre: F. Boucher.
319 : 219 mm.
Inv. no. 12137 (L. 174).
A remarkable ease of invention made this extremely prolific artist the dictator of French Rococo taste. His decorative imagination dominated not only fresco and wall painting, tapestry and easel painting, but also every kind of applied art from furniture to the snuffbox. He was, moreover, when faced with the task, an excellent portraitist, and could, as a draughtsman, become engrossed in some plain bit of nature (see no. 217). Thus it is not surprising that his influence on the development of French eighteenth-century painting was stronger than any other except that of Watteau. Boucher became the epitome of French Rococo. He was, like Natoire, a pupil of Le Moyne and in his youth he was one of the engravers whom De Julienne employed for his publication of engravings after the works of Watteau. The easy and fluid style of his work can be judged from a drawing like the present one. The flow of the gliding chalk strokes lets the figures emerge effortlessly from an undulant maze of lines. The occasional application of the stump lends softness and atmosphere to the modeling.
I. Fenyö draws our attention to an unknown, closely related drawing in Budapest, Museum of Fine Arts (I. Fenyö, Acta Historiae Artium, Academiae Scientiarum Hungaricae, 1965, Tome XI, Fasc. 3—4, p. 352).

JEAN-ÉTIENNE LIOTARD
Born Geneva 1702, died there 1789.

XXII Portrait of the Wife of the Painter Natoire.
Black and white chalk, red chalk, pink crayon on light red paper.
256 : 194 mm.
Inv. no. 12097 (L. 174).
Schönbrunner-Meder 491.
Exhibition: Meisterwerke aus Frankreichs Museen, Albertina, Vienna, 1950, no. 100.

This drawing was probably made between 1729, the year of Natoire's return to Paris, and 1736, the date of Liotard's departure for Rome. It displays the full charm and freshness of the artist in the youthful vigor of his creative activity. Liotard, who had first unsuccessfully tried his hand in the field of historical painting, on Le Moyne's advice took up portraiture, which brought him numerous commissions for pastel and miniature portraits. The delicate modeling of the attractive face clearly reveals the masterly miniature painter. The broader outline of the rest of the body in three chalks still shows the influence of Watteau's drawings. The widely-traveled artist gained that lucidity and almost photographic fidelity in portraiture so characteristic for him only after his successes in Constantinople and Vienna; they permitted him to appear — except in Paris — as a representative of the art of his native Switzerland.

ÉTIENNE JEAURAT
Born Vermenton 1699, died Versailles 1789.

219 The Chinese T'Sao.
Black and white chalk on bluish-green paper; on the parapet the name of the sitter; lower left later inscription in pencil: Watteau.
510 : 323 mm.
Provenance: Chevalier Damery (L. 2862).
Inv. no. 12014 (L. 174).
Schönbrunner-Meder 232; K. T. Parker, Old Master Drawings V, London, 1930, p. 52, plate 33.

Exhibitions: London, 1948, no. 119; Meisterwerke aus Frankreichs Museen, Albertina, Vienna, 1950, no. 98a.

The present drawing was traditionally attributed to Watteau until Parker succeeded in convincingly identifying its author on the basis of a critical comparison of style. Jeaurat as a draughtsman belonged to the followers of Watteau — he was a pupil of Watteau's friend Vleughels — while in his genre paintings he is closer to Chardin. Parker pointed out that the "chinoiseries", so popular in the Rococo, are repeatedly found in his works.

JEAN-BAPTISTE GREUZE
Born Tournus 1725, died Paris 1805.

220 Head of a Young Girl.
Pastel and red chalk, white bodycolor on reddish tinted paper.
342 : 262 mm.
Inv. no. 12771 (L. 174).
Schönbrunner-Meder 289; J. Meder, Albertina-Facsimile, Handzeichnungen französischer Meister des XVI.—XVIII. Jahrhunderts, Vienna, 1922, no. 21; C. Mauclair, J. B. Greuze, Paris, 1906, p. 8 (plate); Jean Martin, Oeuvre de J. B. Greuze, Paris, 1908, p. 11, at no. 136.

Exhibitions: French Art, Royal Academy, London, 1932, no. 1016, Commemorative Catalogue, p. 150, no. 695; Le dessin français dans les Collections du XVIIIe siècle, Wildenstein, Paris, 1935, no. 209; Chefs d'oeuvre de l'art français, Paris, 1937, no. 549; Paris, 1950, no. 147; Meisterwerke aus Frankreichs Museen, Albertina, Vienna, 1950, no. 110.

Study for the head of the mother in the painting "Le Repas partagé" (The Shared Meal), formerly belonging to the Duc de Praslin, engraved by Maleuvre, 1772.
In the history of painting Greuze marked the turning away from the decorative and erotic ideals of the Rococo to a bourgeois range of subjects, whereby his art became the propagator of the morally good as understood by Diderot. His moralizing themes have, in addition to the genuine simplicity of Chardin whom he admired, a certain literary emphasis and stage-like arrangement, against which his masterly portrait studies form a pleasant contrast. A drawing like the present one, with its verve and freshness of observation and its grasp of the human element, surpasses most of his paintings.

FRANÇOIS GUÉRIN
Born Paris, admitted to the Académie Royale in 1761, died Strasbourg after 1791.

XXIII Lady Reading, with a Little Girl.
Black chalk and pastel in red and blue, heightened with white bodycolor. Lower right later inscription: fait pour Mme de Pompadou(r) chardin.
248 : 287 mm.
Inv. no. 12266 (L. 174).
Schönbrunner-Meder 790; J. Meder, Albertina-Facsimile, Handzeichnungen französischer Meister des XVI.—XVIII. Jahrhunderts, Vienna, 1922, no. 15; J. Mathey, Old Master Drawings VIII, June 1933, p. 8, plate 10 (as E. Jeaurat); O. Benesch, Die Österr. Nationalbibliothek, Festschrift J. Bick, Vienna, 1948, p. 239 ff. (Guérin); O. Benesch, Gazette des Beaux-Arts XXXVII, Paris—New York, Janvier—Juin 1950, pp. 125 to 129.

Exhibitions: London, 1948, no. 117; Paris, 1950, no. 145; Meisterwerke aus Frankreichs Museen, Albertina, Vienna, 1950, no. 112 (Guérin).

Guérin was not one of the leading French artists of the Dixhuitième, but one of the petits maîtres. That he was nevertheless able to create two of the most beautiful drawings of this era (the present sheet and its companion piece representing the same lady writing, also in the Albertina), is a manifestation of the period's extraordinary artistic culture. He was a pupil of Natoire and covered a full range of subjects. In his paintings he favored the small format. Madame de Pompadour was his patroness and in the Salon of 1761 he exhibited several genre paintings in her possession.

The unusually high quality of both drawings was the reason for giving credence to the inscription in pencil (in an eighteenth-century hand) and considering them works by Chardin. But two circumstances were disturbing: nothing is known about Madame de Pompadour's having been a patroness of Chardin, and the style of the drawings follows Boucher, which is inconceivable for Chardin. One consequence of such doubt was J. Mathey's attempted attribution to Jeaurat, but this was not a satisfactory solution either.
The solution of this problem was found by the present author in Guérin's sketch for the portrait of the Marquise de Pompadour and her little daughter, Alexandrine Lenormand d'Etiolles (Collection Edmond de Rothschild, Paris). This sketch was discovered by Michel N. Benisovich in the Crocker Art Gallery at Sacramento, California (Gazette des Beaux-Arts 87, 1945, pp. 31—42). Although it is a sketch for a painting and not a study from life like the two drawings in the Albertina, the identity of artist and sitters is apparent. Alexandrine was born in 1744; the drawings were thus made about 1750. The dedication to Madame de Pompadour is therefore correct. The drawings do represent her and her little daughter. That the famous name of Chardin was substituted for the comparatively little known name of Guérin may be due to the writer's mistake in hearing or a slip of memory, if not to the desire to increase the value of the drawings.

HUBERT ROBERT
Born Paris 1733, died there 1808.

221 The Temple of Jupiter Serapis at Pozzuoli near Naples.
Red chalk.
329 : 460 mm.
Inv. no. 12738 (L. 174).
E. Hempel, Die Graphischen Künste 47, Vienna, 1924, I, pp. 15 and 20.

Exhibitions: Hubert Robert, Paris, 1933, no. 34; Paris, 1950, no. 156; Meisterwerke aus Frankreichs Museen, Albertina, Vienna, 1950, no. 114.

Etching in reverse by J. B. Cl. Richard, Abbé de Saint-Non, 1762, Vue de l'entrée du Temple de Sérapis à Pozzuolo près de Naples (Le Blanc, Manuel de l'Amateur 3, p. 413, no. 18).
Robert and Fragonard (see no. 222), favored by external circumstances and their own gifts, developed along surprisingly parallel lines during their years in Italy, a development resulting in mutual influence and even occasional collaboration. Robert, landscape painter and chronicler of contemporary events, went to Italy in 1754 as a "pensionnaire" at the French Academy. The Roman landscapists, particularly Piranesi and Pannini, inspired in him a new style of landscape painting, heroically dramatic in its composition, but without abandonment of any of the highly pictorial qualities of the Rococo. By the middle of the century the imminent turn to Neo-Classicism was already making itself felt. In addition to the assistance of the Academy, Robert and Fragonard found a patron in the Abbé (Claude Richard) de Saint-Non, who traveled through South Italy and Sicily with Robert in the spring of 1759. The landscape sketches made by Robert during this journey were etched by De Saint-Non himself and published in the work "Voyage Pittoresque dans les royaumes de Naples et des Deux Siciles". The present drawing was utilized in this publication.

JEAN-HONORÉ FRAGONARD
Born Grasse 1732, died Paris 1806.

222 Young Bull in a Stable.
Brush and bistre over preparatory drawing in leadpoint; inscription on the back of the mount: Cabinet Puisegur.
319 : 437 mm.
Provenance: Leroy de Senneville (Paris, Sales, April 5—11, 1780, no. 145, April 26, 1784, no. 106; Chabot et De La Mure, December 17—22, 1782, lot 291).
Inv. no. 12734 (L. 174).
A. Ananoff, L'Oeuvre dessiné de J.-H. Fragonard, I, Paris (1961), no. 285, fig. 101.

Exhibitions: Dessins de Fragonard, J. Seligmann & Fils, Paris, May 1931, no. 49; Paris, 1950, no. 151; Meisterwerke aus

Frankreichs Museen, Albertina, Vienna, 1950, no. 128; French Drawings from Fouquet to Gauguin, The Arts Council, London, 1952, no. 65, plate XII; Fragonard, Musée des Beaux-Arts de Berne, Berne, 1954, no. 119.

Fragonard was a pupil of Chardin, Boucher and Van Loo. Among his teachers, the main influence was exerted by Boucher, whose works he copied, but it was with Van Loo that he prepared for his Roman scholarship. He thus combines the élan and the high pictorial qualities of the Dix-huitième with the "maniera grande" of Roman Classicism. He was as prolific and important a draughtsman as he was a painter. His drawings were mostly made for their own sake, even if their ideas were subsequently used for paintings. With regard to technique he cultivated both drawing with the brush, full of an incredible boldness and freedom, as well as drawing in chalk, revealing a more careful graphic discipline, especially after his friendly relationship with Robert (see no. 221). Many of the drawings exist in several versions, demonstrating their independent importance.

The present drawing is based on a study from nature in black chalk in the Musée Fragonard at Grasse (Ananoff 278). There are two more versions in brush with slight variations: with a young girl asleep in the right corner (Wildenstein Collection, New York, Ananoff 281) and with a barrel on the same spot (Abdy Collection, London, Ananoff 283). There is also a painting of the same subject (Le Taureau Blanc, Georges Wildenstein, The Paintings of Fragonard, London, 1960, cat. no. 115).

The sheet in its masterly handling of light reveals the influence of Rembrandt on Fragonard, who repeatedly copied his works.

223 Scene in a Roman Park with a Fountain.
Brush and bistre over slight preparatory drawing in leadpoint; inscription by the artist's own hand: Rome 1774; upper right collector's inscription: Fragonard du Cabinet de M. De Levi.
289 : 368 mm.
Inv. no. 12736 (L. 174).

J. Meder, Handzeichnungen französischer Meister des XVI. bis XVIII. Jahrhunderts, Vienna, 1922, no. 32; E. Hempel, Die Graphischen Künste 47, Vienna, 1924, I, p. 22, fig. 8.

Exhibitions: Dessins de Fragonard, J. Seligmann & Fils, Paris, 1931, no. 76; Paris, 1950, no. 153; Meisterwerke aus Frankreichs Museen, Albertina, Vienna, 1950, no. 124; Fragonard, Musée des Beaux-Arts de Berne, Berne, 1954, no. 56.

In the summer of 1760 the Abbé de Saint-Non (see no. 221) rented the Villa d'Este at Tivoli and invited Fragonard to be his guest. There are accordingly from this time a series of drawings of Italian gardens. In 1761 the Abbé traveled with Fragonard to Naples. As a result of this journey the volume of De Saint-Non's etchings entitled "Différentes vues dessinées d'après nature dans les environs de Rome et de Naples par Robert et Frago" appeared in 1761—1763.

In 1773—1774 Fragonard visited Italy for a second time accompanied by a patron, the Receveur Général Bergeret de Grancourt. Fragonard drew diligently during this journey; later there was a lawsuit between Bergeret and the artist concerning the drawings he had made. The months from December to April were spent in Rome. In the spring of 1774 Fragonard's finest drawings of Roman parks were made. Most of them are drawings done with the brush in a pointillist technique, full of Roman grandeur and majesty of vision and pervaded with a magic silvery light recalling the works of the great Dutch masters.

224 Young Woman Drawing (Marguerite Gérard, the Artist's Sister-in-Law).
Brush and bistre over preparatory drawing in leadpoint; signed: H Fragonard.
451 : 338 mm.
Inv. no. 12731 (L. 174).
Schönbrunner-Meder 749; J. Meder, Albertina-Facsimile, Handzeichnungen französischer Meister des XVI.—XVIII. Jahrhunderts, Vienna, 1922, no. 26.

Exhibitions: Dessins de Fragonard, J. Seligmann & Fils, Paris, May 1931, no. 58; London, 1948, no. 114; Paris, 1950, no. 154; Meisterwerke aus Frankreichs Museen, Albertina, Vienna, 1950, no. 131; Fragonard, Musée des Beaux-Arts de Berne, Berne, 1954, no. 75.

Marguerite Gérard, the sister of Marie-Anne, Fragonard's wife, eleven years her junior and also a painter, was born at Grasse in 1761. As a young girl she became the pupil and assistant of her brother-in-law, who used her as a model for some of his finest drawings. This drawing consequently must have originated in the second half of the 1770's. The artist here combined a composition in the severe Roman style — a large triangle and a small subordinate one — with an attractive genre representation: a young artist drawing the Holy Family. The result is a drawing of intimate charm, remarkable in its effects of brilliant light and deep colorful shadows. The artist at work was a favorite subject of the French in the eighteenth century, allowing them to express their enthusiasm for artistic activity and their love for the representation of the most subtle psychological tensions.

XXIV The Girl with the Marmot (Rosalie Fragonard, the Artist's Daughter).
Watercolor.
259 : 212 mm.
Inv. no. 17543 (L. 174).

Schönbrunner-Meder 362; J. Meder, Albertina-Facsimile, Handzeichnungen französischer Meister des XVI.—XVIII. Jahrhunderts, Vienna, 1922, no. 25.

Exhibitions: Dessins de Fragonard, J. Seligmann & Fils, Paris, May 1931, no. 61; London, 1948, no. 116; Meisterwerke aus Frankreichs Museen, Albertina, Vienna, 1950, no. 120; Fragonard, Musée des Beaux-Arts de Berne, Berne, 1954, no. 78, plate XVIII.

Rosalie was born in 1769, which fixes the date of this watercolor at about the middle of the 1780's. There are two versions in oil of this watercolor: a larger one on canvas in the Museum of Portland, Oregon (Wildenstein, op. cit., cat. no. 507), and a smaller one on copper in the Pushkin Museum in Moscow (Wildenstein, op. cit., cat. no. 508). The companion pieces of these two paintings are two representations of a Savoyard boy, with a peepshow, who is supposed to be the artist's son Evariste.

This watercolor is undoubtedly the original version and artistically the most valuable one.

JEAN MICHEL MOREAU, called Moreau le Jeune
Born Paris 1741, died there 1814.

225 The Young King Louis XVI of France Accepts the Homage of the Peers of the Realm in the Cathedral of Reims.
Pen and brush and bistre over preparatory drawing in leadpoint; signed and dated lower left: J M Moreau Le jeune 1775, below once more the letters "Mor".
420 : 558 mm.
Inv. no. 15388 (L. 174).

His extensive engraved oeuvre made this artist one of the liveliest and most informative chroniclers of customs and events in the eighteenth century. He devoted several drawings and prints to the coronation ceremony of Louis XVI; of these, his etching "Le Serment de Louis XVI à son Sacre" (Mahérault 81) is the most famous. The polycephalous crowds depicted in the print with the most painstaking exactitude were rendered in his washed pen drawings in a sort of shorthand which created a heightened impression of vibrant life.

JACQUES LOUIS DAVID
Born Paris 1748, died Brussels 1825.

226 Diomedes Wounds Aphrodite in the Battle against Aeneas and Pandarus (Homer, Iliad, Book V).
Pen and brush and Indian ink, heightened with white bodycolor, on bluish-gray paper; signed and dated: L. David. f. Roma. 1776.
1840 : 865 mm.
Inv. no. 17428.

W. Hofmann, Gazette des Beaux-Arts LI, Paris, March 1958, pp. 157—168, fig. 1.

This drawing is an important example of David's early work, dating from the second year of his first stay in Rome (1775—1780). The traditional Baroque style is transformed under the influence of the Cinquecento masters and is given a monumental heaviness which presages the future realist. This development from Baroque to Classicism creates a strange anticipation of Géricault's art, in which the process is reversed, that is, a turning from Classicism to Baroque.

This drawing had been unknown to the scholars for a long time, as, owing to its unusual size, it had been hidden away in a supplementary portfolio of the Albertina, from which the present author first brought it to light again in 1951. The old handwritten catalogue ("Cahier") mentions it as a "Dessin Capital". W. Hofmann in his publication expresses the convincing opinion that it was acquired by Duke Albert of Sachsen-Teschen on his journey to Italy in 1776. It is quite conceivable that this example of the talent of the French Academy's scholar was submitted to him in Rome.

PORTUGUESE AND SPANISH MASTERS

NUÑO GONÇALVES (Gonzalves)
Portuguese painter. documented from 1450 to 1472, appointed Court Painter to King Alfonso V in 1450.

227 Male Portrait, Three-Quarters to the Right.
Silverpoint, brush and bistre on white prepared paper.
147 : 108 mm.
Inv. no. 4842 (L. 174).

O. Benesch, Annuaire des Musées Royaux des Beaux-Arts de Belgique, Éditions de la Connaissance, Brussels, 1938, p. 42, fig. 13.

Old attribution: Israel van Meckenem.

This remarkable drawing has been attributed in turn to the German, Netherlandish, and French schools, yet these attributions did not grasp the essence of this study which is as solemn in attitude as it is stirringly realistic in execution. It was obviously made from the living model. All the areas in silverpoint are genuine; only the strand of hair has been added with the brush by another hand.

A comparison with the expressive and realistic portraits in the polyptych dedicated to St. Vincent, from the Cathedral of Lisbon (now in the Museu Nacional de Arte Antiga), led the present author to attribute the drawing to this rare artist. Although no other panel by his hand has been preserved, he stands out as one of the greatest artists of the fifteenth century. There is no painted work which comes closer to this drawing, which is equally deliberate and relentlessly realistic in its modeling, than the powerful portrait heads in Gonçalves' altarpiece.

VICENTE CARDUCHO (Vincenzo Carducci)
Born Florence 1578, died Madrid 1638.

228 The Meeting of Joachim and Anna at the Golden Gate.
Black chalk, washed with bistre and heightened with white bodycolor on brown paper; signed with pen and bistre along lower margin: Vicencio Carducho.
393 : 251 mm.
Inv. no. 25428 (acquired 1927).

Design for an altarpiece.

The name of this artist, who was born in Italy, was Carducci. He was the younger brother and pupil of Bartolomé Carducho, a pupil and assistant of Federico Zuccari (see no. 43), who followed his teacher when the latter was summoned in 1585 by Philip II to execute some frescoes and altarpieces in Spain. Both Bartolomé and his brother Vicente, whom he induced to accompany him, settled for some time in Spain. Vicente sought to hispanize himself and succeeded his brother as court painter after the latter's death. He painted numerous altarpieces and frescoes for churches, these representing Late Mannerism in Spain. Although the derivation of the present altar design from Florentine and Roman Late Mannerism is obvious in the forms of its style,

the muted solemnity and rapture of this Meeting at the Golden Gate definitely exudes a completely Spanish religious atmosphere.

JUSEPE DE RIBERA (Lo Spagnoletto)
Born Játiba about 1590, died Naples 1652.

229 The Crucifixion of St. Peter.
Pen and bistre, washed; signed lower left: Jusepe Rivera.
329 : 226 mm. (upper left corner missing).
Inv. no. 13072 (L. 174).
Schönbrunner-Meder 1206; E. Gradmann, Spanische Meisterzeichnungen, Frankfort-on-Main, 1939, no. 8.

Ribera was a pupil of Ribalta in Valencia. He emigrated to Italy in his youth and came into contact with Venetian painting during his stay in Parma and Padua; in Rome, Caravaggio's art exerted a decisive influence upon him. From 1616 onward he lived in Naples. The present drawing belongs to the early period of the master, during which he painted St. Andrew Preparing for his Crucifixion, Budapest (1628). The realistic composition of the nude with the rough executioners is quite Caravaggesque in character. The technique of drawing with its modeling of the half-shadows in light derives from Venice and is reminiscent of followers of Veronese and Tintoretto like Palma Giovane.

FRANCISCO DE HERRERA EL MOZO (the Younger)
Born Seville 1622, died Madrid 1685.

230 Apotheosis of Maria Anna of Austria, Widow of King Philip IV, and of her Son, King Carlos II.
Pen and bistre, washed, over preparatory drawing in black chalk; damaged at lower left margin; signed on the lion's skin held by angel-putti: D. franco de Herrera. ft ... 1668.
314 : 219 mm.
Inv. no. 13093 (L. 174).

Design for a Title-Page.

The younger Herrera was the pupil of his father Francisco Herrera the Elder. He soon went to Rome, where he lived until 1656. The impression made on him by Roman Baroque art at its height was decisive. He displayed a sparkling imagination in his designs, which included architectural and decorative elements, as can be seen from this spirited drawing. He was also active as an architect. He was the drawing teacher of Carlos II and later his court painter.

FRANCISCO JOSÉ DE GOYA Y LUCIENTES
Born Fuendetodos 1746, died Bordeaux 1828.

231 The Blind Workman.
Brush and Indian ink; inscribed below in black chalk: el ciego trabajador.
238 : 171 mm.
Provenance: A. Beurdeley (L. 421).
Inv. no. 23431 (acquired 1925).

Exhibition: Francisco de Goya, Albertina, Vienna, 1961, no. 2.

It was Goya's habit, especially from 1800 onward, to group his drawings in series, which he sometimes provided with their own numbers. In so doing he linked the thoughts of a great artist and a thinker about life and the relativity of all human values in a spiritual and human unity. He often provided these drawings with his own aphorisms and inscriptions expressing in pithy form his criticism and his unshakable faith in the good and the right.

The present drawing belongs to a late series depicting the life of the humble, the oppressed and the disinherited toiling for a scant livelihood. By drawing a frame around the individual scenes Goya made them appear as a pictorial whole and gave them their definitive character. Here the destitute blind cobbler carries on his work while his customers wait. He has moreover to look after a baby which he holds close to his chest—a picture of human misery.

In his late years Goya—the greatest etcher and draughtsman after Rembrandt—with a minimum of graphic means imbued these brush drawings with the deepest and most moving human expression.

SIR JAMES THORNHILL
Born Malcombe Regis 1675, died Weymouth 1734.

232 Design for a Decorative Wall Painting with Scenes from the Story of Hercules.
Pen and bistre, washed; the lower third at the left corrected with a diagonally trimmed overlay which is pasted down.
266 : 390 mm.
Inv. no. 900 (L. 174).
Wickhoff Sc. R. 1005 ("Later than Pietro da Cortona").
Old inventory: Pietro Berettini da Cortona.
Attribution by the present author.

Thornhill is the typical representative of Baroque decorative painting in England in the era of Queen Anne, whose court painter he was. The most important royal and ecclesiastical buildings were decorated with paintings by his hand. His style developed on international lines by reason of the contacts he made with the art of France, Italy and the Netherlands during his extensive journeys. He made careful preparatory drawings for his projects, intended primarily to give his patrons an idea of the projected work. The correction of the present drawing in the form of a pasted overlay shows that it served such a purpose.

THOMAS GAINSBOROUGH
Born Sudbury (Suffolk) 1727, died London 1788.

233 Mountainous Landscape with Houses by a River.
Charcoal, stumped, and white chalk on bluish paper.
259 : 356 mm.
Inv. no. 24458 (acquired 1925).

In his youth Gainsborough was the pupil of the talented illustrator Gravelot, a circumstance that imbued his draughtsmanship with an ineradicable dash of French Dixhuitième. In other respects, the eminent portraitist owed his formation more to the study of the works of art in the possession of the English aristocracy than to instruction or travel. In his landscapes he followed the style of the Netherlanders (Wijnants, Teniers, Hobbema). In particular he studied the works of Van Dyck, to whose drawings and watercolors of English landscapes he is greatly indebted in his studies of similar subjects.

GEORGE ROMNEY
Born Dalton-le-Furness (Lancashire) 1734, died Kendal 1802.

234 Figure Study of a Tragedienne on the Stage.

Brush and bistre over preparatory drawing in pencil.
370 : 204 mm.
Inv. no. 24255 (acquired 1925).

The pictorial objectivity of the great English portraitists changes with Romney, particularly after his stay in Rome (1773—1775), into romantic neo-classic pathos, in which elements of the Gothic Revival and of Füssli's and Blake's art are foreshadowed. He took a great interest in the stage and made several paintings for Boydell's Shakespeare Gallery.

JOHANN HEINRICH FÜSSLI THE YOUNGER
(after 1770 he called himself Henry Fuseli or Fusely).
Born Zurich 1741, died Putney Hill near London 1825.

235 Odysseus Questions the Shadow of Tiresias.
Pen and brush and Indian ink, watercolor and gouache, highlights scratched in; signed lower right in pen and Indian ink: H. Fuseli.
915 : 628 mm.
Inv. no. 17299 (L. 174).
Exhibition: Goethe-Ausstellung, Österreichische Nationalbibliothek, Vienna, 1949, p. 230, no. 27.

The composition appears to have been prepared in a pen and wash sketch in the Kunsthaus, Zurich (A. Federmann, J. H. Füssli, Zurich, 1927, plate 46). In the present watercolor, made during Füssli's English period, it has undergone strong dramatization and unification. Shining in a spectral light, the procession of shadows rises like a flame behind Tiresias, repeating the outline of his figure. The Michelangelesque and the Gothic dominate Füssli's fantastic art which is full of demoniacal storm and stress. He inspired artists like Sergel and Blake as well as poets like Herder and Goethe.

JOHN HOPPNER
Born London 1758, died there 1810.

236 Portrait of a Gentleman, in Profile, Half-Length.
Pen and brown ink.
235 : 181 mm.
Inv. no. 24418 (acquired 1925).

While Hoppner as a painter must be classified among the group of Reynolds' pupils at the Academy, in his spirited pen sketches he preserves a considerable degree of independence from their style. A portrait study like the present one is comparable in handling rather to the lively line of the humorous illustrators and cartoonists like Rowlandson. It is a line also found in the drawings of sculptors of this period, revealing considerable experience in the use of the stippling technique in the modeling of the face.

INDEX OF ARTISTS